$1—
A

RSVP

An Invitation From
The Junior League of Portland, Maine

Cover Design and Illustrations by
Shirley Leighton

The Junior League of Portland, Maine, Inc.
Portland, Maine

If you wish to order additional copies, use the order blanks in the back of the book or write to:

R.S.V.P.
The Junior League of Portland, Maine
P.O. Box 677
Portland, Maine 04104

The price of each book is $14.95 plus $3.00 for postage and handling. Maine residents please add $.90 sales tax per book. Checks should be made payable to R.S.V.P., The Junior League of Portland, Maine, Inc.

Organizations and retail stores wishing to purchase R.S.V.P. please write the above address.

The Junior League of Portland, Maine, Inc. has no reason to doubt that recipe ingredients, instructions and directions will work successfully. However, the ingredients, instructions, and directions have not necessarily been thoroughly or systematically tested, and the cook should not hesitate to test and question procedures and directions before preparation. The recipes in this book have been collected from various sources, and neither the Junior League of Portland, Maine, Inc., nor any contributor, publisher, printer, distributor or seller of this book is responsible for errors or omissions.

Library of Congress Catalog Card No.: 81-71437
ISBN: 0-939114-55-0

First Edition
First Printing: 10,000 copies
Second Printing: 10,000 copies
Third Printing: 10,000 copies
Fourth Printing: 7,000 copies
Fifth Printing: 10,000 copies

Printed in the USA by

WIMMER
The Wimmer Companies, Inc.
Memphis • Dallas

TABLE OF CONTENTS

Menus 5

Beverages 31

Appetizers and Hors d'Oeuvres 39

Soups 63

Salads and Dressings 77

Brunch 93

Vegetables 107

Seafood 133

Poultry 147

Meats 165

Breads 189

Cookies 209

Desserts 229

Gifts from your Kitchen 269

Index 288

Order Form 303

COOKBOOK COMMITTEE

Chairman and Editor	Carol Day
Food Editor	Patti Britt
Copy Editor	Rebecca Sweeney
Test Kitchens Editors	Priscilla Connard
	Sue Kimble
Chapter Coordinators	Nancy Beebe
	Carol Bouton
	Patti Britt
	Betty Cimino
	Mel Coles
	Priscilla Connard
	Nancy Cragin
	Carol Day
	Bonnie Dowling
	Lee Edwards
	Helen Kleiber
	Luranna Marzilli
	Susan Oestreicher
	Caroline Pratt
	Gretchen Ramsay
	Gail Robinson
	Kathleen Sardegna
Treasurer	Rebecca Sweeney
Typist	Katie Freilinger

The purpose of the Junior League is exclusively educational and charitable and is to promote voluntarism, to develop the potential of its members for voluntary participation in community affairs and to demonstrate the effectiveness of trained volunteers. Proceeds from the sale of R.S.V.P. will finance projects and community activities of the Junior League of Portland, Maine.

MENUS

NEW YEAR'S EVE GALA

La Cuisine Soupe À L'Oignon Gratinée
Filet of Beef
Baked Stuffed Potatoes
Broccoli with Lemon Butter
Spinach Salad
Popovers with Sweet Butter
Reine De Saba
Champagne
Coffee

SUPER BOWL PARTY

Cousin Molly's Pepper Jam with Cream Cheese
Fish Dip
Raw Vegetables with Curry Dip
Greek Zucchini
Joe's Yummy Special
Tossed Salad with Italian Dressing
French Bread
Tollhouse Brownies
Apricot Bars
Coffee, Tea

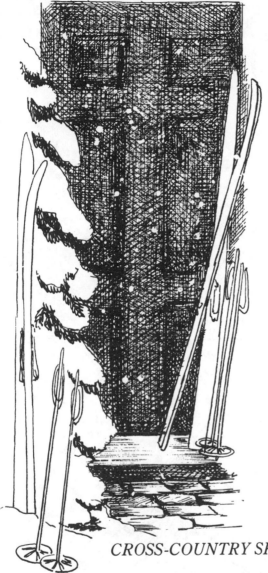

CROSS-COUNTRY SKI DINNER

Fishmonger's Kettle with Linguini
Spinach Salad with Oil and Vinegar
Angel Biscuits
Tray of Fresh Fruits (Apples, Pears, Green Seedless Grapes)
Bel Paese Cheese
Chinese Almond Cookies
Coffee

BEFORE THE HOCKEY GAME SUPPER

Guacomolé
Nasty Nachos
Beer
Tossed Salad with Oil and Vinegar Dressing
Key Lime Pie
Coffee, Tea

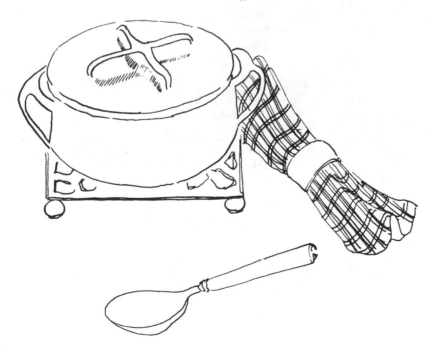

EIGHTEENTH CENTURY TAVERN DINNER

Smoked Trout
Liver Paté
Cheddar Cheese
Ale
Brunswick Stew
Salmagundi (This is the 18th Century version of Chef's Salad)
Spider Corn Bread
Maine Potato Bread
Crocks of Sweet Butter
Perfect Poundcake with Fresh Strawberries and Whipped Cream
Tea, Coffee

GREEK DINNER
Dolmathes
Athenian Leg of Lamb
Baked Vegetable Casserole
Spinach Pie
Galactoburiko
Cherry Liqueur Salonika
Coffee

FIRESIDE DINNER

Winter Wooly Soup
Oatmeal Sesame Bread
Cheddar Cheese
Indian Pudding with Vanilla Ice Cream
Coffee

ITALIAN DINNER

Cantaloupe with Prosciutto
Lasagna Alla Carola
Antipasto with Caponata Alla Siciliano
Italian Bread
Cassata Torte
Espresso

11

OPENING NIGHT BUFFET

Cheese Canapés
Chicken Mushroom Crêpes with Mock Mornay Sauce
Spinach Filled Tomatoes
Romaine Salad with Vinaigrette Dressing
Lemon Sherbet with Vodka
Pecan Crisps
Coffee, Tea

MIDNIGHT BUFFET AFTER THE SYMPHONY

Salty Topaz
Crocked and Sherried Crab
Rice, Patty Shells, or Toast Points
Broiled Tomatoes
Cucumber Ring Supreme
Lemon Lovenotes, Sir Walter Raleighs
Coffee, Tea

CUPID'S CHOICE

Oysters on the Half Shell
Chicken Geraldine
Fresh Green Beans with Toasted Slivered Almonds
Hearts of Lettuce Salad
Dinner Rolls
Chocolate Ripple Cheesecake
Coffee, Tea

REHEARSAL DINNER

Melon Balls with Rum Lime Sauce
Chicken in Puff Pastry
Braised Celery and Carrots
Cranberry Salad
Ellen's Herbert Hotel Rolls
Chocolate Hungarian Torte
Coffee, Tea

ENGAGEMENT CHAMPAGNE BUFFET

Crudités with Surprise Dip
Smoked Turkey with Honey Mustard
Cold Filet on Miniature Rolls with Herb Butter
Stuffed Mushrooms
Lobster Dip
Chocolate Covered Potato Chips
Compote of Fresh Minted Melon
(Cantaloupe, Honeydew and Watermelon)
Frosted Almond Cookies
Champagne

SPRING FEVER or EASTER BRUNCH

Bloody Mary's
Whiskey Sours
Oeufs Avec Crabe
Tomatoes with Spinach Mornay
Quartered Fresh Pineapple with Fresh Strawberries
Wine Jelly Ring with Seedless Grapes
Lemon Tea Bread
English Muffins with Homemade Jam
Sugared Nuts
Coffee, Tea

GRADUATION DINNER

Spicy Cheese Twists
Chicken Breasts with Mushrooms in Madeira
Rice and Pecan Casserole
Fresh Garden Peas
Tossed Green Salad
Blueberry Mousse

SPECIAL OCCASION DINNER

Champagne
Potted Shrimp
Chicken Chablis
Sweet Peas with Pearl Onions
White or Wild Rice
Champagne Mold
Dinner Rolls
Lime Soufflé
Coffee, Tea

BRIDAL SHOWER

Champagne Punch
Chicken Divan
Cherry Jubilee Ring
Rolls
Vanilla Almond Crunch with Hot Fudge Sauce
Mints
Coffee, Tea

ANNIVERSARY PARTY BUFFET

Chocochip Paté
Peach Melba
Smoked Turkey with Champagne Mustard
Curried Cheese on Rye
Cheese Platter with Fresh Fruit
Cold Tenderloin
Lobster Newburg on Toast Points
Barbecued Pork Leg
Rolls
Rice Giralda
Tania's Broccoli Salad
Salad with Oranges and Red Onions in Vinaigrette Dressing
Wedding Cake
Champagne

COCKTAILS FOR 24—A DOUBLE DOZEN

Poor Man's Salmon Mousse
Chicken Livers Hollister
Treasure Bits
Vegetable Platter
Green Pelican Cheese
Chinese Barbecued Ribs
Jane's Cheese Puffs
Assorted Crackers

JUBILEE DINNER

Purée of Carrot Soup
Contrefilet with Bernaise Sauce
Asparagus Au Naturel
Rice
Salade Vinaigrette
Oranges Supreme
Lemon Zucchini Cookies
Coffee, Tea

INDEPENDENCE DAY DINNER

Cantaloupe with Blueberries
Grilled Salmon Steaks
Herbed New Potatoes
Fresh Buttered Peas
Hundred Dollar Chocolate Cake with Fudge Frosting

SUMMER LUNCHEON

Cucumber Soup
Favorite Quiche
Grapefruit and Orange Sections
with Classic White French Dressing
Almond Tortoni Frenning
Iced Tea and Iced Coffee

SUMMER BRUNCH

Peach Fuzzies
Magic Morning Surprise
Spinach Quiche
French Doughnut Muffins
Blueberries Aragonaise
Coffee, Tea

SUPPER AFTER THE MONHEGAN RACE

Cheese Bombay
Hobo Steak
Corn-on-the-Cob
Seven Layer Salad
Mom's German Potato Salad
Chocolate Zucchini Cake with Cream Cheese Frosting

PATIO SUPPER

Best Marinated Mushrooms Ever
Grilled Chicken with Pughie's Seasoned Salt
Onions Au Gratin
Sautéed Cherry Tomatoes
Caesar Salad
Crusty Bread
Great Vanilla Ice Cream
Frosted Praline Bars

CAPE SHORE LOBSTER BAKE

Steamed Clams
Steamed Lobsters
Corn-on-the-Cob
Hot Dogs
Hard-Boiled Eggs
Corn Bread
Deb's Blueberry Buckle

AFTER THE GAME DINNER

Cocktail Cauliflower
Ratatouille with Sausage
Tossed Green Salad with Vinaigrette Dressing
French Bread
Serendipity Cake
Coffee, Tea

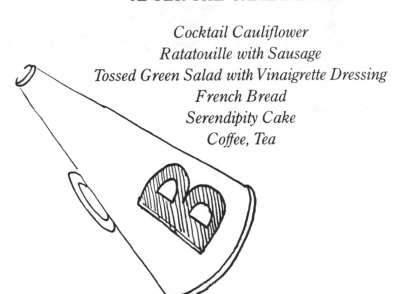

HARVEST DINNER

Consommé
Pot Roast Autrichienne
Parsleyed Noodles
Glazed Carrots
Hard Rolls
Harvest Apple Pie

HOLIDAY FAMILY BRUNCH

Cranberry Damsel
Croissants with Strawberry Butter
Danish Coffee Cake
Eggs-A-Plenty
Baked Ham with Honey Mustard
Fruit Compote
Coffee, Russian Tea

CHRISTMAS DINNER

Cranberry Rosé Soup
Standing Rib of Roast Beef
Yorkshire Pudding
Spinach Casserole
Saint Nick Salad Ring
Plum Pudding with Eggnog Custard Sauce

CHRISTMAS PARTY

Father Kerr's Christmas Punch
Peanut Kisses
Cocktail Kielbasa
Bacon Date Roll-Ups
Baked Brie
Three Cheese Squares
Marinated Broccoli
Party Punch
Coconut Crisps
Holiday Billy Goats
Pumpkin Cookies
Thumb Cookies
Cathedral Windows
Crunchy Chip Cookies
Finnish Sour Cream Rings
Coconut Butter Balls
Lemon Bonbon Cookies
Henry Bars
Christmas Chocolates

BEVERAGES

MAGIC MORNING SURPRISE

Serves: 1

2 ounces rum
4 drops orange liqueur
Juice of 2 oranges or 4 ounces
    orange juice

1 teaspoon powdered sugar

Mix in blender with ice.

Judith Bishop Condron
(Mrs. Arthur)

PEACH FUZZIES

Serves: 4 to 6

6 peaches, peeled and sliced
1 (6-ounce) can frozen lemonade
    concentrate

18 ounces fresh orange juice
6 ounces vodka or gin (to taste)

Combine all ingredients in blender. Blend until smooth. Pour over ice in tall glasses.

Karen Axelsen Maxell
(Mrs. Bruce)

LEMON COCONUT COOLER

Serves: 2

2 teaspoons grated lemon peel
2 cups cold milk
¼ cup coconut

¼ cup sugar
¼ cup lemon juice
6 ice cubes

Combine all ingredients in blender and blend until ice is completely puréed and drink is frothy. Garnish with grated lemon peel and slices.

Lee Morse Edwards
(Mrs. Dwight H.)

PLAZA SUITE

Serves: 2

2 ounces coffee liqueur
2 ounces white crème de menthe

2 ounces heavy cream

Combine and serve over ice.

The Committee

GOOMBAY SMASH

Serves: 2 (13-ounces)

2 ounces rum
2 ounces coconut rum
½ ounce lemon juice

½ ounce sugar syrup
8 ounces pineapple juice

To make sugar syrup: boil equal parts of sugar and water for 5 minutes. Chill and store in covered bottle. Combine all ingredients in blender or shaker. Mix thoroughly. Pour over crushed ice.

Sara Koirth Boxer
(Mrs. Daniel)

MORNING CUP

Serves: 4

4½ ounces gin
9 ounces fresh orange juice
1½ ounces lemon juice
3 dashes bitters

3 egg whites, beaten until frothy
4½ ounces Chablis
2 tablespoons honey

Combine all ingredients, shake well. Serve over crushed ice. Garnish with orange slice.

Carol Such Bouton
(Mrs. Dale C., Jr.)

CRANBERRY DAMSEL

Serves: 2

2 ounces cranberry liqueur
1 ounce white rum
2 ounces unsweetened orange
  juice

Dash lemon juice
½ ounce sugar syrup

Combine all ingredients in shaker with ice. Shake and serve with the ice in large stemmed glasses.

Lee Morse Edwards
(Mrs. Dwight H.)

BARTENDER'S RUM COLLINS

1½ ounces rum, silver or white
  label
1½ ounces lemon juice
½ ounce sugar syrup

½ ounce water
Slice of lemon
Slice of orange
Maraschino cherry

Combine rum, lemon juice, sugar syrup and water in shaker with ice. Shake and pour into tall glass with the ice. Garnish with lemon and orange peels and cherry.

Sugar Syrup

1 cup water   1 cup sugar

Combine water and sugar. Boil for 3 minutes. Chill. Store in covered jar.

Lee Morse Edwards
(Mrs. Dwight H.)

BLOODY MARY MIX

Serves: 6 to 8

1½ teaspoons celery salt
6 drops hot pepper sauce
¾ teaspoon dried parsley
3 to 5 tablespoons
  Worcestershire sauce

1 (46-ounce) can tomato juice
2 pinches dill seed

Combine all the above ingredients; refrigerate at least 12 hours before serving. Mix with vodka for super Bloody Mary's or serve as spiced tomato juice.

Patricia Pugh Britt
(Mrs. Michael E.)

FATHER KERR'S CHRISTMAS PUNCH

Yield: 9½ cups

1 fifth Southern Comfort
48 ounces cranberry juice

¼ cup lemon juice

Combine all ingredients and add lots of ice just before serving.

Deborah Snite Bates
(Mrs. Daniel W.)

TWENTY-FOUR HOUR COCKTAIL

Yield: 42 ounces
(Approximately)

1 cup water
1 fifth bourbon
½ cup sugar

8 lemons, quartered
Pinch of whole cloves

Combine all ingredients in a glass container and let stand for 24 hours at room temperature. Squeeze lemons to extract all juice. Strain and chill. Serve icy cold.

Eileen A. Pugh
(Mrs. Richard F.)

MULLED WINE

Serves: 12

½ gallon red wine
6 tablespoons sugar
2 cinnamon sticks

4 to 6 whole cloves, to taste
4 oranges, halved and sliced
2 cups orange juice

Heat all ingredients until warm, but do not boil. Put in large punch bowl. When pouring, try to put fruit in each cup served.

Doris Martineau Stevens
(Mrs. Paul S.)

BRANDIED CHAMPAGNE PUNCH

Yield: 96 servings

2 cups vodka, chilled
1 quart apricot brandy, chilled

3 quarts gingerale, chilled
4 fifths champagne, chilled

Combine all ingredients and serve immediately. If not possible to have all the ingredients chilled, make an ice ring using one of the quarts of gingerale. Garnish with orange and lemon slices.

Patricia Pugh Britt
(Mrs. Michael E.)

CHAMPAGNE PUNCH

Serves: 50 to 60
2½ gallons

¾ cup cognac
¾ cup yellow chartreuse
¾ cup orange liqueur
3 quarts club soda

Sugar to taste (about 1 cup)
Slices of orange, lemon and
  pineapple
10 fifths champagne

Mix all but champagne together. Chill until ready to serve. Add champagne and serve immediately.

Kathleen Foshay Hanson
(Mrs. Robert)

FISH HOUSE PUNCH

Serves: 30

12 ounces very fine sugar
2 quarts water
1 quart lemon juice

2 quarts dark rum
1 quart cognac
6 ounces peach brandy

Dissolve sugar in water. Add remaining ingredients and stir well. Then add large chunk, or mold, of ice. Mellow for 2 hours, stirring often.

Nancy Montgomery Beebe
(Mrs. Michael)

SPARKLING RUM FRUIT PUNCH

Yield: 10 quarts

6 ounces frozen lemonade
6 ounces frozen limeade
6 ounces frozen orange juice
12 ounces apricot nectarine
  juice, chilled
½ cup grenadine

1½ cups white rum
5 cups crushed ice
5 cups club soda
1 quart raspberry or pineapple
  sherbet

Mix undiluted frozen juices together. Add next three ingredients and mix well. Refrigerate until ready to serve. Add ice and soda water; float large spoonfuls of sherbet on top and serve immediately.

Jeri Dyer Edgar
(Mrs. Joseph H., Jr.)

PARTY PUNCH

Serves: 20
3½ quarts

1 quart cranberry juice
1 quart unsweetened pineapple
  juice
1 (6-ounce) can frozen orange
  juice, defrosted

1 (6-ounce) can frozen lemonade,
  defrosted
1 quart ginger ale
Ice cubes

Mix all ingredients together, except ginger ale and ice cubes. Add ginger ale and ice cubes just before serving.

Susan Messia Harrod
(Mrs. Peter E.)

STRAWBERRY WINE SLUSH

Serves: 4 to 6

6 ounces frozen lemonade
1⅓ cups sauterne
16 ice cubes

8 ounces frozen strawberries
  (whole and unsweetened) or
1 pint fresh strawberries

Place all ingredients in blender and blend at high speed until thick. Can be made one week in advance and frozen until ready to use. Serve in wine glasses with a sprig of mint.

Kathleen Foshay Hanson
(Mrs. Robert)

EGG NOG

Yield: 1½ gallons

12 eggs, separated
½ cup sugar
2 quarts medium cream
1 quart milk
1½ cups sugar
26 ounces whiskey

8 ounces rum
6 ounces brandy
6 ounces sherry
½ cup sugar
Nutmeg

Beat egg yolks. Continue beating continuously while slowly adding the milk, cream, sugar and liquor. Beat egg whites until stiff. Add the additional ½ cup sugar to egg whites. Fold into first mixture. Refrigerate and keep indefinitely. Serve cold with a shake of nutmeg.

Alden Horton

RUSSIAN TEA

Serves: 8
20 cups

10 tea bags
8 cups water
8 cups water
1 to 1½ cups sugar
1 tablespoon cloves
1 tablespoon crushed cinnamon
   sticks

Juice of one lemon
Juice of six oranges or
1 (6-ounce) can of diluted orange
   juice

Pour eight cups of boiling water over tea bags. Steep at least three minutes. In a separate pan, add sugar to the other eight cups of hot water. Wrap cloves and cinnamon sticks in cheesecloth and add to pan of sugar and water. Bring to a boil. Remove spices and combine all ingredients.

Antoinette Figuers Pierce
(Mrs. Thomas)

YARMOUTH SPICED TEA

Serves: 50
40 cups

5 cups sugar
2 quarts water
2 cinnamon sticks
12 ounces frozen orange juice
6 ounces frozen orange juice

6 ounces frozen lemonade
6 quarts water
1 cup tea leaves
4 cups boiling water

Make syrup.

Boil sugar, two quarts water and cinnamon sticks for five minutes; add orange juice and lemonade, then six quarts water.

Steep tea leaves in four cups boiling water for five minutes. Add this mixture to the above mixture just before serving.

Candy MacDonald Gibbons
(Mrs. Albert E., Jr.)

HORS D'OEUVRES

ASPARAGUS CANAPÉS

Serves: 25

20 slices thin white bread
3 ounces bleu cheese
1 (8-ounce) package cream
  cheese

1 egg
20 spears canned asparagus
½ cup melted butter

Trim crusts from bread and flatten with rolling pin. Blend cheeses and egg to workable consistency and spread evenly on each slice of bread. Place one asparagus spear on each slice; roll and secure with toothpicks. Dip in melted butter to coat thoroughly, place on cookie sheet and freeze. When firmly frozen, slice into bite size pieces. Place on cookie sheet and bake at 400 degrees for 15 minutes or until lightly browned. Can be cut and frozen in bags until ready to cook.

Susan Lechman Oestreicher
(Mrs. Charles R.)

ARTICHOKE SQUARES

Yield: 40 squares

2 (6-ounce) jars marinated
  artichoke hearts
1 small onion, finely chopped
5 eggs
½ cup seasoned bread crumbs
⅛ teaspoon pepper
1 clove garlic, crushed

¼ teaspoon salt
3 tablespoons chopped parsley
  (or 1 tablespoon dried)
Dash hot pepper sauce
2 cups shredded cheese, Cheddar
  or Monterey Jack

Drain artichokes, reserving marinade from 1 jar. Sauté onion in marinade. Cut up artichokes. Beat eggs and add crumbs and seasonings. Stir in cheese, sautéed onion and artichokes. Turn into greased 11 x 7-inch baking pan. Bake at 325 degrees for 30 minutes. Cool slightly before cutting into squares.

Nancy Montgomery Beebe
(Mrs. Michael)

CALIFORNIA CRISPIES

Yield: 18 pieces

3 medium cucumbers
1 avocado
1 (3-ounce) package cream
cheese, softened
2 tablespoons finely chopped
onions
2 tablespoons finely chopped
radishes or water chestnuts

1 tablespoon toasted sesame
seeds
1½ teaspoons seasoned salt
1 tablespoon wine vinegar
¼ teaspoon ginger
Chopped parsley or paprika

Peel cucumbers and score with a fork. Slice into 1-inch pieces. Scoop out some of seeds. Cut, peel and mash avocado, then blend with cheese. Mix remaining ingredients, except cucumber, with cheese and avocado. Spoon into center of cucumber slices. Chill. Just before serving sprinkle with parsley or paprika.

Nancy Montgomery Beebe
(Mrs. Michael)

MINI-QUICHE APPETIZER

Yield: 24

3 ounces cream cheese, softened
½ cup butter or margarine,
softened
1 cup flour
¼ teaspoon salt
4 to 6 slices bacon

1 small onion, chopped
½ cup shredded Swiss cheese
2 eggs
½ cup milk
Dash of nutmeg
Dash of pepper

Cut cream cheese and butter or margarine into flour. Add salt, blend well and chill 1 hour. Divide into small balls and press into miniature muffin tins. These shells can be refrigerated and filled later. When ready to fill, cook bacon until crisp, drain well and dice. Using a little bacon fat sauté onion until limp. Put a few pieces of bacon and onion into shell and add a pinch of Swiss cheese. Beat eggs, milk and spices together. Pour about 1 tablespoon into each shell and bake in 450-degree oven for 10 minutes; then reduce temperature to 350 degrees and bake 10 more minutes. These can be baked and frozen and reheated in a 350-degree oven.

Susan Welky Corey
(Mrs. John B.)

ANTIPASTO

Serves: 10

1 (12-ounce) bottle chili sauce
1 (14-ounce) bottle catsup
½ tablespoon Worcestershire sauce
Juice of ½ lemon
1 tablespoon prepared horseradish
1 tablespoon vinegar
2 (7-ounce) cans white tuna, broken, drained

1 (8-ounce) jar sweet pickles, drained, chopped
1 (4½-ounce) jar pickled cocktail onions, drained
1 (4-ounce) can button mushrooms, drained
1 (8-ounce) jar hot dill cauliflower, drained, chopped
1 (4½-ounce) jar stuffed olives, drained

Mix all ingredients in a large bowl with tight fitting lid. Taste. Can add more lemon juice, catsup or chili sauce to taste.

Sara Koirth Boxer
(Mrs. Daniel)

ANTOJITOS
(STUFFED TORTILLAS)

Yield: 32 pieces

6 (8-inch) flour tortillas
2 (3-ounce) packages cream cheese, softened
4 ounces Monterey Jack cheese, shredded

½ cup diced green chilies
¼ cup chopped, pitted black olives
2 tablespoons butter or margarine, melted

Spread tortillas with about 2 tablespoons cream cheese and 2 tablespoons shredded Monterey Jack cheese. Sprinkle with chilies and olives. Stack tortillas in twos, one on top of the other. Preheat oven to 400 degrees. Roll each stack tightly like a jelly roll, cut into 1-inch thick slices and place on cookie sheet. Brush with butter and bake for 10 minutes or until lightly browned. They freeze well.

Kathleen Foshay Hanson
(Mrs. Robert)

PEANUT KISSES

Yield: 36

1 (8-ounce) package cream
  cheese, softened
½ cup creamed cottage cheese
3 tablespoons drained pickle
  relish

4 to 5 midget gherkin pickles,
  cut into ¼-inch pieces
1 cup coarsely chopped salted
  peanuts

Beat cream cheese until smooth. Add creamed cottage cheese and relish. Chill until firm enough to handle. Using a heaping teaspoon of the cheese mixture, shape it into a ball around a piece of gherkin. Roll each ball in the peanuts. Refrigerate until serving time.

Gertrude Lane Potter
(Mrs. Charles W.)

BACON DATE ROLL-UPS

Serves: 8 to 10

1 (8-ounce) package pitted
  whole dates

Brown sugar
Bacon

With a small teaspoon, stuff each date with brown sugar. Cut each slice of bacon into 4 pieces and wrap 1 piece around stuffed date and secure with toothpick. Broil until sugar melts and bacon is crisp.

Carol Potter Day
(Mrs. Richard B.)

CHILI RELLENOS

Serves: 6

4 to 6 ounces longhorn or
  Cheddar cheese
2 (4-ounce) cans whole green
  chili peppers, peeled
1 egg
¼ cup milk

½ cup flour
⅛ teaspoon salt
⅛ teaspoon pepper
Dash garlic powder
Oil

Cut cheese into 3-inch strips and stuff each chili pepper with one strip. Beat the egg with milk. Add flour and spices. Mix well. The batter should have a heavy consistency so it will cling to the peppers. Dip the stuffed peppers into the batter and place in 1 to 2 inches of hot oil. Fry until both sides are deep golden brown and cheese is melted. Drain well and serve immediately.

Julianne Radkowski Opperman
(Mrs. John R.)

SALMON PARTY LOG

Serves: 8 to 10

2 cups canned salmon
1 (8-ounce) package cream
cheese, softened
1 tablespoon lemon juice
2 teaspoons grated onion
1 teaspoon prepared horseradish

¼ teaspoon salt
1 teaspoon liquid smoke
seasoning (optional)
½ cup chopped walnuts or
pecans
3 tablespoons snipped parsley

Drain and flake salmon, removing skin and bones. Combine salmon with next 6 ingredients and mix well. Chill several hours. Combine nuts and parsley. Shape salmon mixture into 8 x 2-inch log and roll in nut mixture. Chill well. Serve with crisp crackers.

Lisabeth Lepoff

SWEET AND SOUR MEATBALLS

Yield: 6 dozen

2 pounds ground round steak
6 tablespoons chopped parsley
2 cups buttered bread crumbs
2 tablespoons grated onion
2 eggs, well-beaten

Salt, to taste
Pepper, to taste
2 tablespoons butter or
margarine

Combine first 7 ingredients, shape into 1-inch balls and sauté in butter or margarine.

3 tablespoons cornstarch
1 cup vinegar
1 cup sugar
3 drops hot pepper sauce
1 tablespoon Worcestershire
sauce

2 green peppers, diced
1 red pepper, diced
1 (20-ounce) can pineapple
chunks, undrained
1 (12-ounce) jar of pickled
cauliflower, drained

Combine cornstarch, vinegar and sugar and cook until clear. Add remaining ingredients, mix well and pour over meatballs. Bake in 300 to 325-degree oven for 30 minutes. Serve hot in chafing dish.

Kathleen Foshay Hanson
(Mrs. Robert)

TREASURE BITS

Yield: 3 dozen

1 pound ground beef
½ teaspoon salt
¼ teaspoon pepper
¼ cup minced onions

1 egg
½ cup Italian bread crumbs
¼ to ½ pound bleu cheese

Break up meat with a fork in a mixing bowl, add remaining ingredients except cheese and mix well. Set aside. Shape bleu cheese into 20 tiny balls, then shape beef mixture around them. Bake in 375-degree oven until done, about 30 minutes.

Sauce

¼ cup juices from meatball
   cooking
1 tablespoon flour

¼ cup water
½ cup sour cream

Stir flour into meat juices and mix until smooth. Stir in water and cook until slightly thickened. Stir in sour cream and cook until hot, but not boiling. Add meatballs and serve. Serve these in a chafing dish with cocktail picks. Meatballs freeze well. Do not freeze sauce.

Gail Young Robinson
(Mrs. David E.)

PEACH MELBA

Yield: 2½ cups

2 (8-ounce) packages cream
   cheese, softened
1 (16-ounce) can peaches,
   drained

2 Kiwi
Swedish gingersnaps

In a food processor or blender, combine cream cheese and peaches. Garnish with sliced kiwi and serve with Swedish gingersnaps.

Carol Potter Day
(Mrs. Richard B.)

DOLMATHES
(Stuffed Grapevine Leaves)

Serves: 16 to 18

⅓ cup rice
½ cup chicken, beef or lamb
   broth
2 pounds lean ground lamb or
   1 pound lean ground beef and
   1 pound lean ground pork
1 large onion, chopped
2 cloves garlic, finely minced
½ cup chopped fresh parsley
2 tablespoons chopped fresh mint
   or 1 teaspoon dried mint

¼ teaspoon ground allspice
1 teaspoon salt
½ teaspoon pepper
Juice of 1 lemon
¼ cup catsup
1 large jar grapevine leaves
   (California)
2 cups meat broth

Soften rice by letting it come to a boil in ½ cup of chicken or any meat broth. Set aside to cool while preparing meat mixture. Combine cooled rice and remaining ingredients except grape leaves and the 2 cups meat broth. Remove grape leaves from jar and thoroughly rinse them several times in hot water. Drain in colander. Snip stems with scissors. Take about one tablespoon of meat mixture and lay it on a grape leaf. Fold over the sides and roll up snugly. Arrange in bottom of a 6-quart Dutch oven. Continue rolling leaves until all meat mixture is used up. There will be several layers of rolled leaves in the pot. Place a heavy plate on top of leaves, pour about 2 cups of meat broth over all. Cover tightly and cook on medium-low heat for 1 hour. Serve with sauce if desired. Freezes well; may be prepared a couple of days in advance.

Sauce for Dolmathes

3 eggs, separated
Juice of 1 lemon

Broth from cooking dolmathes

Beat egg whites until stiff, add yolks and beat until well blended. Slowly add the juice of the lemon and continue beating. Gradually add hot broth and stir over low heat until sauce thickens.

Helene M. Giftos
(Mrs. Sarando P.)

COUSIN MOLLY'S PEPPER JAM

Serves: 12 to 16

1 (10-ounce) jar pineapple
  preserves
1 (10-ounce) jar apple jelly
2½ ounces prepared horseradish

1 ounce dry mustard
½ teaspoon cracked pepper
2 (8-ounce) packages cream
  cheese, softened

Mix first 5 ingredients together and pour over cream cheese. Serve with crackers or use as a sauce with ham. This is enough jam to cover 32 ounces of cream cheese. The recipe keeps well in the refrigerator.

Pamela Merkel Whipple
(Mrs. James C.)

JALAPEÑO PEPPER SPREAD

Yield: 2½ cups

2 (8-ounce) packages cream
  cheese
1 shallot, minced
1 clove garlic, minced
1 tablespoon chopped parsley

1 jalapeño pepper, seeded
  and minced
1 egg yolk
Salt and pepper, to taste

Mix all ingredients together and serve with crackers.

Judith Bishop Condren
(Mrs. Arthur)

POOR MAN'S SALMON MOUSSE

Serves: 12

1 (10¾-ounce) can tomato soup
1 (8-ounce) package cream
  cheese
½ ounce gelatin dissolved in
  ⅓ cup hot water
1 (7-ounce) can light tuna in oil,
  drained

1 cup chopped celery
1 teaspoon steak sauce
Salt, to taste
Pepper, to taste
1 cup mayonnaise
Cucumber slices

Mix soup, cheese and gelatin in pan over low heat until cream cheese has melted. Add tuna, celery, steak sauce, salt, pepper, and mayonnaise. Grease 4-cup mold with mayonnaise; add mixture and chill. Decorate with slices of cucumber.

Barbara Morris Goodbody
(Mrs. James B.)

THREE CHEESE SQUARES

Yield: 40 squares

½ cup butter
½ cup flour
6 large eggs
1 cup milk
1 teaspoon salt
1 teaspoon sugar

1 teaspoon baking powder
1 (3-ounce) package cream
cheese, softened
2 cups cottage cheese
16 ounces Monterey Jack cheese,
cubed

Melt butter in small saucepan. Add flour and cook until smooth. Beat eggs in large bowl. Add milk, salt, sugar, baking powder and butter-flour mixture. Add cheeses and stir until well blended. Pour into well greased 13 x 9 x 2-inch baking pan. Bake at 350 degrees for 45 minutes.

Nancy Montgomery Beebe
(Mrs. Michael)

SPICY CHEESE TWISTS

Yield: 3½ dozen

1½ cups flour
1 teaspoon dry mustard
½ teaspoon baking powder
½ teaspoon salt
½ cup shortening

1 cup shredded Cheddar cheese
¼ teaspoon hot pepper sauce
⅓ cup cold water
2 tablespoons flour
2 teaspoons paprika

Sift first 4 ingredients together; cut in shortening, then beat in next 3 ingredients, mixing well. Sprinkle work area with flour and paprika, place dough on top of flour and paprika and roll out into a 10 x 15-inch rectangle; turn dough rectangle over and cut in half. Cut the halves in ¾-inch wide strips. Twist each strip 2 or 3 times and place on ungreased baking sheet, pressing down the end of each strip. Bake in 450-degree oven 8 to 10 minutes. May be frozen and reheated.

Helen Koniares Cleaves
(Mrs. Robert E., III)

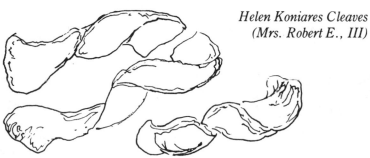

CURRIED CHEESE ON RYE

Yield: 36

13 ounces sharp Cheddar cheese,
  shredded
6 medium green onions, chopped
  (tops included)
1 (4.2-ounce) can ripe olives,
  sliced

¼ to ½ teaspoon curry powder
  (to taste)
Mayonnaise (enough to obtain
  spreading consistency)
1 (8-ounce) loaf party rye bread,
  sliced

Mix first 5 ingredients. Spread on rye slices. Bake at 350 degrees for 5 to 10 minutes or until cheese melts. Serve hot.

Rebecca Bilbrey Sweeney
(Mrs. Eugene G., Jr.)

JANE'S CHEESE PUFFS

Yield: 100

2 (8-ounce) packages cream
  cheese
½ cup mayonnaise
8 scallions, including stems,
  chopped
¼ cup grated Parmesan cheese

Dash of hot pepper sauce
1 (20-ounce) loaf firm bread
Butter
Additional grated Parmesan
  cheese

Mix first 5 ingredients together and refrigerate. Cut out rounds of bread with small 1-inch cookie cutter, butter one side and brown under broiler. Generously spread cheese mixture on unbuttered side and dip in more Parmesan cheese. Broil and serve. Can be made ahead and frozen, thaw slightly before broiling.

Dee-Dee Dana Bradford
(Mrs. John W.)

BAKED BRIE

Serves: 4

1 (4½-ounce) can Brie
1 tablespoon butter

2 tablespoons toasted slivered
  almonds

Place Brie in a small soufflé dish (approximately the same size as the cheese). Place butter on top of Brie. Sprinkle the almonds on top. Bake at 325 degrees for 15 to 20 minutes. Stir and serve with thinly sliced French bread like fondue.

Patricia Pugh Britt
(Mrs. Michael E.)

CHEESE BOMBAY

Serves: 6 to 8

1 (8-ounce) package cream
  cheese
1 (6-ounce) package Cheddar
  cheese, shredded
2 teaspoons sherry wine

½ teaspoon curry powder
½ cup chopped chutney
2 tablespoons minced fresh
  scallions

Mix softened cheeses together until well blended. Add wine and curry powder
and mix well. Place on platter and arrange into a pie-shaped wedge about 1-inch
high. Frost completely with chutney. Sprinkle scallions over the top. This can
be made several days ahead and refrigerated.

Kathleen Foshay Hanson
(Mrs. Robert)

GREEN PELICAN CHEESE

Yield: A Lot

2 pounds Cheddar cheese,
  shredded
1 pound bleu cheese, shredded
1 pound cream cheese, softened
2 cups dry sherry

5 tablespoons Worcestershire
  sauce
1½ garlic cloves (or more,
  to taste), crushed

Blend cream cheese with sherry. Add shredded cheese to cream cheese mixture. Add Worcestershire sauce and garlic. Pack in jars or crocks. Refrigerate
2 weeks to age. Serve with crackers. Cheese can be frozen.

Jean Potter Benton
(Mrs. Don Carlos III)

YOUNGSTOWN CLUB CHEESE

Yield: 3 pounds

2 pounds 13 ounces cold pack
  Cheddar cheese food
3 ounces prepared horseradish

4 tablespoons dry mustard
2½ ounces Worcestershire sauce
2½ ounces port wine

Allow the Cheddar cheese food to stand in a warm place until soft. Add the
horseradish and dry mustard and mix at low speed until combined. Combine the
Worcestershire sauce and the port and very slowly add to the cheese mixture.
Continue mixing on low speed until well blended. Pack in crocks and refrigerate.
Serve with crackers.

Patricia Pugh Britt
(Mrs. Michael E.)

GREEK ZUCCHINI

Yield: 48 (2-inch) squares

3 cups finely diced zucchini
1 cup biscuit mix
½ medium onion, chopped
⅓ cup grated Parmesan cheese
2 tablespoons parsley
½ teaspoon salt

½ teaspoon oregano
1 garlic clove, minced
½ cup vegetable oil
4 eggs, beaten
8 ounces feta cheese, crumbled

Mix first 9 ingredients; add eggs and feta cheese and mix well. Spread mixture into a buttered 9 x 13 x 2-inch pan and bake in a 350-degree oven for 40 minutes. Cool slightly and cut into 2-inch squares and serve warm. Can be cut into larger pieces and used as an entree or can be served as a vegetable with a roast. Can be baked and frozen ahead of time. To serve, place frozen squares in 350-degree oven for 15 minutes.

Joan Paradis Fortin
(Mrs. Roger)

MARINATED BROCCOLI

Serves: 24

3 bunches fresh broccoli
1 cup cider vinegar
1½ cups vegetable oil
1 tablespoon sugar

1 tablespoon dill weed
1 teaspoon salt
1 teaspoon pepper
½ teaspoon garlic powder

Cut broccoli heads into bite-size pieces with 1-inch stems, discard remaining stems. In a bowl combine oil, vinegar and spices. Place broccoli in a large plastic bag, pour in the marinade and seal bag tightly. Place bag in a bowl, in case it leaks, and refrigerate 24 hours, turning the bag frequently to distribute the marinade. Drain well and blot with paper towel to absorb excess oil. Serve chilled.

Mary Beth Christman Sweeney
(Mrs. John J.)

CHINESE BARBECUED SPARERIBS

Yield: About 20 ribs

2 pounds lean spareribs, cut
 into 2-inch lengths
Salt
½ cup water
⅓ cup soy sauce
⅓ cup light brown sugar
2 tablespoons cider vinegar

¼ teaspoon freshly grated
 ginger root
1 to 2 cloves garlic, very
 finely minced
1 tablespoon cornstarch
2 tablespoons water

Place the lightly salted ribs in a roasting pan with the ½ cup of water. Cover and bake at 350 degrees for 1¼ hours. Drain off all water and grease, cool slightly, and cut into individual ribs. Can do this several days ahead. Combine the soy sauce, sugar, vinegar, ginger and garlic in a saucepan and bring to a boil stirring constantly. Boil one minute. Combine cornstarch and water well and add to the sauce. Cook over medium heat stirring constantly until sauce is thick and clear. Cool slightly and then pour over ribs to coat completely. Place coated ribs in a flat baking dish and bake for 20 minutes at 350 degrees.

Patricia Pugh Britt
(Mrs. Michael E.)

CHINESE CHICKEN WINGS

Serves: 8 to 10

½ cup soy sauce
1 cup pineapple juice
1 garlic clove, mashed
2 tablespoons minced onion

1 teaspoon ginger
¼ cup brown sugar
1 cup beer
36 chicken wings

Mix all the above ingredients, except wings, until sugar is dissolved. Split chicken wings at joints, do not use tips (can be used for stock) and add to marinade. Marinate for one hour at room temperature. Place on buttered baking sheet, 1-inch apart, and bake for 30 minutes in 375-degree oven.

Merryl Gillespie Hodgson
(Mrs. Donald G.)

CHINESE DELIGHTS

Yield: 4 dozen

Pastry

1 cup butter	2 cups flour
1 (8-ounce) package cream cheese	1 egg yolk
	2 teaspoons cream or milk
Pinch of salt	

Mix butter, cream cheese and salt until well blended and smooth, then work flour in with hands. Chill dough several hours or overnight.

Filling

1 pound lean ground pork	2 teaspoons freshly grated ginger root
½ cup finely chopped cooked shrimp or crabmeat	2 tablespoons soy sauce
1 teaspoon salt	1 small garlic clove, crushed
½ cup minced water chestnuts	1 egg
2 green onions, minced	¼ cup fine breadcrumbs

Cook and stir pork until whitish in color; add remaining ingredients and mix well. Chill several hours. Roll pastry out into 16 x 12-inch rectangle and cut into 2-inch squares. Place teaspoon of filling on one edge of pastry; roll, seal and crimp edges. Mix egg yolk and cream or milk together and brush tops of Chinese delights. Place on ungreased baking sheet and bake in 375-degree oven for 25 to 30 minutes.

Hope Palmer Bramhall
(Mrs. Peter T. C.)

PICKLED PINEAPPLE

Yield: a lot

2 (20-ounce) cans pineapple chunks	1¼ cups sugar
	8 cloves
¾ cup reserved syrup	1 cinnamon stick
¾ cup vinegar	

The day before serving drain pineapple and set aside. Mix syrup, vinegar, sugar, cloves and cinnamon stick and simmer 10 minutes. Add pineapple and bring to a boil. Refrigerate mixture 24 hours. Drain before serving.

Mary Jane Shaw
(Mrs. Bradley T.)

EGGROLLS

Yield: 24 large eggrolls

Filling

1 cup small tofu cubes, ground pork, shrimp or diced chicken	2 garlic cloves, minced
3 cups shredded Chinese cabbage	1 cup chopped fresh spinach
1 cup chopped mushrooms	2 tablespoons sesame oil
2 cups mung bean sprouts	1 tablespoon ginger
½ cup diced celery	¼ cup soy sauce
1 large onion, chopped	1 tablespoon cornstarch
1 cup oil	1 (16-ounce) package eggroll wrappers

Cook your choice of tofu, pork, shrimp or chicken; drain and combine with next 11 ingredients in a large pot. Cook on high heat, stirring often until cabbage wilts, about 5 minutes. Heat ½-inch of oil in electric frypan or use deep fryer. While oil is heating, assemble eggrolls. Moisten the wrapper with water. Place filling in center of wrapper, fold in sides and roll. Fry until evenly brown. Drain on paper. Keep warm until ready to serve or freeze. Reheat frozen eggrolls in 375-degree oven. Filling can be made ahead of time, but do not assemble eggrolls until ready to fry or they will get soggy.

Nina Vasques Kosack
(Mrs. Richard J.)

CHEESE STUFFED MUSHROOMS

Serves: 6 to 8

40 medium-size fresh mushroom caps	5 tablespoons milk
½ cup butter	½ teaspoon garlic powder
8 ounces cream cheese, softened	2 tablespoons finely chopped, fresh chives
¾ cup grated Parmesan cheese	

Wash and dry mushrooms. Melt butter in small saucepan. Dip each mushroom in butter, coating well. Place the buttered caps on a cookie sheet and set aside. In a medium-size mixing bowl add remaining ingredients and mix well. Place a generous teaspoon of mixture in each mushroom cap, letting it mound instead of tapping it down. Bake in a preheated 350-degree oven for 15 minutes or until browned. Serve at once. May be prepared ahead and frozen. To serve, bake the mushrooms while still frozen. Add about 5 more minutes to baking time.

Linda Frinsko
(Mrs. Paul)

BEST MARINATED MUSHROOMS EVER

Serves: 8

2 pounds large mushrooms,
  washed and halved
1½ cups water
1 cup cider vinegar
½ cup oil
1 clove garlic, halved
2 tablespoons salt

1 teaspoon oregano
1 teaspoon thyme
1 teaspoon basil
1 or 2 teaspoons ground
  peppercorns
2 tablespoons dried parsley

Place mushrooms in a large casserole. Pour water and vinegar over mushrooms; add spices and oil. Stir and mix well. Cover and refrigerate. Marinate two full days, stirring occasionally each day. Drain off liquid and serve.

Karen Ker Day
(Mrs. Thomas)

STUFFED MUSHROOMS

Yield: 16

16 large mushrooms, caps and
  stems
2 anchovies, finely chopped
1 onion, finely chopped
2 teaspoons chopped parsley
2 tablespoons olive oil

4 tablespoons cracker crumbs
1 egg, slightly beaten
⅔ cup olive oil
½ teaspoon salt
½ teaspoon pepper

Chop mushroom stems and set aside. Sauté anchovies, onion, and parsley in olive oil until onions are limp; add stems and cook slowly 5 minutes more. Remove from heat and cool; add egg and crumbs and mix thoroughly. Fill mushroom caps with mixture and place in shallow baking pan. Pour olive oil over caps and sprinkle with salt and pepper. Place in 400-degree oven for 20 minutes.

Sandra Edson Tuttle
(Mrs. Richard)

RUSSIAN CHICKEN LIVERS

Yield: 4 to 5 dozen

Pastry

1 (8-ounce) package cream
  cheese, softened
1 cup butter or margarine,
  softened
2¼ cups flour

1 teaspoon salt
1 egg white
1 egg, slightly beaten
1 tablespoon water

Beat cream cheese and butter or margarine with mixer until smooth and creamy. Gradually mix in flour and salt with mixer on low speed. On lightly floured board, knead dough until it just clings together. Place dough in waxed paper and refrigerate 3 to 4 hours or overnight. If overnight, let stand at room temperature at least ½ hour before rolling. Prepare filling. Assembly: On floured board, roll out ¼ of dough at a time into a 20 x 4-inch rectangle. Place 1 cup of filling in a row ¾ to 1-inch thick down center of dough. Draw one edge over the filling and press slightly. Moisten the other edge with egg white and draw up to seal the filling in. This should form a roll 20-inches long. Roll the filled pastry onto a cookie sheet seam side down. Repeat until all the dough and filling are used up. (4 rolls). Chill at least 1 hour. Cut slantwise into 1-inch slices, separating slightly. Mix water and slightly beaten egg. Brush on pastry. Bake in 325-degree oven for 25 to 30 minutes or until lightly browned. These turnovers may be frozen and then baked while still frozen; allow extra baking time if frozen.

Filling

1 cup butter
2 onions, finely chopped
1 clove garlic, minced
1 pound chicken livers
2 eggs, hard-boiled

2 tablespoons cognac
¼ cup finely chopped parsley
Salt and freshly ground pepper,
  to taste

Sauté onions and garlic in butter until tender; increase heat and add chicken livers. Brown quickly and cook 3 minutes, stirring frequently. Chop livers and eggs until very fine. Add cognac, parsley, salt and pepper. Mix well.

Hope Palmer Bramhall
(Mrs. Peter T.C.)

CHOPPED CHICKEN LIVERS HOLLISTER

Serves: 6 to 8

1 pound chicken livers
2 medium onions, divided
2 eggs, hard boiled
1 garlic clove, minced
1 or 2 tablespoons sour cream

1 teaspoon salt
¼ teaspoon freshly ground black
   pepper
Watercress, cherry tomatoes,
   hard-boiled egg yolks

Wash the livers and place in a pan with 1 onion and enough water to cover. Bring the water to a boil, lower heat and cook 10 minutes. Drain and discard the onion. Peel and chop the hard boiled eggs. Chop the other onion. Place the liver, eggs, onion, and garlic in a large wooden chopping bowl. Chop until smooth and blend in the sour cream, salt and pepper. Chill. Garnish with watercress, cherry tomatoes, and sieved egg yolk. Can be made 1 day ahead.

The Committee

LIVER PATÉ

Serves: 6 to 8

½ teaspoon unflavored gelatin
½ cup chicken broth
½ pound chicken livers
½ cup butter, softened
2 tablespoons chopped onion
¼ teaspoon nutmeg
½ teaspoon dry mustard

⅛ teaspoon cloves
¼ cup liquid drained from
   cooking livers
1 teaspoon brandy
Salt
Lettuce leaves

Soften gelatin in chicken broth, heat over hot water until dissolved. Pour into 1½ cup mold, chill until firm. Cook livers in salted water to cover about 10 minutes, drain, reserving liquid. Cut liver into small pieces and put in blender with butter, onion, nutmeg, mustard, cloves, liquid and brandy. Blend until smooth. Season to taste with salt. Pour over firm gelatin, chill. Unmold to serve. Serve at room temperature on a bed of lettuce leaves.

Kathleen Crowe Sardegna
(Mrs. Carl)

CHOCOCHIP PATÉ

Yield: 2 cups

2 (8-ounce) packages cream
  cheese, softened
1 (12-ounce) bag semi-sweet
  chocolate chips

Dark cherries, to garnish
Parsley, to garnish

In a food processor or blender, combine cream cheese and chocolate chips. Garnish with dark cherries and parsley. Serve with stoned wheat cracker.

Carol Potter Day
(Mrs. Richard B.)

CHESTNUT BACON ROLLS

Serves: 6 to 8

1 pound bacon
1 (6-ounce) can whole water
  chestnuts

½ cup mayonnaise
4 tablespoons chili sauce
4 tablespoons brown sugar

Cut bacon strips in half. Roll a piece of bacon around a water chestnut and secure with toothpicks. Place side by side in an 8 x 8 x 2-inch baking dish. Combine remaining ingredients and mix well. Pour over bacon and chestnut rolls. Bake in 300-degree oven for 1 hour. Drain excess fat before serving.

Sharon Staples Alexander
(Mrs. Alan R.)

SURPRISE DIP

Yield: 2½ cups

1 (10-ounce) package frozen
  chopped spinach, thawed
1 pint sour cream
1 (8-ounce) package cream
  cheese, softened

⅓ to ½ cup chopped onion
¼ teaspoon Worcestershire
  sauce
½ teaspoon seasoned salt

Drain all moisture from spinach, squeezing with hands, if necessary. In blender or food processor mix sour cream and cream cheese until well blended. Add remaining ingredients including spinach and mix well. Refrigerate for several hours in covered container before serving. Serve with corn chips or salted wheat crackers.

Mary Beth Christman Sweeney
(Mrs. John J.)

CURRY DIP FOR RAW VEGETABLES

¾ cup mayonnaise
4½ teaspoons grated onion
4½ teaspoons catsup

4½ teaspoons honey
1½ teaspoons fresh lemon juice
1½ teaspoons curry powder

Combine all the ingredients and refrigerate overnight. Serve with raw vegetables as an hors d'oeuvre. This dip can also be used as a dressing for crabmeat and avocado salad.

Eileen A. Pugh
(Mrs. Richard F.)

VEGETABLE PLATTER

Serves: 12

1 loaf round rye bread, unsliced

Vegetables

Brussels sprouts, cooked
Carrots
Cucumber
Turnip
Cauliflower
Green peppers
Red peppers

Celery
Cherry tomatoes
12 deviled eggs
Black olives
Fresh parsley
Nasturtium blossoms

Dip

1 cup mayonnaise
1 cup sour cream
1 teaspoon Beau Monde
   seasoning

1 teaspoon dill weed
1 teaspoon minced parsley
1 tablespoon minced onion

Hollow out bread to resemble a bowl. Set in center of large platter, tray or flat basket and arrange vegetables around the bread; place Brussels sprouts and halved deviled eggs around edges. Mix all dip ingredients together and place in hollowed out bread. Remaining bread can be cut into bite-size pieces and used as dippers along with the vegetables. Garnish as desired with olives, parsley and nasturtium blossoms.

Linda Armstrong Andrews
(Mrs. Richard C.)

COCKTAIL CAULIFLOWER

Serves: 8 to 12

1 medium size head fresh
   cauliflower
1 egg, additional egg may be
   needed

2 cups cornflake crumbs

Cut cauliflower into flowerettes and discard stem. Beat egg lightly. Dip flowerettes into egg and then into cornflake crumbs. Place on lightly greased cookie sheet and bake at 350 degrees for 20 minutes or until crisp.

Tanya Fogelsohn Shapiro
(Mrs. Gregory)

POTTED SHRIMP

Serves: 4 to 6

2 medium onions, thinly sliced
⅓ cup fresh lemon juice
2 cups salad dressing (not
   mayonnaise)
1 cup sour cream

1½ tablespoons sugar
1 pound bag small frozen shrimp
   (cleaned and precooked)
Paprika
Cocktail rye

Mix first six ingredients together and place in a covered casserole. Put in the refrigerator and stir daily for 3 days. Garnish with paprika and serve with cocktail rye.

Patricia Pugh Britt
(Mrs. Michael E.)

HOT CRABMEAT DIP

Yield: 1½ cups

8 ounces cream cheese, softened
1 tablespoon chopped chives
2 (6½-ounce) cans crabmeat,
   drained
2 tablespoons finely chopped
   onion
½ teaspoon prepared horseradish

½ teaspoon garlic salt
Pepper, to taste
Hot pepper sauce, to taste
½ cup chopped walnuts or
   pecans
Butter

Blend first 8 ingredients together and spoon into a greased 1-quart baking dish. Top with nuts that have been sautéed in butter until brown. Bake in 375-degree oven for 25 minutes or until bubbling. Can be frozen; thaw before baking.

Jeri Dyer Edgar
(Mrs. Joseph H., Jr.)

FISH DIP

Serves: 12

1 pound haddock
2 tablespoons chopped pimento
2 teaspoons prepared horseradish
½ cup chili sauce
1 cup mayonnaise

1 cup sour cream
¼ cup chopped celery
¼ cup chopped onion
Salt and pepper, to taste

Boil and flake haddock and allow to cool. Add remaining ingredients and refrigerate until ready to use. Serve with chips or crackers.

Joan Paradis Fortin
(Mrs. Roger)

LOBSTER DIP

Serves: 6

1 (8-ounce) package cream
  cheese
¼ cup mayonnaise
1 clove garlic, minced
1 teaspoon grated onion
1 teaspoon prepared mustard

1 teaspoon sugar
Salt, a pinch
1 (5-ounce) can lobster, flaked
3 tablespoons sherry

Melt the cream cheese over very low heat. Add the mayonnaise, garlic, onion, mustard, sugar and salt. Blend well and heat. Add lobster and sherry. Heat thoroughly and serve hot with melba toast.

Patricia Pugh Britt
(Mrs. Michael E.)

SMOKED OYSTER DIP

Yield: 2 cups

1 (8-ounce) package cream
  cheese, softened
1 tablespoon mayonnaise
1 tablespoon lemon juice

Dash of garlic salt or powder
1 (3⅔-ounce) can smoked oysters
½ cup minced ripe olives

Mix cheese and mayonnaise until creamy; add remaining ingredients and mix well. Refrigerate in covered container at least 1 hour before serving. Serve with plain crackers.

Jane Hatch Peterson

HOT ARTICHOKE DIP

Serves: 8 to 10

2 (14-ounce) cans artichoke
  hearts
1 cup mayonnaise

1 cup grated Parmesan cheese
Garlic powder, to taste (optional)
Paprika

Drain artichokes and cut into quarters. Add mayonnaise and cheese and mix together. Place in a shallow baking dish and refrigerate until ready to bake. Sprinkle with paprika for color. Bake in 400-degree oven uncovered for 30 minutes. Serve with king-size corn chips or melba rounds.

Mary Kay Durland
(Mrs. Lawrence W.)

CHILI CON QUESO

Serves: 6 to 8

1 small onion, chopped
1 garlic clove, minced
2 pound box of pasteurized,
  processed cheese spread

2 (4-ounce) cans chopped green
  chilies
1 (28-ounce) can tomatoes,
  chopped, well-drained

Sauté onion and garlic; add cheese. When cheese is melted, add chilies and tomatoes. Serve with tortilla chips or bread cubes.

Anne Stockmar Upton
(Mrs. John)

HUMMUS

Serves: 6

2 cups garbanzo beans or chick
  peas
Juice of 1 lemon
6 tablespoons Sesame Tahini
1 or 2 garlic cloves, finely
  chopped

3 tablespoons olive oil
Flour tortillas, Lebanese bread
  or pita
3 lemons, cut into wedges
2 red onions, sliced

Beat first 5 ingredients in blender. Spread on tortillas, Lebanese bread, or pita and place a slice of onion on each piece after squeezing juice from lemon wedge. Roll up like jelly roll and serve.

Anne Stockmar Upton
(Mrs. John)

SOUPS

CRANBERRY ROSÉ SOUP

Serves: 6

16 ounces fresh or frozen
    cranberries
2 cups water, brought to boil
1 cup rosé wine
¾ to 1 cup sugar

1 to 1½ teaspoons allspice
1 to 2 inches cinnamon stick
1 tablespoon grated lemon rind
6 tablespoons sour cream
Toasted slivered almonds, to
    taste

Add cranberries and wine to boiling water. Cover and cook until berries pop, about 20 minutes. Stir in sugar, allspice, cinnamon stick and lemon rind and cook, stirring constantly until sugar is dissolved. Remove the cinnamon stick. Press the mixture through sieve or food mill. Return purée to pan, stirring constantly until mixture comes to a boil. If soup is too thick, add more wine. Serve hot with a tablespoon of sour cream and a sprinkle of toasted slivered almonds on top.

Shirley Thompson Leighton
(Mrs. Thomas M.)

COLD CUCUMBER SOUP

Serves: 12

5 cucumbers
Salt
½ cup chopped parsley
6 scallions, chopped
2 tablespoons dried dill

½ cup lemon juice
1 quart buttermilk
1 pint sour cream
White pepper and salt, to taste

Peel cucumbers, cut in half lengthwise, remove seeds, sprinkle with salt and drain 30 minutes. Chop cucumbers. Put in blender with parsley, scallions, dill and lemon juice. Slowly add buttermilk and sour cream. Add salt and pepper. After all ingredients are blended, chill.

Doris Martineau Stevens
(Mrs. Paul S.)

SOUPE AUX CERISES

Serves: 6

3 cups cold water
½ cup sugar
1 cinnamon stick
4 cups pitted cherries

1 tablespoon arrowroot
  (thickening agent)
⅓ cup heavy cream
¾ cup very dry red wine, chilled

Combine water, sugar and cinnamon stick in pan. Bring to boil. When sugar dissolves, add cherries. Simmer 35 minutes. Remove cinnamon stick. Add a little cold water to arrowroot and mix into a paste. Stir into soup. Bring soup almost to a boil, stirring constantly, until it is clear and slightly thickened. Chill. Stir in cream and wine just before serving.

Roselle Flynn Johnson
(Mrs. Steven M.)

CREAM OF ASPARAGUS SOUP

Serves: 4

2 pounds asparagus
1 small onion or several shallots,
  chopped
4 tablespoons butter
2 cups chicken broth

1 tablespoon lemon juice
1 cup milk or cream
1 teaspoon chopped tarragon
Salt and white pepper, to taste

Steam or boil asparagus. Cut off tips and reserve. Chop stalks into 1-inch pieces, place in blender and purée. Sauté onions in butter until soft. Purée in blender the onions, chicken broth and lemon juice. Add to blender milk or cream, tarragon, salt and pepper. Gently heat soup or chill. Carefully arrange tips on top of soup before serving.

Susan Hall Haynes
(Mrs. J. David)

AVOCADO SOUP

Serves: 4

1 (13-ounce) can vichyssoise soup
1 avocado, peeled and sliced
1 handful fresh or frozen peas,
  cooked

Shake of pepper
Shake of curry powder

Put all the ingredients in the blender and blend. Chill.

Barbara Morris Goodbody
(Mrs. James B.)

SAVORY MINESTRONE

Serves: 4

3 slices bacon, finely chopped
1 cup chopped onion
½ cup chopped celery
1 teaspoon crushed basil leaves
1 (10½-ounce) can beef broth
1 (11-ounce) can bean with bacon
  soup
1½ soup cans of water

1 (16-ounce) can tomatoes,
  undrained
½ cup uncooked ditali (small
  tube macaroni)
½ teaspoon salt
1 cup cabbage, cut into long,
  thin shreds
1 cup cubed zucchini

In large pan brown bacon. Add onion, celery and basil. Cook until tender. Stir in soups, water, tomatoes, ditali and salt. Bring to boil. Cover and reduce heat. Simmer 15 minutes. Add cabbage and zucchini. Cook 10 minutes, or until tender, stirring occasionally. It is even better reheated.

Barbara Gee Chellis
(Mrs. Thomas)

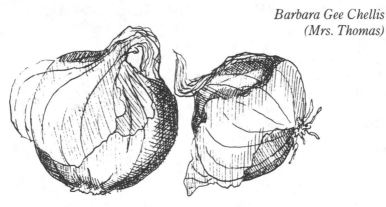

SOUPE A L'OIGNON GRATINÉE

Serves: 8

½ cup peanut oil
6 large onions, sliced
1 teaspoon thyme
1 bottle dry red wine

10 cups beef consommé
8 slices stale French bread
1½ pounds Swiss cheese,
  shredded

Heat oil in large pan. Add onions and sauté until cooked, but not brown. Add thyme and stir in wine. Bring to a boil and let soup reduce for a few minutes. Add consommé and cook uncovered for 20 minutes. Pour into 8 large ovenproof soup bowls. Top each with a slice of French bread. Sprinkle with cheese. Broil quickly until bubbling and golden. Serve at once.

Judith Bishop Condron
(Mrs. Arthur)

VEGETABLE SOUP NIVERNAISE

Serves: 6

½ cup butter
1 cup sliced carrots
1 cup sliced turnips
1 cup sliced leeks
1 cup sliced celery

1 cup sliced potatoes
1 teaspoon salt
4 cups water
1 cup heavy cream

Melt butter in deep heavy pan. Add vegetables and cover. Stew for 20 minutes. With food processor's chopping blade chop vegetables almost to purée stage. Return vegetables to pan. Add water and salt. Bring to a boil and simmer 20 minutes. Before you serve, add cream and adjust seasonings.

Roselle Flynn Johnson
(Mrs. Steven M.)

CANADIAN SPLIT PEA SOUP

Serves: 8

1 pound dried split peas
  (yellow or green)
¼ cup diced salt pork
½ cup chopped onion
2 cloves garlic, crushed
2 quarts water
2 stalks celery with leaves,
  chopped

1 ham bone or small smoked
  ham hock
1 bay leaf, crushed
2 teaspoons salt
½ teaspoon pepper
Croutons, optional

Cover peas with water and soak overnight. For a quicker method cover peas with water, bring to boil, cover pan, remove from heat and soak one hour. Sauté salt pork in large pan until crisp and browned. Remove pork and set aside. Add onion and garlic to remaining fat and sauté until golden. Add to pan the drained peas and remaining ingredients. Simmer 2 hours or until peas are tender. Strain through a food mill. Reheat, and if necessary, thin with hot water. Sprinkle with reserved diced pork when served. Add croutons if desired.

India Horton Weatherill
(Mrs. Robert H.)

MUSHROOM CHOWDER

Serves: 4

6 tablespoons butter
1 large onion, chopped
1 pound fresh mushrooms, sliced
1 quart chicken stock
2 carrots, grated
1 large potato, diced

2 celery stalks, chopped
Salt
Fresh pepper
Garlic salt
4 tablespoons barley, soaked in
   1½ cups stock

Sauté onions and mushrooms in butter until golden (about 5 minutes). Add 1 quart boiling chicken stock, carrots, potatoes, celery, salt, pepper, garlic salt and barley in stock. Boil 5 minutes. Reduce heat. Simmer 1 hour or until barley is tender.

Carol Such Bouton
(Mrs. Dale C., Jr.)

PURÉE OF CARROT SOUP

Serves: 8

3 tablespoons unsalted butter
2 pounds carrots, chopped
2 large onions, sliced
2 large potatoes, peeled and
   chopped

1 bay leaf
6 cups (or more) chicken stock
Salt and freshly ground pepper,
   to taste
Fresh parsley, minced

Melt butter in large pan over low heat. Add carrots and onions, cover with circle of waxed paper and let sweat for 8 minutes. Add potatoes and bay leaf and cover ingredients with stock. Cover and simmer until vegetables are tender, about 40 minutes. Discard bay leaf. Purée soup in batches in food processor or blender. Return to pan, season with salt and pepper and bring to boil, stirring occasionally. Garnish with parsley when served.

Sharon Smith Bushey
(Mrs. Donald J.)

SOUPE PROVENCE

Serves: 8

4 to 5 garlic cloves, minced
1 tablespoon oil
8 cups chicken broth
¾ teaspoon salt
⅛ teaspoon thyme
⅛ teaspoon sage

⅛ teaspoon pepper
3 egg yolks
½ cup light cream
Toast rounds
Parmesan cheese, grated

Sauté the minced garlic in the oil until golden. Add the broth, salt, thyme, sage and pepper and simmer for 1 hour. Beat the egg yolks and combine with the cream. Gradually add the hot soup to the egg yolk and cream mixture. Do not boil, but keep warm. Place toast rounds in the bottom of each bowl. Pour hot soup over toast rounds. Sprinkle with grated Parmesan and serve.

Eileen A. Pugh
(Mrs. Richard F.)

ZUCCHINI SOUP WITH SAUSAGE

Serves: 9

1 pound Italian sweet sausage
2 cups celery, cut into ½-inch
  angled pieces
2 pounds zucchini, cut into
  ½-inch pieces
1 cup chopped onions
2 (28-ounce) cans tomatoes

2 teaspoons salt
1 teaspoon oregano
1 teaspoon sugar
½ teaspoon basil
¼ teaspoon garlic powder
2 green peppers, cut into ½-inch
  pieces

Remove the casing from the sausage and brown in a large pan, breaking the sausage into small pieces with a fork. Drain sausage. Add celery and cook 10 minutes, stirring often. Add all remaining ingredients except green peppers. Simmer covered for 20 minutes. Add green peppers and cook for 10 more minutes.

Martha Butler Dudley
(Mrs. Richard A.)

PARSNIP CHOWDER

Serves: 6

½ cup cubed salt pork or bacon
2 cups minced onion
2 cups diced parsnips
1 cup diced potatoes
1 cup canned Italian tomatoes
  (plus liquid)

Water or vegetable juice
1 cup milk
1 cup light cream
Salt and pepper, to taste
Butter

In large pan sauté pork until brown. Remove pork and set aside. Cook onions in fat until soft. Add parsnips, potatoes, tomatoes and pork. Cover with water or juice. Simmer for 30 minutes. Stir in milk, cream, salt and pepper. Heat to boiling point. Put 1 tablespoon butter in each bowl when serving.

Cynthia Goodwin Riley
(Mrs. Brook)

FISHMONGER'S KETTLE

Yield: 10 servings

1 pound scallops
1 pound haddock
1 pound shrimp, small to
  medium size
3 quarts cold water
1 pound lobster meat, can use
  body meat
1 pound crabmeat
½ cup butter
1 pound mushrooms, sliced

3 green peppers, sliced
6 to 8 large cloves garlic
Salt and pepper, to taste
⅛ teaspoon crushed red chili
  peppers (or more, to taste)
2½ quarts marinara sauce
½ pound steamed clams,
  optional, for garnish
Linguine

Cut scallops and haddock into bite size pieces. Put scallops, haddock, shrimp into a large pot with 3 quarts cold water. Parboil until half cooked, about 15 minutes. Add the lobster and crabmeat. Remove from the heat and let stand 2 minutes. Drain the fish and reserve 1½ quarts of fish stock. In a skillet, melt butter and sauté mushrooms, green peppers and garlic. When the vegetables are barely tender, add the drained fish, salt and pepper and crushed red chili peppers. Sauté together for 5 more minutes. Return to a large pot and add approximately 1 to 1½ quarts of fish stock and 2½ quarts of marinara sauce. Heat through and serve or refrigerate. If this is made 2 or 3 days ahead of time the flavor is much improved. Before serving, steam clams and garnish each serving with at least 2 steamers. Serve over a small amount of linguine in a soup bowl.

Louie Della Valle, Jr.

FISH CHOWDER

Serves: 8

2 pounds fresh or frozen fish
    fillets (haddock, cod, halibut)
¼ pound salt pork, diced
1 cup chopped onions
6 medium potatoes, peeled and
    cubed
2 cups water

2 teaspoons salt
¼ teaspoon pepper
2 cups milk
2 tablespoons flour
1 (13-ounce) can evaporated milk
Parsley, garlic powder, celery
    salt (optional)

If using frozen fish, thaw. In large pan sauté pork until brown; drain all but 1 to 2 tablespoons fat and set aside cooked pork. Add onion to fat and cook until tender. Add potatoes, water, fish, salt and pepper. Bring to boil, reduce heat, cook 15 to 20 minutes or until potatoes are tender and the fish flakes. Remove fish and break into bite-size pieces and return to pan. Combine milks and flour, whisk well and add to fish mixture. Add salt pork and cook over low heat until heated, but do not boil. Parsley, garlic powder and celery salt may also be added. Best if made a day ahead.

Nancy Armbruster Cragin
(Mrs. Charles L., III)

PANTRY CLAM CHOWDER

Serves: 8 to 10

8 slices bacon, diced
2 large onions, diced
3 (8-ounce) bottles clam juice
2 (16-ounce) cans potatoes, sliced
3 (6½-ounce) cans whole clams
    with juice

2 (6½-ounce) cans minced clams
    with juice
1 (13-ounce) and 1 (5½-ounce)
    can evaporated milk
1 cup whole milk
¼ cup fresh minced parsley

Sauté the bacon and onions. Drain off most of the grease and add the bottled clam juice to the bacon and onions. Drain the potatoes, slice, and cook 5 minutes in the clam juice. Add the whole clams and the minced clams. Heat thoroughly and then add the evaporated milk, the whole milk, and fresh parsley. Heat very gently over low heat. Do not allow to boil! Refrigerate overnight if possible as the flavor improves on standing.

Eileen A. Pugh
(Mrs. Richard F.)

SALMON CHOWDER

Serves: 8

4 cups peeled and diced potatoes
1 cup diced carrots
½ cup chopped green pepper
1 cup chopped celery
3 cups water
1 tablespoon salt
1 (10-ounce) package frozen peas
1 onion, chopped
⅓ cup butter or margarine
¼ cup flour
5 cups milk (or use 2 cups
   evaporated milk or light cream
   as part of the 5 cups)

1 (1-pound) can salmon,
   undrained and flaked or 1
   pound fresh salmon, simmered
   in a pan with a small amount
   of water until flaked
½ teaspoon Worcestershire
   sauce
1 teaspoon dried parsley
½ teaspoon thyme

Put potatoes, carrots, pepper and celery in large pan; add water and salt, bring to a boil. Lower heat and simmer until vegetables are tender, about 15 minutes. Add peas and simmer 5 minutes. Remove from heat. To prepare sauce, sauté the onions in butter until tender. Gradually add flour, stirring until smooth. Cook 1 minute. Slowly stir in 2½ cups of milk, stirring constantly over low heat until mixture is thickened. To the vegetables add salmon with liquid; add sauce, Worcestershire sauce, parsley and thyme. Add remaining milk. Reheat gently before serving. May be made ahead.

Lee Morse Edwards
(Mrs. Dwight H.)

CHEDDAR CHEESE SOUP
(AS SERVED AT PORTLAND COUNTRY CLUB)

Serves: 4

1 cup grated carrots
1 cup finely diced celery
2 cups boiling water
1 small onion, grated
   or finely diced
½ cup butter

¾ cup flour
1 cup chicken stock or bouillon
1 cup milk
¾ pound sharp Cheddar cheese,
   shredded
¼ pound American cheese, diced

Simmer carrots and celery in water until tender, about 10 minutes. Sauté onion in butter until soft. Add flour and blend well. Cook for 5 minutes over low heat. Do not brown. Place onion in double boiler. Add chicken stock and milk. Cook until thickened, stirring constantly. Add cheeses, stir until melted. Add cooked vegetables, including water. Blend and heat thoroughly.

CLARKE'S CORN AND CHEDDAR CHEESE CHOWDER

Serves: 4 to 6

1 large potato, peeled and diced
2 cups water, boiling and salted,
  to taste
1 bay leaf
½ teaspoon cumin seeds
  (ground okay)
¼ teaspoon dried sage
3 tablespoons butter
1 onion, finely chopped
3 tablespoons flour

1¼ cups heavy cream
1 (10-ounce) package frozen shoe
  peg corn
Salt and pepper, to taste
Chopped chives, to taste
2 cups shredded sharp Cheddar
  cheese
½ cup dry white wine
Parsley

Boil potato in salted water with bay leaf, cumin and sage until just tender, about 20 minutes. Melt butter and sauté onion until tender. Stir in flour and add cream, stirring with a whisk. Pour this into the potatoes and the water. After corn has been cooked according to package directions, add to the chowder. Add the seasonings and simmer 10 minutes. Stir in the cheese and wine. Mix well until cheese is melted, but be careful not to burn. Serve with a sprig of parsley on top. This chowder can be made in advance without adding cheese and wine until preparing to serve.

Mallory Marshall Hambley
(Mrs. Clarke)

CORN CHOWDER

Serves: 8 to 10

½ cup or more chopped ham
  or crumbled bacon
2 tablespoons bacon fat or
  margarine
3 medium onions, chopped
4 or 5 stalks celery, chopped
1½ quarts chicken stock

4 medium potatoes, cubed
3 (20-ounce) bags frozen corn
  (thawed)
1 cup heavy cream
Salt, to taste
Freshly ground black pepper,
  to taste

Sauté ham in the margarine or fry cut up bacon. Remove meat and set aside. Cook onions and celery in the fat until just tender. Set aside. Pour chicken stock into a large kettle. Add potatoes and cook until tender. Purée 2 packages of the corn in the blender, using some of the hot stock to moisten. Add the blended corn and the whole kernels to the stock in the kettle. Add cream, salt, pepper, celery and onions, and the ham or bacon. Heat to serving temperature. This soup is better the next day. It freezes well.

Bonnie Bonjean Dowling
(Mrs. Patrick)

ART'S ELEGANT POTATO SOUP

Serves: 6

3 cups potatoes, scrubbed,
  unpeeled and cut up
4 tablespoons butter or
  margarine
6 scallions, sliced or 1 onion,
  finely chopped

2 tablespoons flour
3 cups chicken broth
1 teaspoon salt
⅛ teaspoon white pepper
2 cups light cream
Parsley

Cover potatoes with water and cook until tender. Meanwhile, sauté onions in butter until golden. Gradually add flour and simmer gently for 1 to 2 minutes. Gradually add broth, salt and pepper. Simmer 10 minutes, stirring frequently. Drain potatoes, reserving the liquid. Put potatoes in blender, about ¼ to ⅓ at a time. Blend, adding the cooking liquid from the potatoes, the broth mixture and the cream as necessary to blend (be sure to use in that order). Place mixture in large heavy pan, heat gently and stir frequently. Do not boil. Advisable to use a heat dissipator to avoid scorching and/or lumping. This is a thick soup, but cream may be added to thin. When served, garnish with parsley. May be prepared in advance and gently reheated.

Variations: 2 (10-ounce) packages of frozen vegetables or comparable amount of fresh vegetables may be substituted for potatoes.

Lee Morse Edwards
(Mrs. Dwight H.)

LENTIL SOUP

Serves: 8

1 (16-ounce) package lentils
1½ to 2 quarts chicken broth
6 to 8 cups chopped Swiss chard
⅔ cup olive oil
2 cups chopped onions

2 cups chopped celery
10 garlic cloves, chopped
½ cup lemon juice (5 to 6
  lemons)
Salt and pepper, to taste

In large pot, cook lentils in chicken broth until tender. Add Swiss chard, and more water, if necessary. Cook until tender. Meanwhile sauté onion, celery, and garlic in olive oil. When soft and golden, add to chard and lentils. Stir in lemon juice. Add more salt and pepper, if necessary.

Nancy Montgomery Beebe
(Mrs. Michael)

BOHEMIAN VEGETABLE SOUP (CREAM)

Serves: 6

¼ to ½ pound bacon
1 teaspoon butter
1 large onion, chopped
1½ quarts water
1 large potato, diced
2 carrots, diced

2 celery stalks, diced
2 to 3 parsnips, diced
½ teaspoon nutmeg
Salt and pepper, to taste
2 to 3 chicken bouillon cubes
½ to 1 cup cream

Cook bacon, remove from skillet and crumble. Melt butter in bacon fat. Add onion and cook until light brown. Add water, vegetables, spices, bacon and bouillon cubes. Bring to boil. Reduce heat and simmer 30 minutes. Purée in blender and add desired amount of cream.

Merryl Gillespie Hodgson
(Mrs. Donald G.)

SATURDAY NIGHT SOUP

Serves: 6 to 8

2 pounds lean ground beef
2 teaspoons seasoned salt
⅛ teaspoon pepper
2 eggs, slightly beaten
¼ cup chopped parsley
⅓ cup cracker crumbs
2 tablespoons milk
3 tablespoons flour
1 tablespoon salad oil
4 onions, sliced
6 cups water

6 cups tomato juice
6 beef bouillon cubes
3 cups sliced carrots
3 to 4 cups sliced celery
2 to 3 cups diced potatoes
¼ cup long grain rice
1 tablespoon sugar
2 teaspoons salt
2 bay leaves
1 teaspoon marjoram

Combine and mix thoroughly the ground beef, salt, pepper, eggs, parsley, cracker crumbs and milk. Form into small balls (walnut size). Dip balls into flour and put in 8 to 10-quart pan with oil. Brown lightly. Add remaining ingredients. Bring to boil and cover. Reduce heat. Cook 30 minutes. This recipe tastes better the second day. It freezes well.

Karen Gorham Hibyan
(Mrs. Roy P.)

SQUASH SOUP
AS SERVED AT COUNTRY MILE RESTAURANT AT SUGARLOAF

Serves: 6

1 butternut squash, peeled,
  seeded and diced
4 cups chicken broth or stock
1 tablespoon tarragon
1 tablespoon minced parsley
1 medium onion, chopped
1 clove garlic, minced

2 tablespoons butter
2 tablespoons sherry
4 tablespoons flour
Celery salt, to taste
Salt and pepper, to taste
1 cup medium cream

Cover squash with broth. Add tarragon and parsley and cook until tender. Sauté onions and garlic in butter and sherry; cook until soft. Add flour to onions. Mix well. Whisk squash mixture until smooth. Add onion mixture to squash and stir. Simmer until mixture is slightly thickened. Purée in blender or food processor. Season to taste, adding the celery salt first, and then salt and pepper. Add cream shortly before serving.

Lorraine Petrio-Gorski Shuman
(Mrs. Michael)

WINTER WOOLY SOUP

Yield: 8 to 10 servings

Meaty bone from a roasted leg
  of lamb
1 cup or more lamb, leftover
4 quarts water
6 carrots, sliced
3 potatoes, peeled and cubed
2 white turnips, peeled and
  cubed
2 stalks celery, sliced

2 onions, chopped
1¼ cups dried split peas
2 teaspoons salt
1 teaspoon freshly ground black
  pepper
½ teaspoon thyme
½ teaspoon rosemary
1 bay leaf

Simmer bone in water for 1 hour. Add remaining ingredients and simmer for another hour. Remove bone. Best made a day ahead and gently reheated. Freezes well.

Carol Potter Day
(Mrs. Richard B.)

SALADS

MELON BALLS WITH RUM LIME SAUCE

Serves: 10

⅔ cup sugar
⅓ cup water
1 teaspoon grated lime rind
½ cup light rum

6 tablespoons lime juice
2 quarts melon balls—any
  assortment
Fresh mint

Mix sugar and water in saucepan. Bring to boil, reduce heat and simmer for 5 minutes. Add lime rind and cool at room temperature. Stir in rum and lime juice. Pour over melon balls. Chill covered for 3 to 5 hours. Garnish with mint.

Merryl Hodgson
(Mrs. Donald G.)

CUCUMBER RING SUPREME

Serves: 8 to 10

1 (3-ounce) package lemon
  gelatin
1 cup boiling water
¾ cup water
3 tablespoons lemon juice
1 cucumber, unpeeled, sliced thin
1 envelope unflavored gelatin
3 tablespoons sugar
¾ teaspoon salt
¾ cup water

2 tablespoons lemon juice
1 (8-ounce) package cream
  cheese, cubed and softened
4 cucumbers, pared, seeds
  removed, and shredded
1 cup mayonnaise
3 tablespoons finely chopped
  onion
¼ cup snipped parsley

Dissolve lemon flavored gelatin in boiling water. Add the first ¾ cup of water and 3 tablespoons lemon juice. Pour into a deep 6½ to 7-cup mold and chill. When partially set, arrange overlocking slices of cucumber in bottom. Press into gelatin and chill until almost firm. Mix the unflavored gelatin, sugar and salt in saucepan. Add the second ¾ cup water. Stir over low heat until gelatin and sugar dissolve. Stir in the 2 tablespoons lemon juice. Beat hot gelatin into cream cheese with beater until smooth. Add shredded cucumber, mayonnaise, onion and parsley to cream cheese. Pour over almost firm gelatin in mold. Chill until firm.

Sally Grindell Vamvakias
(Mrs. James)

FROZEN FRUIT SALAD

Serves: 6 to 8

1 (3-ounce) package cream
   cheese
2 tablespoons milk
2 tablespoons lemon juice
⅓ cup mayonnaise
¼ teaspoon salt
1 cup crushed pineapple, drained
1 can white pitted cherries
1 cup green seedless grapes

1 can apricots, drained and
   sliced
1 cup miniature marshmallows
½ cup pecans
1 cup whipped heavy cream
2 tablespoons sugar
A few sliced red tart cherries ·
Lettuce

Blend cream cheese and milk. Add lemon juice, mayonnaise and salt. Mix well. Combine cream cheese mixture with pineapple, white cherries, grapes, apricots, marshmallows and nuts. Fold in whipped cream. Pour into an 8 x 8-inch pan. Sprinkle with sugar and arrange tart cherries on top. Freeze. Remove from freezer 1 hour before serving. Place in refrigerator and cut into serving squares. Serve on lettuce.

Lorraine Petrio-Gorski
(Mrs. Michael)

WINE JELLY RING WITH SEEDLESS GRAPES

Serves: 6

2 envelopes unflavored gelatin
1½ cups cold water
1½ cups boiling water
1 cup sugar
1 cup sherry

⅓ cup orange juice
3 tablespoons lemon juice
Seedless green grapes
½ pint sour cream
Light brown sugar

Soften gelatin in cold water. Dissolve gelatin in boiling water. Add sugar, sherry, orange and lemon juice. Strain into ring mold (11½-inch) and chill. Wash and dry grapes well. Mix with sour cream. Unmold wine jelly. Pile grapes in center of ring. Just before serving, sprinkle grapes with strained brown sugar.

Jean Potter Benton
(Mrs. Don Carlos, III)

CHAMPAGNE MOLD

Serves: 10

2 envelopes unflavored gelatin
1 cup water
1 cup sugar
1 bottle champagne or fruity
white wine
1 cup seedless grapes
1 (10-ounce) can pitted bing
cherries

1 (11-ounce) can mandarin
oranges
Water
1 (6-ounce) package raspberry
gelatin
½ cup port wine
½ cup coarsely chopped walnuts
Sour cream

In a small saucepan, sprinkle the gelatin over 1 cup of water to soften. Place over low heat, stirring until gelatin dissolves. Add champagne. Chill until it is the consistency of unbeaten egg whites, about 45 to 50 minutes, stirring occasionally. Fold in grapes. Place in bottom of 5½-cup mold. Chill. Drain cherries and oranges. Reserve liquid and pour into 1-quart measuring cup. Add enough water to make 3¼ cups liquid. Heat and add raspberry gelatin, stirring to dissolve. Add port wine. Chill until thickened but loose. Add fruit and nuts. Spread sour cream over the top of the first gelatin layer in the mold. Top with second gelatin mixture. Chill until firm.

Doris Martineau Stevens
(Mrs. Paul S.)

DELICIOUS MOLDED FRUIT SALAD

Serves: 15

1 (6-ounce) package lime gelatin
2 cups hot water
1 (14-ounce) can crushed
pineapple, drained
2 diced unpeeled apples
15 small marshmallows

1 (13-ounce) can evaporated milk
1 cup chopped pecans or walnuts
2 cups sugar
1 cup mayonnaise
1 (16-ounce) carton cottage
cheese

Dissolve gelatin in hot water. Chill until almost set. Add all of the remaining ingredients to gelatin. Chill until firm. Prepare in 9 x 13 x 2-inch dish. Cut into squares and serve.

Mary Jane Shaw
(Mrs. Bradley T.)

ORANGE PINEAPPLE DELIGHT

Serves: 10

1 (6-ounce) package orange
   gelatin
1 (11-ounce) can mandarin
   oranges, drained
1 (20-ounce) can crushed
   pineapple, drained

1 pint cottage cheese
1 (9.6-ounce) package frozen
   whipped topping

Mix gelatin according to package directions. Chill until almost firm. Add cottage cheese and whipped topping to the gelatin, mixing well. Add drained pineapple and mandarin oranges. Mix well and chill for at least 3 hours.

Linda Armstrong Andrews
(Mrs. Richard C.)

SAINT NICK SALAD RING

Serves: 14 to 16

2 (3-ounce) packages cream
   cheese
½ cup chopped fresh parsley
3 (3-ounce) packages strawberry
   gelatin
4½ cups boiling water
2½ tablespoons lemon juice

1 tablespoon vinegar
1 teaspoon salt
1 tablespoon grated onion
2 grapefruits, sectioned
1 cup diced celery
1 apple, diced
1 avocado, sliced (optional)

Cut cream cheese into squares (about 6 squares from each package). Roll in chopped parsley and set aside. Make gelatin using the boiling water. Add lemon juice, vinegar, salt and grated onion. Arrange cream cheese squares in large ring mold. Pour in a small amount of gelatin. Chill until set. When set, add more gelatin on top to cover cream cheese. Chill until set. Place grapefruit sections on top. Add more gelatin and chill until set. Add celery and apple to remaining gelatin and put on last. Chill until firm. Garnish with avocado.

Joyce Sarat White
(Mrs. David W.)

MUSTARD RING

Serves: 10 to 12

4 eggs
¾ cup sugar
1 envelope unflavored gelatin
1½ tablespoons dry mustard
½ teaspoon turmeric

¼ teaspoon salt
1 cup water
½ cup cider vinegar
1 cup whipping cream

Beat eggs in top of double boiler. In bowl, mix sugar and gelatin thoroughly; stir in mustard, turmeric and salt. Add water and vinegar to eggs, and then stir in sugar mixture. Cook over boiling water until slightly thickened, stirring constantly (very important). Cool until thickened. Whip cream and beat into cooled mixture. Turn into 1½-quart, lightly oiled ring mold and refrigerate until firm. Unmold and fill center with fresh fruit, or coleslaw. Garnish with greens.

Deborah Snite Bates
(Mrs. Daniel W.)

CHERRY JUBILEE RING

Serves: 6

1 (1-pound) can pitted bing
  cherries
½ cup currant jelly
¾ cup sherry
1 (3-ounce) package black cherry
  gelatin

¼ cup lemon juice
¼ cup chopped pecans
¼ cup sour cream
¼ cup mayonnaise

Drain cherries, reserve ¾ cup syrup. Combine syrup, jelly and sherry. Bring to boil and remove from heat. Add gelatin, dissolve. Add cherries and lemon juice. Chill until partially set. Add nuts. Chill in 3 to 4-cup ring overnight. Unmold on greens. Mix ¼ cup each sour cream and mayonnaise. Put in center of ring.

Nancy Armbruster Cragin
(Mrs. Charles L., III)

CRANBERRY SALAD

Serves: 8 to 10

3 oranges
2½ cups fresh cranberries
3 (3-ounce) packages orange
   gelatin
3 cups boiling water
2 tablespoons lemon juice

1 cup sugar
Pinch salt
1½ cups finely chopped celery
1 cup drained, crushed pineapple
½ cup chopped walnuts

Peel oranges. Chop the peelings of one orange and the cranberries in a food processor or blender. Remove the white membrane from oranges and section them. Break into small pieces. Dissolve gelatin in boiling water. Add lemon juice, sugar and salt. Stir until dissolved. Add orange pieces, the chopped orange and cranberry mixture, celery, pineapple and nuts. Pour into mold and chill until set.

Karen Gorham Hibyan
(Mrs. Roy P.)

FROZEN LIME MINT SALAD

Serves: 16

1 (8¼-ounce) can crushed
   pineapple
1 (20-ounce) can crushed
   pineapple
1 (3-ounce) package lime gelatin

1 (6½-ounce) package miniature
   marshmallows
1 cup crushed butter mints
4 cups whipped cream
Fresh mint, garnish

In large bowl, combine both cans undrained pineapple, dry lime gelatin, marshmallows and mints. Cover and refrigerate for several hours. Fold in whipped cream. Spoon mixture into sherbet glasses and freeze overnight. Garnish with fresh mint.

Sally Lunan Trussel
(Mrs. David)

SHRIMP SALADE BOMBAY

Serves: 8 to 10

2 pounds small shrimp, cooked
   and shelled
1 cup vinaigrette dressing (see
   index)
2 cups long grained rice

¾ cup mayonnaise
3 tablespoons diced onion
2 tablespoons curry powder
1 tablespoon Dijon mustard
Salt and pepper

Marinate shrimp in ½ cup vinaigrette for 30 minutes. Cook rice in 4 cups of water for 14 minutes. Rinse under cold water. Toss the rice with remainder of vinaigrette, mayonnaise, onion and seasonings. Add shrimp and chill. Serve on bed of lettuce.

Roselle Flynn Johnson
(Mrs. Steven M.)

TANIA'S BROCCOLI SALAD

Serves: 6 to 8

2 pounds fresh broccoli, chopped
   or 2 (16-ounce) packages
   frozen chopped broccoli,
   thawed
Salt
Dash of lemon juice
Freshly ground black pepper

1½ to 2 cups mayonnaise
3 shallots, finely minced
½ cup white wine
1 tablespoon chopped chives
Hard-boiled egg, sliced
   (optional)

Parboil broccoli until tender crisp. Drain and dry on paper towel. Sprinkle broccoli with lemon juice, salt and pepper. Combine shallots and wine in saucepan. Cook until wine has evaporated. Add shallots to mayonnaise and chives. Pour mayonnaise mixture over broccoli and refrigerate 2 to 3 hours. If desired, garnish with egg slices.

Jane (Ba) Davidson Kopp
(Mrs. Donald)

ARTICHOKE PIMENTO SALAD

½ cup salad oil
⅓ cup vinegar
2 tablespoons water
4 thin slices onion
1 tablespoon sugar
1 garlic clove, crushed
¼ teaspoon celery seed
½ teaspoon salt

Pepper, to taste
1 (9-ounce) package frozen
  artichoke hearts
1 (4-ounce) jar pimentos,
  drained and chopped
Iceberg lettuce
Spinach leaves

In saucepan, combine oil, vinegar, water, onion, sugar, garlic, celery seed, salt and pepper. Bring mixture to boil. Add artichoke hearts. Cook until tender, 5 to 8 minutes. Cool and stir in pimento. Chill until serving time. Place artichokes, onion and pimento over a bed of variety greens. Toss with enough of remaining marinade to coat.

Hope Palmer Bramhall
(Mrs. Peter T.C.)

KOREAN SALAD

Serves: 8

1 bag spinach
1 (8-ounce) can sliced water
  chestnuts
5 strips bacon, fried and crushed
1 (16-ounce) can bean sprouts,
  drained

1 (8-ounce) can mandarin
  oranges, drained
2 hard-boiled eggs, sliced for
  garnish

Toss salad ingredients together with part of dressing. Garnish with sliced hard-boiled eggs.

Dressing

¾ cup sugar, or ½ cup honey
2 teaspoons Worcestershire
  sauce
1 cup salad oil (¾ cup if honey is
  used)

⅓ cup catsup
¼ cup vinegar
1 large onion, grated
Salt, to taste

Combine all ingredients. Use part of dressing for salad; reserve remainder for another salad.

Judith Bishop Condron
(Mrs. Arthur)

SEVEN LAYER SALAD

Serves: 14 to 16

1 head lettuce, broken into
    pieces
1 cup diced celery
1 green pepper, diced
1 (16-ounce) package frozen
    peas, defrosted and drained

1 purple onion, diced
1½ to 1¾ cups mayonnaise
2 tablespoons sugar
1 cup grated Parmesan cheese
8 slices bacon, cooked and
    crumbled

In a large glass bowl, alternate the following ingredients: lettuce, celery, green pepper, peas and onions. Spread the mayonnaise over the top of these layers. (Only on the top of the completed layers). Sprinkle sugar, Parmesan cheese and bacon bits over the mayonnaise. Prepare 24 hours ahead and refrigerate. Add a layer of meat (ham, beef, etc.) and use as a main course for 6 to 8 people.

Helen Koniares Cleaves
(Mrs. Robert E., III)

CAESAR SALAD

Serves: 6 to 8

2 heads Romaine lettuce,
    washed, dried, chilled and
    torn in pieces
⅔ cup olive oil
1 clove garlic, crushed
Juice of 1 large lemon
1 teaspoon salt
¼ teaspoon freshly ground
    pepper

¼ teaspoon dry mustard
Worcestershire sauce, dash
1 extra large egg, lightly beaten
½ cup grated Parmesan cheese
1 cup croutons
1 tin, flat anchovy filets

Crush garlic clove into olive oil. Pour olive oil over lettuce pieces. Mix well to thoroughly coat all pieces. Sprinkle lettuce with lemon juice, salt, pepper, dry mustard, and Worcestershire. Toss gently. Pour beaten egg over lettuce. Toss lightly. Sprinkle grated cheese and croutons over lettuce. Mix. Top each serving with an anchovy filet.

Paul Frinsko

MOM'S GERMAN POTATO SALAD

Serves: 12

5 pounds potatoes
2 eggs, beaten
1 teaspoon pepper
1½ teaspoons salt
1 cup mayonnaise
1 teaspoon sugar
2 tablespoons dry mustard

2 tablespoons vegetable oil
½ cup white vinegar
½ pound bacon, fried crisp
¼ cup warm water
1 large onion, chopped
Optional: 3 to 4 tablespoons
    bacon grease

Boil potatoes until slightly firm. Do not overcook. Cool, peel and slice potatoes. Mix remaining ingredients and blend well. Pour over potatoes. Gently blend. Serve at room temperature.

Priscilla Taggart Connard
(Mrs. G. Baer, Jr.)

ZESTY SLAW

Serves: 12 to 14

1 large cabbage, chopped
1 green pepper, chopped
1 large onion, chopped
1 cup vinegar, heated
1 cup sugar

1 teaspoon celery seed
1 tablespoon salt
1 teaspoon dry mustard
¾ cup salad oil

Combine cabbage, pepper and onion. Pour hot vinegar over sugar, celery seed, salt and dry mustard. Add salad oil and pour all of the above ingredients over slaw while hot. Do not stir. Refrigerate overnight. Recipe keeps up to one week.

Suzanne Studley Megathlin
(Mrs. Keith)

TABBOULEH

Serves: 4 to 6

½ to ¾ cup fine bulgar wheat
6 firm tomatoes, cut small
1 bunch parsley, chopped
1 bunch scallions, chopped
8 to 10 stems fresh mint leaves,
  chopped
1 teaspoon dried mint

½ teaspoon cinnamon
¼ teaspoon allspice
¼ cup lemon juice, fresh
  preferred
¼ cup oil
Salt and pepper, to taste
Romaine lettuce

Measure bulgar wheat into large bowl, add enough water to cover the wheat. Let stand until wheat has expanded and is light and fluffy (about 1 hour). Drain off excess water by removing wheat from bowl and squeezing between hands. Transfer back to bowl. Add remaining ingredients except lettuce. Mix well. Cover and marinate at least 10 to 15 minutes before serving. To serve, mound tabbouleh in center of large platter on top of Romaine lettuce. Serve with pita bread.

Susan Welky Corey
(Mrs. John B.)

SPINACH AND BLEU CHEESE SALAD

Serves: 12 to 14

10 cups fresh spinach, bite-size
  pieces
2 cups sliced fresh mushrooms
5 strips bacon, fried and
  crumbled

½ cup crumbled bleu cheese
¼ cup thinly sliced green onion
Dressing, recipe below

Place spinach in large salad bowl. Add mushrooms, bacon, cheese and green onions. Toss, cover and chill. To serve, shake dressing, pour over salad. Toss.

Dressing

1 cup salad oil
2 tablespoons lemon juice
1 egg yolk
¼ teaspoon garlic powder
¾ teaspoon salt

½ teaspoon dry mustard
½ teaspoon dried, crushed thyme
¼ teaspoon sugar
⅛ teaspoon freshly ground
  pepper

In blender, combine all ingredients and blend until smooth. Put in a covered jar and chill well.

Mrs. Fran Barnes

CHEDDAR SPINACH SALAD

Serves: 6

1 pound fresh spinach
1 (10-ounce) package sharp
   Cheddar cheese, shredded

2 hard-boiled eggs, grated

Wash spinach, remove stems, break up into pieces. Add cheese and eggs. Before serving, pour dressing over salad and toss lightly.

Dressing

1 pint sour cream
½ teaspoon dry mustard
Garlic salt, to taste

2 tablespoons wine vinegar
2 to 3 tablespoons sugar
Salt

Combine all ingredients.

Susan Hall Haynes
(Mrs. David J.)

MEXICAN CHEF SALAD

Serves: 12

1 head lettuce, broken in
   bite-sized pieces
1 onion, chopped
4 medium tomatoes, cut into
   bite-sized pieces
4 ounces sharp Cheddar cheese,
   shredded

¾ pound ground beef
1 (15-ounce) can kidney beans,
   drained
½ to 1 teaspoon chili powder
¼ teaspoon salt
French dressing, recipe below

Break lettuce into large bowl. Add chopped onion and tomatoes. Add shredded cheese. Brown ground beef and add beans to it. Add chili powder and salt. Simmer for 10 minutes. Add hot bean mixture to cold salad with French dressing. Toss to blend ingredients. Serve immediately.

French Dressing

⅓ cup wine vinegar
1 teaspoon salt
1 cup salad oil

1 clove garlic, minced
¼ teaspoon freshly ground
   pepper

Dissolve salt in vinegar. Add salad oil, garlic and pepper. Shake well.

India Horton Weatherill
(Mrs. Robert H.)

BEAN SALAD

Serves: 10

1 (16-ounce) can cut green beans, drained
1 (16-ounce) can red kidney beans, drained
1 (16-ounce) can pitted ripe olives, drained
1 (8-ounce) can sliced mushrooms, drained
1 (4-ounce) can diced pimento, drained
1 (9-ounce) can marinated artichoke hearts, drained

1½ cups sliced celery
1 medium onion, thinly sliced
¼ cup tarragon vinegar
1¼ teaspoons salt
1 teaspoon sugar
1 tablespoon mixture of parsley, chives and tarragon
¼ cup chopped parsley
¼ teaspoon hot pepper sauce
½ cup salad oil

Mix all ingredients together and refrigerate. Recipe is better if prepared the day before it is served.

Lorraine Petrio-Gorski Shuman
(Mrs. Michael)

MARGE'S BLEU CHEESE DRESSING

Yield: 3 cups

1 cup crumbled bleu cheese
2 cups mayonnaise
¼ cup vinegar

2 tablespoons sugar
½ cup dairy sour cream
1 clove garlic, minced

Mix together. Beat until fluffy. Chill.

Jane Hatch Peterson

CELERY SEED DRESSING

Yield: 2 cups

⅔ cup sugar
1 teaspoon dry mustard
1 teaspoon paprika
1 teaspoon celery seed
¼ teaspoon salt

⅓ cup honey
⅓ cup vinegar
1 tablespoon lemon juice
1 teaspoon minced onion
1 cup salad oil

Mix well in blender.

Martha White Nichols
(Mrs. Christopher)

CHEESE DRESSING

Yield: 3 cups

2 eggs
2 teaspoons brown sugar
1½ teaspoons salt
1 teaspoon dry mustard
1 teaspoon Worcestershire sauce
2 teaspoons prepared horseradish
2 cups salad oil

¼ cup cider vinegar
¼ cup lemon juice
4 ounces Cheddar cheese,
   shredded
¼ cup finely chopped green
   onions

In a processor or blender, combine eggs, sugar, salt, mustard and Worcestershire. Mix well. Add horseradish. With machine running, slowly add ½ cup of the oil. Add vinegar and lemon juice alternately with remaining oil and blend 1 minute longer. Add cheese and onion and blend to mix. Best made day before.

Carol Such Bouton
(Mrs. Dale C., Jr.)

ROQUEFORT SALAD DRESSING

1 cup mayonnaise
4 tablespoons olive oil
1 tablespoon vinegar
1 teaspoon Worcestershire sauce
1 (8-ounce) carton sour cream

Salt and pepper
1 clove garlic, minced
4 to 6 ounces Roquefort or bleu
   cheese, crumbled

Mix all ingredients and refrigerate. Best made a day ahead as flavor improves with age.

Susan Wilson Starbuck
(Mrs. Gary W.)

NEW ORLEANS SALAD DRESSING

Yield: 1 cup

1 teaspoon salt
½ teaspoon sugar
¼ teaspoon pepper
½ teaspoon paprika
½ teaspoon dry mustard

¾ cup salad oil
¼ cup vinegar
½ teaspoon Worcestershire
   sauce

Add in given order and shake well.

Mrs. Betty Harrod

VINAIGRETTE DRESSING SUPREME

Yield: 3 cups

3 eggs at room temperature
½ cup tarragon vinegar
½ teaspoon minced garlic
1 teaspoon dried tarragon
1 teaspoon sweet basil
1 tablespoon chopped shallots

1½ teaspoons black pepper
1½ teaspoons salt
1 cup olive oil, room temperature
1 cup peanut oil, room
  temperature

In food processor or blender, place eggs, vinegar, garlic, spices, shallots, salt and pepper. Blend for 20 seconds. Slowly add oils, ¼ cup at a time, blending after each addition. Stop machine when a creamy consistency is formed. Chill at least 2 to 3 hours.

Mary Beth Christman Sweeney
(Mrs. John J.)

VINAIGRETTE DRESSING

Yield: ½ cup

2 tablespoons fresh lemon juice
6 tablespoons olive oil

1 tablespoon Dijon mustard
1 clove garlic, finely minced

Combine all ingredients in a blender or processor and blend a few seconds to combine thoroughly.

Patricia Pugh Britt
(Mrs. Michael E.)

GRANDMOTHER OLSON'S FRENCH DRESSING

Yield: 1½ cups

½ cup sugar
¼ cup vinegar
1 tablespoon lemon juice
1 small onion, chopped

2 tablespoons catsup
½ cup salad oil
1 teaspoon salt
1 teaspoon paprika

Put all ingredients in a jar and shake. Use a blender for more creamy dressing.

Mrs. Elizabeth Baird

LUNCH & BRUNCH

S. Leighton

CHICKEN MUSHROOM CRÊPES
WITH MOCK MORNAY SAUCE

Serves: 12 to 14

1½ cups whole milk
3 large eggs
2 tablespoons melted butter,
   cooled
1 teaspoon sugar

¼ teaspoon salt
2 tablespoons fresh parsley,
   finely minced
1½ cups flour

Put the milk, eggs, butter, salt, sugar and parsley into blender. Add the flour and blend at high speed for 1 minute. Stop the blender, scrape sides with spatula and blend briefly until all the flour is incorporated and the batter is smooth. Cover and refrigerate overnight. Stir batter gently before making crêpes. The batter should be the consistency of heavy cream. If batter is too thick add a few teaspoons of water, if too thin whisk in a tablespoon of flour. Heat a 5-inch crêpe pan and brush lightly with oil until very hot, but not smoking. Pour 1½ to 2 tablespoons of batter into the pan and quickly rotate pan to coat entire surface with batter. Cook the crêpe over medium high heat for 60 seconds (or until browned on underside). Turn crêpe and brown on other side for an additional 30 seconds (this will be the side on which filling is placed). Remove crêpe to a plate and repeat the process until all the batter is used. Grease the crêpe pan only when necessary. Makes 28 to 32 crêpes 5-inches in diameter. Unfilled crêpes may be frozen or refrigerated between layers of waxed paper.

Chicken Mushroom Filling

5 cups cooked chicken
½ cup butter
2 medium onions, finely chopped
1 clove garlic, finely minced
2 pounds mushrooms, chopped

¼ cup sherry
6 cups Mornay sauce, divided
Salt and pepper, to taste
1 cup shredded Gruyere

Cut the chicken into bite-size pieces and put aside. Melt the butter in a large skillet and sauté the onion and garlic until transparent. Add the mushrooms and cook over medium heat for 3 minutes, add the chicken and the sherry. Stir well to combine, reduce heat, add 2 cups of the mock mornay sauce and cook over low heat until thickened. Adjust seasoning to taste. Cool slightly. Fill crêpes and roll, place seam side down in a 7 x 11 x 2-inch glass casserole. The 32 crêpes will fill 2 casseroles. Divide the remaining sauce in half and pour 2 cups of sauce over each casserole. Sprinkle the shredded cheese on top. Bake in a preheated 375-degree oven for 15 minutes and serve immediately.

Mock Mornay Sauce

¾ cup butter
¾ cup flour
4 cups milk, heated
2 cups chicken stock, heated

5 tablespoons brandy
2 pound box of pasteurized
  processed cheese spread,
  shredded

Melt the butter and stir in the flour, cook over medium heat until the flour is slightly browned. Very slowly add the heated liquids and stir constantly until thickened. Add the brandy and the shredded cheese spread and cook over low heat until the cheese melts.

*Patricia Pugh Britt
(Mrs. Michael E.)*

CHICKEN LIVERS AND MUSHROOMS IN MADEIRA SAUCE

Serves: 6 to 8

Sauce

2 tablespoons butter
½ pound fresh mushrooms,
  thinly sliced
2 tablespoons shallots, chopped
⅓ cup Madeira wine

1 cup chicken broth
2 teaspoons tomato paste
1 teaspoon arrowroot (can use
  cornstarch)
1 tablespoon Madeira wine

Melt butter in skillet and add mushrooms. Cook for 2 minutes, stirring constantly. Add shallots and cook 5 minutes. Add Madeira, chicken broth and tomato paste. Simmer 5 to 10 minutes. Blend arrowroot with 1 tablespoon Madeira wine and add to sauce to thicken.

2 pounds chicken livers, trim
  away veins and tissues
4 tablespoons flour

½ cup oil
Salt and pepper, to taste
Fresh parsley, chopped, to taste

Coat chicken livers with flour. Heat oil and cook chicken livers over high heat for 2 minutes, stirring constantly. Doing this in two batches is better. Drain livers and add to sauce. Add salt, pepper and parsley. If not thick enough, add more arrowroot to thicken.

*DoDo Martineau Stevens
(Mrs. Paul S.)*

BLUEBERRY-CORN CAKES

Yield: 20 (3½-inch) cakes

1 slice bacon, diced (reserve fat)
1 egg
1¼ cups buttermilk
½ teaspoon baking soda
¼ cup flour
1 teaspoon sugar

1 teaspoon baking powder
½ teaspoon salt
¾ cup corn meal
2 tablespoons liquid shortening
   (added to reserved bacon fat)
½ cup blueberries

Cook bacon slowly, drain, reserve melted fat. Heat griddle slowly while mixing batter. Beat egg. Add buttermilk and mix well. Sift together soda, flour, sugar, baking powder and salt and add to above mixture. Mix in cornmeal and liquid shortening (added to reserved bacon fat). Fold in diced bacon and blueberries. Cook on griddle. Serve with real maple syrup or the following syrup.

Syrup

1 pound brown sugar
1 cup water

3 tablespoons light corn syrup
¼ teaspoon maple flavoring

Place brown sugar and water in saucepan. Add corn syrup, bring to a boil and let simmer uncovered 5 minutes. Add maple flavoring. Yield: 1½ cups.

India Horton Weatherill
(Mrs. Robert)

EGGS AUGENSTEIN

Serves: 12 to 15

2 (4-ounce) cans chopped green
   chili peppers
1 (8-ounce) package, mild
   Cheddar cheese, sliced
1 (8-ounce) package sharp
   Cheddar cheese, sliced

12 eggs
1 pint sour cream
1½ teaspoons salt

Cover bottom of a 9 x 13-inch pan with cheeses. Sprinkle chili peppers on cheese in pan. Beat eggs, sour cream and salt until light. Pour over cheese. Bake at 350 degrees about 35 to 45 minutes. Let stand 10 minutes before serving. Cut into squares. Can be frozen before baking.

Carol Potter Day
(Mrs. Richard B.)

BREAKFAST SOUFFLÉ

Serves: 6

¼ cup onions, chopped
2 tablespoons butter
2 cups cooked ham
1 cup sharp Cheddar cheese,
  shredded

⅔ cup butter crackers, crushed
4 eggs, beaten
½ cup milk
1 cup green pepper, chopped
  (optional)

Sauté onions in butter until transparent. Combine all other ingredients. Bake at 325 degrees for 45 minutes in a 10 x 6 x 1½-inch pan. Cover with foil half-way through baking.

Cynthia Craig Harwood
(Mrs. William)

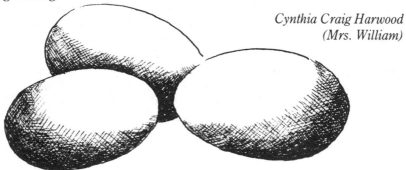

OEUFS AVEC CRABE

Serves: 10 to 12

2½ cups milk
3 ounces cream cheese
12 eggs
1 to 1½ teaspoons salt
Pepper, to taste
½ cup melted butter

1 large onion, chopped and
  sautéed in a small amount of
  butter
Hot pepper sauce, a few drops, to
  taste
12 ounces flaked crabmeat,
  canned or fresh

Heat the milk and blend in the cream cheese stirring until cheese melts. Beat eggs slightly and add the milk-cream cheese mixture, salt, and pepper. Pour the melted butter into a greased 2-quart glass casserole. Add the sautéed onion and the hot pepper sauce to the egg mixture and pour into the casserole. Bake in a preheated 350-degree oven for 20 minutes, remove from oven and stir. Return to oven and bake 20 more minutes. Remove from oven, stir in the flaked crabmeat and continue baking an additional 15 minutes. Total baking time is 55 minutes. Stir once when removing from oven and serve immediately.

Patricia Pugh Britt
(Mrs. Michael E.)

AUSTRIAN HAM STRUDELS

Serves: 6

6 frozen patty shells

Filling

2 cups finely chopped or ground ham	2 tablespoons sweet pickle relish
⅔ cup finely chopped onion	1 tablespoon sharp mustard
2 hard-cooked eggs, chopped	2 tablespoons chopped parsley
	Dash pepper

Mix filling together. Divide filling into 6 parts. Place portions in center of pastry rounds, which have been thawed completely, then rolled out to approximately 6-inch circles. Lift two sides toward center, making boat shapes and pinch together to seal. Bake on ungreased cookie sheet for 20 minutes in 450-degree oven. May be frozen before baking.

Betty Muzzey
(Mrs. Clifford L.)

EGGS-A-PLENTY

Serves: 12

½ pound sweet sausage	1 teaspoon Worcestershire sauce, or to taste
1 medium onion, chopped	¾ pound fresh mushrooms, sliced and sautéed in as little butter as possible
Garlic salt, to taste	
19 eggs, well beaten	
2¾ cups milk	
½ teaspoon thyme, or to taste	8 ounces extra sharp cheese, shredded
Salt and pepper, to taste	

Brown sausage with chopped onion and garlic salt. Beat eggs and add milk and seasonings to form a very thin egg mixture. Combine egg mixture, mushrooms, shredded cheese, and sausage. Grease three 2-quart casseroles. Fill each casserole only half-full. Bake in a preheated 350-degree oven for about 30 minutes or until eggs are fluffy and only slightly moist. After first 15 minutes of cooking, cut through eggs with a knife. Can be prepared ahead of time and refrigerated. Remove from refrigerator 30 minutes before baking, stir, and bake.

Patricia Pugh Britt
(Mrs. Michael E.)

CHRISTMAS BREAKFAST

Serves: 6

7 slices white bread (regular, not thin)
8 ounces Cheddar cheese, shredded
6 eggs
3 cups milk
½ teaspoon salt
¼ teaspoon pepper
1 teaspoon dry mustard
3 strips bacon, cut in half

Trim crusts from bread; crumble bread. Mix bread and cheese, spread on greased 9 x 13 x 2-inch baking dish. Beat eggs and milk; add salt, pepper and mustard; pour over breaded cheese. Lay bacon on top; cover and refrigerate overnight. Next morning (while opening presents) bake uncovered at 350 degrees for 50 to 55 minutes.

Jeri Dyer Edgar
(Mrs. Joseph E.)

KELSEY'S CHRISTENING BRUNCH

Serves: 6 to 8

6 eggs, hard-boiled
½ pound bacon
2 medium onions, chopped
1 (10-ounce) package spinach, cooked and drained
¼ cup butter
¼ cup flour
1 pound cheese (Swiss, Gruyere or Cheddar), shredded
1 cup light cream
1 cup milk
¼ teaspoon each, thyme, marjoram and basil
Grated pepper
Pinch of salt
Buttered bread crumbs
¼ cup chopped parsley

Hard boil eggs; cool and slice thin. Sauté bacon until crisp; drain and crumble. Sauté onions. Make a very thick white sauce with butter, flour, cheese, cream and milk. Add all spices. In shallow 9-inch casserole, layer sauce, eggs, spinach, onion and bacon (2 layers of each ingredient). Spread bread crumbs on top and lay a few pieces of bacon and parsley on top of crumbs. Bake at 350 degrees for 30 to 40 minutes until brown and bubbling.

Mallory Marshall Hambley
(Mrs. Clarke)

CRAB OPEN-FACED SANDWICHES

Yield: 6 open-faced sandwiches

1 (7½-ounce) can crabmeat, or ½ pound fresh or frozen crabmeat, drained, flaked, cartilage removed
¼ cup mayonnaise
1 (3-ounce) package cream cheese, softened
1 egg yolk

1 teaspoon onion, finely chopped
¼ teaspoon prepared mustard
Salt
3 English muffins, split and toasted
2 tablespoons butter or margarine, softened
Paprika

Stir together crabmeat and mayonnaise; set aside. Beat together cream cheese, egg yolk, onion, mustard, and a dash of salt until smooth and creamy. Spread toasted muffin halves with butter or margarine, then with crabmeat mixture. Top with cream cheese mixture. Sprinkle with paprika. Place on baking sheet; broil 5 to 6 inches from heat for 2 to 3 minutes, until tops are golden and bubbly. Ingredients may be prepared ahead, but do not top muffins with mixtures until ready to broil.

Lee Morse Edwards
(Mrs. Dwight H.)

GRILLED APPLE SANDWICHES

Serves: 8

1 (8-ounce) package cream cheese
2 tablespoons mayonnaise
1 cup tart apples, finely chopped

6 slices bacon, cooked and crumbled
16 slices white bread
Butter or margarine, melted

Mash cream cheese; add mayonnaise; beat until fluffy. Stir in apples and bacon. Spread between bread slices. Brush both sides of sandwiches generously with melted butter or margarine; grill until golden brown.

Jean Winn Swan
(Mrs. Robert M.)

PARTY SALAD LOAF

Serves: 8

Egg salad (6 eggs)
Tuna salad (7½-ounce can)
Crabmeat salad (6-ounce can)

Cream cheese (8-ounce package)
Loaf of unsliced bread
Radishes, olives, parsley

Slice bread horizontally into 4 slices; trim crusts. Spread each slice with a salad. Assemble layers. Frost top and sides with cream cheese. Garnish top with vegetables (radishes, olives, parsley) or with colored cream cheese as if decorating a cake. Refrigerate until ready to serve. If making a day ahead, butter each slice of bread on both sides so that fillings will not dry out.

Tanya Fogelsohn Shapiro
(Mrs. Gregory)

ORANGE FRENCH TOAST

Serves: 4 to 5

2 eggs, beaten
½ cup orange juice

10 slices raisin bread
23 graham crackers, crushed

Combine beaten eggs and orange juice. Dip bread into mixture and then into crumbs. Fry on both sides in margarine until brown. Serve with butter and warm maple syrup.

Rho Francke Leavitt
(Mrs. William)

PANCAKES ALLEMAGNE

Serves: 4

2 apples, pared, cored and sliced
1 tablespoon margarine
1 cup flour
4 tablespoons sugar
Pinch salt

2 eggs
½ cup milk
Cinnamon-sugar mixture
3 teaspoons butter or margarine

Cook apple slices with margarine in cast iron frying pan over medium heat until slices are tender. Turn occasionally with spatula. Sift flour, sugar and salt into mixing bowl. Stir eggs and milk together, then blend with dry ingredients. Beat until smooth. Pour over hot apples in frying pan. Place pan in a 425-degree oven and bake for 15 minutes. Sprinkle with cinnamon-sugar mixture. Dot with butter. Bake for an additional 5 minutes. Serve immediately.

Susan Welky Corey
(Mrs. John B.)

SPINACH PIE

Serves: 30

2 pounds fresh spinach
1 bunch parsley
1 bunch green onions
1 pound feta cheese
1 pound cottage cheese

6 eggs
Salt and pepper
1 pound butter, melted
1 pound phyllo dough

Wash spinach and allow to drain. Chop spinach, parsley and green onions. Place in large mixing bowl and add feta cheese, crumbled. Then add cottage cheese, unbeaten eggs, and season to taste with salt and pepper. Pour half of melted butter over spinach mixture and toss lightly to combine all ingredients. Lightly brown 3 sheets of phyllo pastry, individually, in 350 degree oven. Set aside. Place ten pastry sheets in greased 12 x 17-inch pan, spreading each with melted butter. Top with one of the baked pastry sheets, sprinkle with ¼ of the spinach mixture. Alternate rest of pastry sheets and spinach. Cover with 10 more individually buttered pastry sheets. Bake at 350 degrees for approximately 1 hour or until golden brown. Cut in squares. Serve hot or cold.

Amalia Kalyvas

FAVORITE QUICHE

Serves: 6 to 8

9-inch pie crust (deep-dish)
1½ cups shredded Swiss cheese
1 tablespoon flour
½ pound bacon
2 tablespoons butter
1 large onion, thinly sliced

3 eggs
1 cup milk
½ cup light cream
½ teaspoon salt
Cayenne, dash
Nutmeg, dash

Preheat oven to 450 degrees. Prick pie crust and bake 5 minutes. Mix cheese and flour. Fry bacon until crisp. Pour off bacon grease. Add butter to bacon pan and melt over medium heat. Separate onions into rings and cook in butter until limp. Spread cheese in crust; sprinkle with crumbled bacon and top with onion rings. Beat eggs lightly; add milk, cream, seasonings; pour into pie crust. Bake at 450 degrees for 15 minutes; reduce to 350 degrees and bake for 10 to 15 minutes longer until custard sets.

Mary Beth Christman Sweeney
(Mrs. John J.)

SPINACH QUICHE

Serves: 6 to 8

1 baked 9-inch pie shell
1 (10-ounce) package frozen,
  chopped spinach
1 cup cottage cheese
½ teaspoon nutmeg
2 eggs, slightly beaten

Salt and pepper
1 onion, diced
1 cup muenster or Cheddar
  cheese, shredded
Parmesan cheese

Cook spinach slightly; drain. Add cottage cheese, nutmeg, eggs, salt and pepper and mix. Sauté onion and add to spinach mix. Place ½ spinach mix in pie shell. Sprinkle ½ cup muenster or Cheddar cheese over mix in pie shell. Repeat layers. Sprinkle Parmesan cheese over quiche. Bake at 350 degrees for 35 to 40 minutes or until set.

Nancy Benoit
(Mrs. Andre E.)

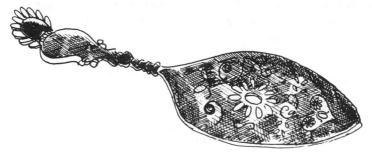

CRAZY QUICHE

Serves: 6 to 8

2 cups milk
4 eggs
2 tablespoons melted butter
½ cup biscuit mix
¼ cup Parmesan cheese, grated
1 (10-ounce) package chopped
  broccoli, thawed`

¼ teaspoon nutmeg
Salt
Optional: chopped ham,
  crabmeat, chopped mushrooms

Put all ingredients in blender, mix thoroughly. Add optional ingredient(s) if desired. Pour into 9 x 2-inch pie pan and bake at 350 degrees for 45 minutes. May double recipe using a 9 x 13 x 2-inch pan which will serve 12.

Deborah F. Hammond

TOMATO PIE

Serves: 6

Crust

1 cup flour	⅛ cup grated Parmesan cheese
¼ teaspoon salt	⅓ cup butter
¼ teaspoon sugar	A squeeze of lemon juice
⅛ cup shredded Cheddar cheese or	½ to 1½ tablespoons cold water

Filling

4 to 5 ripe tomatoes	1 cup mayonnaise
Salt, pepper, basil and chives, all to taste	1 cup shredded Cheddar cheese

Sift flour, salt and sugar together. Stir in cheese. With a pastry blender work in butter. Add a squeeze of lemon juice. Gradually blend in water until the mixture holds together when you gather it into a ball. Roll it out and place in a 9-inch pie plate. Peel and slice the tomatoes. Layer them on the pie crust, sprinkling the spices on top of each layer. Combine the cheese and mayonnaise and spread on top of tomatoes. Bake in a 350-degree oven for 35 minutes, or until brown.

Mary Louise Meyer Dyer
(Mrs. Ralph)

SAUSAGE BISCUITS

Yield: 60 small patties

1 pound pork sausage	2 cups biscuit mix
8 ounces extra sharp cheese, shredded	1 teaspoon crushed red pepper

Cook sausage 2 to 3 minutes to render some of the fat—not all of it. Combine with cheese and biscuit mix, adding red pepper. Shape into balls. Drop on ungreased cookie sheet. Bake at 375 degrees for 20 minutes. These freeze well. Just warm before serving. Accompaniment for scrambled eggs.

Susan Hall Haynes
(Mrs. J. David)

CHRISTMAS SAUSAGE

Yield: 8 patties

1½ teaspoons powdered sage
½ teaspoon summer savory
¾ teaspoon marjoram
¼ teaspoon nutmeg
¼ teaspoon ground cloves
2 teaspoons salt

1 teaspoon fresh ground black
  pepper
¼ cup Madeira
2 tablespoons water
2 pounds lean pork, ground

Mix seasonings with Madeira and water. Add mixture to meat, mixing thoroughly with hands. Form into patties and let stand for 24 hours. To cook place patties in large skillet. Add enough water to barely cover bottom of pan. Cover and cook for 2 minutes. Drain. Cook uncovered over medium heat until patties are browned and meat is completely done. Does not freeze well!

Carol Such Bouton
(Mrs. Dale C., Jr.)

FRUIT COMPOTE

Serves: 16

1 (29-ounce) can peaches
1 (30-ounce) can apricots
1 (20-ounce) can pineapple
1 (29-ounce) can pears
1 (16-ounce) box prunes

1 (21-ounce) can cherry pie
  filling
½ cup sherry
Almonds

Drain all cans of fruit. Mix fruit, prunes, pie filling and sherry. Put in oblong casserole. Top with almonds. Bake at 350 degrees for 20 minutes. Great hot or cold. Can be made in advance. Use for luncheon buffet, side dish or dessert.

Freda Klayman Shapiro
(Mrs. Bernard)

BLUEBERRIES ARAGONAISE

Serves: 12

6 pints blueberries, washed and
   well-drained
Juice of 1 lemon
2 tablespoons grated orange peel

2 tablespoons grated lemon peel
1 cup sugar
Heavy cream (optional)

Pour juice of 1 lemon over blueberries. Add grated orange and lemon peel and
sugar. Mix well. Serve chilled in individual bowls. Pass a pitcher of cream if
desired.

Judith Bishop Condren
(Mrs. Arthur)

BAKED PINEAPPLE

Serves: 6

2 eggs
¼ cup sugar
1 (20-ounce) can crushed
   pineapple (do not drain)

½ cup butter
5 slices white bread, cubed

Beat eggs and sugar until fluffy, add pineapple and mix well. Pour into an 8-inch
square pan. Melt the butter in a skillet, add bread cubes, and cook over medium
heat until cubes are browned, stirring occasionally. Place bread evenly over pineapple mixture. Bake in a preheated 350-degree oven for 30 minutes.

Eileen A. Pugh
(Mrs. Richard F.)

NANA CAREY'S NUTMEG SAUCE

Yield: 2 cups

1 cup sugar
1 tablespoon flour
Pinch of salt

2 cups boiling water
1 tablespoon butter
1 teaspoon nutmeg

Sift together sugar, flour and salt. Add boiling water and stir. Then add butter.
Cook 5 minutes, then add nutmeg. For pancakes, puddings, apple pan dowdies,
etc. For pancake syrup, flour may be omitted.

Alice Tobie Congdon
(Mrs. Allen R.)

VEGETABLES

ARTICHOKE AND SPINACH CASSEROLE

Serves: 10 to 12

4 (10-ounce) packages frozen
  chopped spinach
1 (8-ounce) package cream
  cheese
8 tablespoons margarine
  or butter
1 (10-ounce) can artichoke
  hearts, halved

1 (5-ounce) can water chestnuts,
  sliced
½ cup bread crumbs
4 tablespoons margarine
  or butter

Cook and drain spinach thoroughly. Melt cheese with the margarine and blend
with the drained spinach. Place the cut artichokes and the sliced water chestnuts
in the bottom of a lightly greased 9 x 13 x 2-inch casserole. Pour the spinach
mixture over artichokes and water chestnuts. Sprinkle with bread crumbs and
dot with margarine. Bake uncovered at 350 degrees for 20 minutes or until
mixture bubbles.

Patricia Pugh Britt
(Mrs. Michael E.)

ASPARAGUS PARMESAN

Serves: 4 to 6

2 (10-ounce) packages of frozen
  asparagus, thawed
1 (4-ounce) can mushrooms
¼ cup sliced green onions
2 tablespoons butter or
  margarine

2 tablespoons flour
½ teaspoon salt
½ cup milk
½ cup grated Parmesan cheese
  or
½ cup shredded sharp Cheddar
  cheese

Preheat oven to 400 degrees. Arrange asparagus in a shallow baking dish. Drain
mushrooms, reserving liquid. Chop half of mushrooms. Cook onions in butter
until tender. Add flour and salt and blend well. Stir in milk and mushroom liquid.
Cook until thickened, stirring constantly. Add chopped mushrooms. Pour sauce
over asparagus and sprinkle with cheese. Arrange remaining mushrooms over
top. Bake 25 minutes or until asparagus is tender.

Barbara Gee Chellis
(Mrs. Thomas)

ASPARAGUS AU NATUREL

Serves: 4

2 pounds fresh asparagus, clean
   and snap off tough ends
3 tablespoons butter

Salt, to taste
Pepper, to taste

Place asparagus in 2 layers in a glass 13 x 9 x 2-inch baking dish. Dot with butter and season with salt and pepper. Cover tightly with foil and bake at 350 degrees for 25 to 30 minutes. The asparagus are always perfectly cooked!

Patricia Pugh Britt
(Mrs. Michael E.)

ASPARAGUS-CAULIFLOWER AU GRATIN

Serves: 6

1 (10-ounce) package frozen
   asparagus pieces
1 small cauliflower, cut into
   flowerets
1 (10½-ounce) can cream of
   celery soup

1 cup shredded Cheddar cheese
½ cup milk
1 teaspoon prepared mustard
1 teaspoon Worcestershire sauce
2 tablespoons butter
⅓ cup wheat germ

Cook asparagus according to directions and drain. Cook cauliflower until tender crisp and drain. Combine vegetables in a large bowl. In another pan combine soup, cheese, milk, mustard and Worcestershire sauce. Heat slowly, stirring constantly, until cheese is melted. Pour sauce over vegetables and mix. Transfer to a 1½-quart casserole. Melt butter, add wheat germ and sprinkle around edge of casserole. Bake at 375 degrees for 30 minutes, or until bubbling and brown.

Carol Such Bouton
(Mrs. Dale C., Jr.)

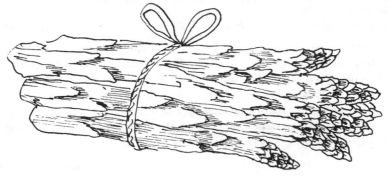

BAKED BEANS

Serves: 8

2 cups yellow eye beans
½ cup brown sugar
½ cup margarine
1 to 3 teaspoons salt

¼ teaspoon pepper
¼ teaspoon dry mustard
Water

Combine all ingredients in a heavy bean pot, using enough water to cover beans. Bake covered in 300-degree oven for 8 to 10 hours. Add water as needed during the day to keep the beans moist.

Sharon Smith Bushey
(Mrs. Donald J.)

SCANDINAVIAN BAKED BEANS

Serves: 8

½ pound bacon, fried and
  crumbled
2 (1-pound) cans baked red
  kidney beans
1 (1-pound) can baked pea beans
½ cup brown sugar
¼ to ½ teaspoon ground
  cinnamon

¼ to ½ teaspoon ground nutmeg
3 tablespoons cider vinegar
¼ teaspoon salt
¼ teaspoon pepper
½ cup sweet relish
½ cup catsup
¼ cup prepared mustard
½ cup finely chopped onion

Preheat oven to 350 degrees. Combine all the ingredients. Put in a bean pot or casserole dish. Bake covered for 30 to 45 minutes until bubbles.

Lee Morse Edwards
(Mrs. Dwight H.)

DILLED GREEN BEANS

Serves: 4

1 pound trimmed green beans
2 tablespoons olive oil
1 tablespoon red wine vinegar

½ teaspoon Dijon mustard
2 teaspoons dried dillweed
6 green onions, sliced

Boil beans 5 to 8 minutes. Drain beans. Beat oil, vinegar, mustard and dillweed together. Add mixture to onions and toss. Pour dressing over beans and toss. This may be served hot or at room temperature.

Anne Reevy Nieman
(Mrs. G. W.)

GREEN BEANS CLARION

Serves: 6 to 8

4 tablespoons vegetable or
  olive oil
3 medium onions, chopped
3 cloves garlic, finely minced
⅓ pound bacon, diced
¾ teaspoon Italian seasoning
¼ teaspoon oregano

Salt, to taste
Pepper, to taste
2 pounds fresh green beans,
  cleaned and cut into
  1½ to 2-inch lengths
¼ cup light brown sugar
2 tablespoons wine vinegar

Sauté the onions and garlic in the oil; add the bacon, cooking until bacon is transparent. Add the seasonings. Cook over medium heat for 3 minutes. Add the green beans and cook over medium heat until slightly tender. Add the brown sugar and vinegar. Cover and cook 6 minutes longer.

Richard F. Pugh

ITALIAN STYLE STRING BEANS

Serves: 8

1½ pounds fresh string beans,
  cut and cooked
¼ cup salt pork, finely chopped
1 clove garlic, minced

¼ cup olive oil
1 (16-ounce) can peeled
  tomatoes, chopped
Salt and pepper, to taste

Chop salt pork and garlic in food processor. Sauté salt pork and garlic in olive oil until light brown. Put tomatoes and liquid in food processor and blend only long enough to break up tomatoes. Add tomatoes, salt and pepper to salt pork mixture. Simmer 2 minutes. Add beans and simmer 60 minutes. Drain beans before serving with a slotted spoon. This recipe tastes better if it is made ahead and is reheated before being served.

Elizabeth King Cimino
(Mrs. Santo A.)

BEETS IN ORANGE SAUCE

Serves: 4 to 6

1 tablespoon flour
3 tablespoons sugar
6 tablespoons orange juice
1 tablespoon butter

¼ teaspoon salt
1 (16-ounce) can beets, sliced,
   drained

Mix flour, sugar, orange juice, butter and salt. Pour this mixture over drained cut beets in a 1-quart casserole. Bake 15 minutes in 350-degree oven.

Clarabell Quick Connard
(Mrs. G. Baer, Sr.)

PICKLED BEETS

Serves: 4

2 cups canned sliced beets,
   drained
6 tablespoons vinegar
¼ cup water
¼ cup sugar

¼ teaspoon ground cloves
½ clove garlic, finely minced
½ teaspoon salt
½ teaspoon dry mustard

Thoroughly blend all ingredients except beets. Pour over beets and allow to marinate in refrigerator for at least 8 hours in a tightly covered container. Keeps 2 weeks.

Patricia Pugh Britt
(Mrs. Michael E.)

BROCCOLI AND BLEU CHEESE

Serves: 6

2 (10-ounce) packages frozen
   chopped broccoli
1 cup milk
1 ounce bleu cheese
3 ounces cream cheese

2 tablespoons flour
2 tablespoons butter
Salt, to taste
1 package buttertype crackers,
   from a 3-package box

Cook broccoli according to directions on package and drain. Place broccoli in a 1¾-quart casserole. Combine milk, cheese, flour, butter and salt. Simmer ingredients until melted and thick. Pour mixture over broccoli. Make crumbs out of the crackers and sprinkle over casserole. Bake in a 350-degree oven for 20 to 30 minutes.

Suzanne Studley Megathlin
(Mrs. Keith N.)

BROCCOLI DELUXE

Serves: 6

1½ pounds fresh broccoli or
1 (10-ounce) package frozen
  chopped broccoli
1 (10¾-ounce) can cream of
  chicken soup
1 tablespoon flour
½ cup dairy sour cream
¼ cup grated carrot

1 tablespoon grated onion
¼ teaspoon salt
⅛ teaspoon pepper
¾ cup herb-seasoned stuffing
  mix
2 tablespoons butter or
  margarine, melted

Remove outer leaves of broccoli and tough part of stalks and discard. Cut remaining broccoli into 1-inch pieces. Cook stalk pieces in boiling, salted water for 5 to 8 minutes. Add flowerets to water and cook until tender, about 5 more minutes. If using frozen broccoli, prepare according to package directions. Blend together soup and flour. Add sour cream, carrot, onion, salt and pepper. Stir in drained broccoli. Turn into 2-quart casserole. Combine stuffing mix and butter and sprinkle around edge of baking dish. Bake in a 350-degree oven for 30 to 35 minutes, or until hot.

Sally Grindell Vamvakias
(Mrs. James G.)

BROCCOLI SURPRISE

Serves: 6 to 8

1 (10-ounce) package frozen
  broccoli, cooked and drained
1 cup shredded sharp Cheddar
  cheese
1 egg, beaten

1 small onion, chopped
½ cup mayonnaise
1 (10¾-ounce) can cream of
  chicken soup

Combine all ingredients and place into a 2-quart greased casserole. Bake in a 350-degree oven for 40 minutes, or until center tests clean with a knife.

Eileen Lechman
(Mrs. Andrew)

HERBED BRUSSELS SPROUTS

Yield: 6 to 8 servings

2 (10-ounce) packages frozen
  Brussels sprouts
3 tablespoons butter or
  margarine
3 tablespoons flour
½ teaspoon salt

⅛ teaspoon black pepper
1½ cups milk
¼ teaspoon ground marjoram
¼ teaspoon ground thyme
Parsley

Prepare Brussels sprouts according to package directions. While they are cooking, prepare sauce. Melt butter in a saucepan. Blend in flour, salt and pepper. Add milk slowly, stirring constantly; cook until sauce thickens. Add herbs. Pour sauce over cooked and drained Brussels sprouts. Garnish with parsley.

The Committee

STUFFED CABBAGE À LA MOOSEWOOD

Serves: 6
(2 rolls each)

1 large head green cabbage
1 medium carrot, diced
1 cup chopped onion
3 tablespoons butter
1 small clove garlic, crushed
¼ cup sunflower seeds
¾ cup raw cashew pieces
1 stalk celery, chopped
Salt and pepper, to taste

2 cups ricotta cheese
¼ cup raisins or currants
1 cup chopped apple
Juice from 1 lemon
1 to 2 tablespoons tamari
1 tablespoon honey
Extra butter
Yogurt or sour cream
Favorite rice

Parboil cabbage in pan of water 10 to 15 minutes, or until outer leaves are easily removed. Remove first 12 leaves. Make sure cabbage is cooked well enough so leaves will not break when rolled, but not so well that they disintegrate. Save cabbage insides to use for another dish. Parboil 2 heads of cabbage if you cannot get enough large leaves from one. Sauté carrots, onions, garlic, seeds, nuts and celery in melted butter until onions are transparent and nuts roasted. Drain the mixture well, and combine it with the salt, pepper, cheese, raisins, apple, lemon juice, tamari and honey. Place 3 to 4 tablespoons of filling near base of each leaf. Roll tightly, folding in sides. Place on buttered sheet and brush with extra butter. Cover and bake in a 325-degree oven for 25 minutes, or until heated through. Serve topped with yogurt or sour cream on a bed of your favorite rice.

M. J. Bailey Larned
(Mrs. F. Stephen)

BELGIAN CARROTS

Serves: 4

1 pound fresh carrots, sliced and
    cooked until barely tender
3 tablespoons butter
1 medium onion, chopped
1 bay leaf

¼ teaspoon thyme
1 teaspoon sugar
3 tablespoons flour
1 cup milk
Salt, to taste

Sauté chopped onion in butter; then add the bay leaf, thyme, and sugar. Reduce heat and add the flour, combining thoroughly. Gradually add the milk, stirring until thickened. Add the cooked carrots and stir to coat carrots with the sauce. Remove from heat and cover for at least one hour. May refrigerate at this point. Just before serving, uncover and reheat over very low heat, stirring often until carrots are heated through. Remove bay leaf before serving. Do not allow to boil. This must be made ahead of time for flavors to blend properly.

Patricia Pugh Britt
(Mrs. Michael E.)

GOLDEN CARROTS

Serves: 8

2 pounds carrots, sliced
1 (10¾-ounce) can tomato soup
1 large onion, sliced
1 cup sugar
¼ cup oil
¾ cup vinegar

1 tablespoon prepared mustard
1 teaspoon Worcestershire sauce
Salt and pepper, to taste

Cook carrots until just tender. Combine remaining ingredients. Pour over carrots and marinate overnight. This keeps for at least two weeks in the refrigerator.

Pamela Rockwell Welsh
(Mrs. Robert H.)

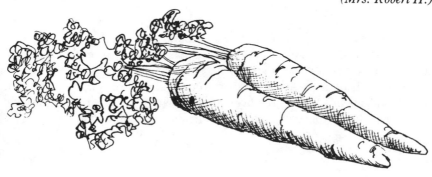

GLAZED CARROTS

Serves: 4 to 6

10 carrots, cut in 2-inch lengths
6 tablespoons butter
3 tablespoons brown sugar

Salt and pepper, to taste
Garlic powder, to taste
Minced parsley

Cook carrots and drain. Melt butter in heavy pan. Add sugar, salt, pepper, garlic powder and carrots and mix. Cover and simmer about 5 minutes. Sprinkle parsley on top before serving.

Sharon Smith Bushey
(Mrs. Donald J.)

CAULIFLOWER SOUFFLÉ

Serves: 6

4 ounces fine noodles, cooked
    according to directions
6 tablespoons chopped parsley,
    divided
3 tablespoons butter
¼ teaspoon salt
1 large cauliflower cut into
    flowerets, cooked, drained,
    and kept warm

½ cup mayonnaise
1 tablespoon grated onion
1 tablespoon lemon juice
Dash of cayenne
1 egg white, stiffly beaten

Mix noodles with 3 tablespoons parsley. Add butter and salt. Turn into 2-quart baking dish. Place cauliflower over noodles. Combine mayonnaise, remaining parsley, onion, lemon juice and cayenne. Fold in egg white. Spoon over cauliflower. Broil for 3 to 4 minutes.

Anne Reevy Neiman
(Mrs. G. W.)

CORN CAKES

Serves: 4

2 (10-ounce) packages frozen
corn, thawed and drained
1 tablespoon flour
2 teaspoons sugar
½ teaspoon salt

Pepper, to taste
2 large eggs, separated
1 tablespoon peanut or
vegetable oil
½ teaspoon baking powder

Combine corn, flour, sugar, salt and pepper. Beat egg yolks until foamy and add to corn mixture. Add the oil. Beat egg whites until stiff and gently fold into corn mixture. Carefully stir in the baking powder. Drop very small spoonfuls onto a lightly oiled griddle and fry until golden on both sides. Do not make cakes too large or they will be difficult to turn.

Patricia Pugh Britt
(Mrs. Michael E.)

VEGETABLE STUFFED EGGPLANT

Serves: 6

1 large eggplant
2 tablespoons butter
1 small onion, chopped
1 small zucchini, chopped
1 small summer squash, chopped

1 tomato, chopped
Oregano, to taste
Salt and pepper, to taste
Dill, to taste
½ cup grated Parmesan cheese

Slice eggplant in half lengthwise. Parboil in salted water for 8 minutes. Let drain on paper towels. Scoop out pulp. Be careful not to puncture eggplant. In a frying pan melt butter. Sauté onions until golden; add zucchini, eggplant pulp and summer squash. Simmer until tender. Add tomato and seasonings. Remove from heat. Stuff the eggplant halves. Sprinkle with cheese. Bake at 350 degrees on cookie sheet until warm and cheese is melted. Remove from oven, slice and serve hot.

Elizabeth A. Cook

117

CAPONATA ALLA SICILIANA

Serves: 8

2 medium sized eggplants, diced into 1-inch cubes
½ cup olive oil
2 onions, sliced
1 cup diced celery
1 (20-ounce) can tomatoes, drained
4 ounces chopped pitted black olives

2 ounces capers, washed (optional)
1 tablespoon pine nuts (optional)
2 tablespoons sugar
4 tablespoons wine vinegar
1 teaspoon mixed Italian spices
Salt and pepper, to taste

Fry diced eggplant in very hot oil about 10 minutes or until soft and lightly browned. Remove eggplant to a saucepan. Fry onion in the same oil about 3 minutes or until golden brown (add more olive oil if necessary). Add tomatoes and celery to the onions and simmer about 15 minutes until celery is tender. Add capers, olives and pine nuts at this point if desired. Stir well to combine and add this mixture to the eggplant. Dissolve sugar in vinegar; add salt and pepper to taste. Heat slightly. Add to eggplant; cover and simmer about 20 minutes over low heat. Stir occasionally to distribute flavor evenly. When done, place in a bowl to cool. This should not be eaten hot. May be used as a side dish with meat or poultry, as a sandwich filling, or in an antipasto. Keeps 1 week in the refrigerator.

Patricia Pugh Britt
(Mrs. Michael E.)

ESCAROLE NAVONNA

Serves: 4

½ pound ground sweet sausage
½ cup bread crumbs
1 clove garlic, minced
2 tablespoons minced parsley
Salt

Pepper
1 medium head escarole, washed, cored, and cut
16 ounces spaghetti sauce, canned or homemade

Brown sausage and drain fat. Combine bread crumbs, garlic, parsley, salt, and pepper with sausage. Place cut up escarole in bottom of 3-quart saucepan and pour sausage mixture over the escarole. Pour spaghetti sauce on top. Cook over medium heat for 30 minutes stirring frequently to prevent sticking. This is best if made early in day or a few days ahead and reheated at serving time.

Patricia Pugh Britt
(Mrs. Michael E.)

MUSHROOM SOUFFLÉ

Serves: 4 to 6

½ pound fresh mushrooms,
  finely chopped
5 tablespoons butter
Shallots, minced (optional)
1 teaspoon salt
Dash cayenne

2 tablespoons flour
1 cup milk
4 egg yolks
4 egg whites
Hollandaise sauce

Sauté mushrooms in butter. If desired, add small amount of shallots. Do not overcook. Season with salt and cayenne. Sprinkle flour over mushrooms and stir slowly. Add milk and simmer until thick. Separate eggs. Lightly beat yolks. Beat egg whites until stiff. After cooling mushrooms, stir in egg yolks and egg whites. Pour mixture into a greased 1-quart soufflé dish. Bake in oven at 375 degrees for 30 minutes. Serve with your favorite hollandaise sauce.

Deborah Snite Bates
(Mrs. Daniel W.)

MUSHROOM ROULADES

Serves: 8 to 10

1½ pounds mushrooms (or any
  cooked vegetable)
6 egg yolks
½ teaspoon salt
½ teaspoon pepper
2 tablespoons lemon juice

Nutmeg, to taste
6 egg whites
Additional whole mushrooms,
  for garnish
Hollandaise sauce or Béarnaise
  sauce

Oil a 15 x 10 x 1-inch jelly roll pan and line with waxed paper. Oil paper. Chop mushrooms very finely and wring in towel. Beat egg yolks until fluffy and combine with mushrooms, salt, pepper, lemon juice and nutmeg. Beat egg whites until peaks form. Fold into mushroom mixture. Pour into jelly roll pan and smooth out. Bake in a 350-degree oven for 15 minutes. Cool and turn onto sheet of waxed paper. Peel off top. Roll from long side by holding waxed paper. Garnish with whole or fluted mushrooms. Serve with your favorite hollandaise or Béarnaise sauce. Can be served either hot or cold.

Roselle Flynn Johnson
(Mrs. Steven M.)

ONIONS AU GRATIN

Serves: 6

6 cups sliced Spanish
  or Bermuda onions
  (¼-inch thick)
1 clove garlic, minced
¼ pound fresh mushrooms,
  sliced
3 tablespoons butter
2 tablespoons flour

½ teaspoon salt
¼ teaspoon pepper
⅓ cup grated Parmesan cheese
⅔ cup shredded Swiss cheese
1 beef bouillon cube
½ cup hot water
Parsley for garnish (optional)

Sauté onions, garlic, and mushrooms in butter until tender. Blend in flour, salt, and pepper. Arrange half of the onion mixture in buttered 2-quart casserole. Combine the two cheeses and sprinkle half the cheese mixture over the onions. Top with remaining onion and cheeses. Dissolve bouillon cube in water and pour over the onion and cheese combination. Bake for 20 minutes at 375 degrees. Garnish with parsley. Leftovers make great onion soup base!

Dorothy B. Ryan
(Mrs. Donald J.)

JULIENNE OF PARSNIP AND LEEK

Serves: 8

1½ pounds leeks
4 medium parsnips
½ cup butter
Peel of 2 lemons, finely grated

¾ teaspoon salt
¼ teaspoon freshly ground
  pepper

Trim leeks so 3 inches of green remain. Wash leeks thoroughly. Cut leeks into 3 x ¼-inch strips. Peel parsnips. Cut in half vertically and discard core if cracked and woody. Cut into strips similar to leeks. Melt butter in 10-inch skillet over medium-high heat. Add lemon peel. When butter is foamy, reduce heat to medium. Add leeks and parsnips. Sauté about 1½ minutes. Reduce heat; cover and simmer until vegetables are tender but still crisp, about 5 minutes. Stir in salt and pepper. Serve immediately in a heated dish.

Sharon Smith Bushey
(Mrs. Donald J.)

CANDIED PARSNIPS

Serves: 4

1 pound parsnips
⅓ cup water

1 cup light brown sugar
Butter

Peel the parsnips and slice into strips. Parboil until tender and drain thoroughly. Place in a buttered 7 x 11-inch glass casserole. Combine the water and brown sugar and pour over the parsnips. Dot with butter and bake for 45 minutes at 350 degrees. May be prepared ahead and put in oven 45 minutes before serving.

Patricia Pugh Britt
(Mrs. Michael E.)

HERBED POTATOES

Serves: 4

16 new potatoes
2 tablespoons rosemary

1 tablespoon thyme
½ cup margarine or butter

Scrub potatoes. Melt butter and add rosemary and thyme. Place potatoes in open baking dish and pour butter mixture over them. Stir several times while cooking. Bake at 350 degrees for 35 minutes, or until potatoes are tender.

Kathleen Foshay Hanson
(Mrs. Robert)

POTATOES O'BRIEN

Serves: 10 to 12

15 potatoes
½ cup butter, more if needed
2 tablespoons chopped
  parsley
1 large green pepper, chopped
1 large onion, chopped

¼ pound Cheddar cheese,
  shredded
3 tablespoons chopped pimento
Parmesan cheese, to taste,
  grated
Butter

Boil potatoes and cool. Peel and cube potatoes. Sauté parsley, green pepper and onion in melted butter. Add to potatoes. Add the cheese and pimento. Mix all ingredients together. Put in buttered 9 x 13-inch pan. Sprinkle with Parmesan cheese and dot with butter. Cover and bake at 350 degrees until bubbly.

Pam Webster
(Mrs. Wayne)

BAKED STUFFED POTATOES

Serves: 8 to 10

6 to 7 large potatoes
¾ cup butter
¾ cup all-purpose cream
2 cups sour cream
Salt and pepper, to taste

1 small onion, grated
⅔ cup shredded longhorn cheese
Chives, to taste
Additional longhorn cheese,
  shredded, to taste

Bake potatoes until done. Cut in half lengthwise (while still hot) and scoop out centers, being careful not to puncture skin of the potato. Put hot potato in mixing bowl and beat with electric beater while adding butter and cream. After mixture is smooth add sour cream, salt, pepper and onion and mix well. Add cheese and mix again. Put spoonfuls of mixture into potato shells. Top with shredded cheese and chives. Bake in a 400-degree oven for 30 minutes, or until cheese melts and mixture is bubbly. This recipe can be made a day ahead.

Mary Carter Anderson
(Mrs. Stephen M.)

HOLIDAY MASHED POTATOES

Serves: 8 to 12

3 pounds (about 12 medium)
  potatoes, peeled, cooked
  and hot
1 (8-ounce) package cream
  cheese, at room temperature
¼ cup butter

½ cup sour cream
½ cup milk
2 eggs, slightly beaten
¼ cup chopped onion
1 teaspoon salt
Dash pepper

In a large mixing bowl, beat hot potatoes until all lumps are removed. Add cream cheese (in small pieces) and the butter. Beat well until cheese and butter are completely melted and mixed. Stir in sour cream. To the milk add the eggs and onion. Add to the potato mixture along with salt and pepper. Beat well until light and fluffy. Place in a greased 9-inch round casserole. Refrigerate several hours or overnight. Bake in a preheated oven at 350 degrees for 45 minutes, or until lightly browned on top. This recipe is delicious left over.

Jane Fauver Acker
(Mrs. Thomas)

BAKED PUMPKIN

Serves: 6

3½ to 4-pound pumpkin
Corn oil
2 cups light cream
½ teaspoon salt (optional)
White pepper, to taste

Fresh ground nutmeg, to taste
1 cup shredded Cheddar or Swiss
  cheese
2 to 3 slices wheat toast (crusts
  removed and cubed)

Wash pumpkin well. Cut the top off as if for a Jack-o-lantern. Scoop out seeds and strings. Rub outside of pumpkin with corn oil. Mix together light cream, salt, pepper, and nutmeg. Place pumpkin in a baking pan and begin layering the cheese and toast cubes ending with cheese. Pack the layers down and pour the cream on top. Put the top back on the pumpkin and bake at 300 degrees for 2 hours. Stir occasionally during the cooking time.

Courtesy of Rebecca
Reilly's Fall Vegetable
Class at the Whip and Spoon

RICE SUPREME

Serves: 8

10 slices bacon
½ cup chopped onion
6 ounces mushrooms, minced
1 teaspoon garlic salt
1½ cups shredded Cheddar
  cheese, divided

1 cup dairy sour cream
½ teaspoon salt
2½ cups cooked brown rice

Cook bacon until crisp. Crumble bacon. Reserve 1 tablespoon drippings. Sauté onion, mushrooms, and garlic salt in drippings until tender. Add rice, 1 cup cheese, sour cream and salt. Mix well. Pour into lightly buttered 2-quart casserole. Sprinkle with remaining cheese and crumbled bacon. Bake in a 350-degree oven for 15 minutes. This recipe does not freeze well.

Kathleen Foshay Hanson
(Mrs. Robert)

RICE AND PECAN CASSEROLE

Serves: 10 to 12

1 pound mushrooms, sliced
4 green onions, sliced
1 clove garlic, minced
1 cup unsalted butter
2 cups uncooked brown rice
½ teaspoon dried thyme
¼ teaspoon turmeric
1 teaspoon salt
¼ teaspoon freshly ground
  pepper

1½ cups chopped pecans
6 cups beef stock or broth or
3 (10¾-ounce) cans condensed
  beef broth mixed with
  2¼ cups water
Whole pecans
Green onions, sliced

Using a large Dutch oven sauté mushrooms, onions and garlic in butter until mushrooms are golden (about 5 to 7 minutes). Stir in rice. Cook, stirring with fork, until rice is hot (about 3 minutes). Add thyme, turmeric, salt and pepper. Stir in chopped pecans. Pour in stock. Bring to a boil. May be frozen at this point, but thaw the mixture completely before using. Bake in a 350-degree oven until all liquid is absorbed and rice is tender, about 1 hour, 20 minutes. Adjust seasonings. Garnish with whole pecans and green onion slices.

Susan Welky Corey
(Mrs. John B.)

RICE GIRALDA

Yield: 12 or more servings

2 (10-ounce) packages yellow
  rice
1 medium onion, chopped
2 cloves garlic, minced
Olive oil—butter
8 ounces Kielbasa, ¼-inch slices

1 (10-ounce) jar salad olives
2 (6½-ounce) jars marinated
  artichoke hearts, quartered
2 cups Parmesan cheese, divided
Salt and pepper, to taste

Cook rice according to package directions. Sauté onion and garlic in olive oil and butter. Add sausage slices and brown lightly. Mix rice, onion, garlic, olives and artichokes together and put in a casserole dish. Season to taste. Cover and bake at 350 degrees for about 20 minutes. Uncover and stir in 1½ cups Parmesan cheese. Sprinkle remaining cheese on top. Bake uncovered for 10 minutes or until cheese is lightly browned.

Carol Potter Day
(Mrs. Richard B.)

FRIED RICE

Serves: 6

½ cup chopped onion
¼ cup chopped green pepper
4 tablespoons vegetable oil
1 teaspoon sesame seed oil
1 cup diced cooked meat
  (beef, pork or chicken)

3 cups cooked rice
3 tablespoons soy sauce, or
  more to taste
¾ cup frozen peas or peas
  and carrots
1 egg slightly beaten

In 10-inch frying pan sauté onion and green pepper in oils until slightly transparent. Add meat, rice and soy sauce. Cook for about 1 minute. Stir in vegetables. Add egg. Cook thoroughly, about 5 minutes.

Cheryl Wetherbee Maisch
(Mrs. Robert)

SAUERKRAUT BAKE

Serves: 4 to 6

1 (27-ounce) can sauerkraut, drained
1 (20-ounce) can tomatoes, undrained

5 thick slices bacon, fried and crumbled
¾ cup light brown sugar
¼ cup margarine

Place sauerkraut and tomatoes in a glass 13 x 9 x 2-inch baking dish. Combine crumbled bacon, brown sugar, and margarine to form a topping. Sprinkle topping over the tomato and sauerkraut mixture. Bake for 1 hour at 350 degrees.

Patricia Pugh Britt
(Mrs. Michael E.)

SPINACH CASSEROLE

Serves: 6 to 8

2 (10-ounce) packages frozen chopped spinach
1 (3-ounce) package cream cheese

¼ cup butter
Salt and pepper, to taste
½ cup chopped pecans
¼ cup grated Parmesan cheese

Cook spinach according to directions. Drain. Melt cheese and butter together and add to spinach. Season to taste. Put in 1-quart casserole. Top with pecans and Parmesan cheese. Heat at 350 degrees for 20 minutes.

Gretchen Harris Ramsay
(Mrs. Scott W.)

MARIA'S SQUASH CASSEROLE

Serves: 8

2 cups mashed cooked squash
¾ cup butter, melted
1 cup shredded Cheddar cheese
2 cups bread crumbs

1½ medium onions, chopped
1 cup evaporated milk
1 teaspoon salt
½ teaspoon pepper
1 or 2 beaten eggs

Mix all ingredients together. Pour into 2-quart casserole. Bake uncovered in a 350-degree oven for 40 minutes.

Mary Rines Thompson
(Mrs. Philip, Jr.)

BAKED ACORN SQUASH

Serves: 2

1 acorn squash, halved and
   cleaned
3 or 4 small apples, peeled
   and chopped
⅓ cup chopped walnuts

⅓ cup raisins
2 tablespoons honey
1 teaspoon cinnamon
Butter

Combine apples, walnuts, raisins, honey and cinnamon. Divide ingredients between squash halves. Dot with butter. Bake in a pan of water at 350 degrees for 30 minutes. Cover with foil and bake another 30 minutes.

Sue Mahan Kimble
(Mrs. John D.)

SPINACH AND CHEESE CASSEROLE

Serves: 3 or 4

1 pound fresh spinach
3 slices bacon, diced
1 small onion, minced
1 egg, beaten
¾ cup cottage cheese
¼ cup shredded Cheddar
   cheese

¼ to 1 teaspoon caraway seeds,
   to taste
½ teaspoon salt
½ teaspoon pepper
Dash of nutmeg
Bread crumbs, to taste
Paprika

Cook spinach until limp. Drain and chop. Cook bacon. Reserve 2 tablespoons of drippings. Sauté onion in drippings until translucent. Combine egg, cheeses, caraway seeds, salt, pepper and nutmeg. Mix with onions and spinach. Turn into shallow, greased 1-quart baking dish. Sprinkle top with bacon. Sprinkle bread crumbs over bacon. Sprinkle paprika over bread crumbs. Bake in 350-degree oven for about 30 minutes. For a more substantial main dish chopped ham may be added.

India Horton Weatherill
(Mrs. Robert H.)

PARTY CASSEROLE

Serves: 12

1 (10-ounce) package frozen French-style green beans
1 (10-ounce) package frozen baby lima beans
1 (10-ounce) package frozen small peas
1¼ cups heavy cream
1¼ cups mayonnaise
¾ cup grated Parmesan cheese or
¾ cup shredded Cheddar cheese
⅛ teaspoon pepper
¼ teaspoon salt
Paprika
Parsley

Preheat oven to 325 degrees. Cook the vegetables in a very small amount of water just until thawed and can be separated with a fork. Drain and cool. Whip the cream. Fold in the mayonnaise, cheese, salt and pepper. Butter a 2-quart casserole. Put in the vegetables. Cover with the cream mixture. Sprinkle with paprika. Bake uncovered about 30 to 40 minutes, or until browned and bubbly. May be prepared ahead and put in the refrigerator until baking time.

Lee Morse Edwards
(Mrs. Dwight H.)

TOMATOES WITH SPINACH MORNAY

Serves: 8 to 10

3 (10-ounce) packages frozen chopped spinach
Salt and pepper
4 tablespoons butter
3 tablespoons flour
Dash salt
Dash cayenne pepper
1 teaspoon Dijon mustard
1 teaspoon dry mustard
1 cup milk
4 tablespoons shredded Swiss cheese
4 tablespoons grated Parmesan cheese
4 tablespoons half and half
8 to 10 medium tomatoes
Grated Parmesan cheese

Cook spinach slowly, without any additional water. Drain thoroughly. Season with salt and pepper. Melt butter in separate pan. Remove from heat and add flour. Season with salt, cayenne, mustards and blend in milk. Stir over heat until it boils, then add cheeses and light cream. Simmer 5 minutes, then combine with spinach mixture. Cut tops off tomatoes and remove seeds and center membranes. Pile spinach into tomato cases and sprinkle with Parmesan cheese. Bake at 350 degrees for 20 minutes.

Nancy Montgomery Beebe
(Mrs. Michael)

TOMATO BLEU CHEESE TIMBALE

Serves: 6

¼ cup minced shallots or onions
2 tablespoons butter
1 pound tomatoes, peeled, seeded
    and chopped
1 tablespoon tomato paste
½ teaspoon sugar

¾ cup cream
½ cup bread crumbs
¼ cup bleu cheese
6 egg yolks
Salt and pepper, to taste

Sauté shallots in butter until soft. Add tomatoes, tomato paste and sugar. Cook, stirring frequently, until all liquid has evaporated. Let cool. Combine cream and bread crumbs in large bowl. Add bleu cheese and yolks. Add tomato mixture, salt and pepper and spoon into 6 buttered custard cups. Cover with buttered waxed paper rounds. Place in pan with boiling water coming up to the middle of cups. Bake in a 350-degree oven for 35 to 40 minutes. Take out of water. Let stand for 5 minutes. Run a knife around edge and unmold. Serve with chive sauce.

Chive Sauce

1 cup cream
2 tablespoons snipped chives or
    dried chives

1 tablespoon butter mixed with
    1 tablespoon flour
Salt and white pepper, to taste

Heat cream and chives to boiling point. Whisk in butter and flour mixture. Stir until smooth. Add salt and pepper. Recipe can also be made in 1-quart buttered mold. Cover mixture with buttered waxed paper round. Place in pan with boiling water coming up to middle of mold. Bake in a 350-degree oven for about 1 hour. Remove from water and follow directions for individual cups.

Elizabeth Strong Mahan
(Mrs. Stuart)

SWEET POTATO SOUFFLÉ

Serves: 6 to 8

3 cups cooked, mashed sweet
  potatoes
1 cup sugar
2 eggs
½ cup milk

1 teaspoon vanilla
1 cup brown sugar
½ cup flour
1 cup chopped pecans
¼ cup margarine

Combine sweet potatoes, sugar, eggs, milk and vanilla. Mix well. Pour into buttered casserole. Combine brown sugar, flour, pecans and margarine. Spread over potatoes. Bake at 400 degrees for 30 to 40 minutes.

Harriet Combs Trafford
(Mrs. Timothy R.)

ITALIAN STUFFED ZUCCHINI

Serves: 4 to 6

2 (10-inch) zucchini, about
  1¼ pounds
4 Italian sausages
1 onion, chopped
1 clove of garlic, minced
1 cup small shell macaroni,
  uncooked
1 tomato, peeled, seeded
  and chopped

1 cup shredded Cheddar cheese
2 tablespoons minced parsley
1 teaspoon dried oregano
Salt and pepper, to taste
2 tablespoons olive oil
¼ cup freshly grated Parmesan
  cheese

Cut zucchini in half lengthwise. Hollow out each half, leaving shell ¼ to ½-inch thick. Chop pulp and measure 2 cups. Remove sausage from casings. Cook in skillet over medium heat, crumbling meat as it cooks. When sausage has rendered some of its fat, add zucchini pulp, onion and garlic. Continue cooking until onion is soft and sausage has lost all of its pink color. Meanwhile, cook macaroni in pot of rapidly boiling water until *al dente,* about 5 minutes. Drain macaroni. Drain fat from sausage mixture. Combine sausage mixture with macaroni, tomato, Cheddar cheese, parsley, oregano, salt and pepper. Blend well. Brush inside of zucchini halves with oil. Mound filling in zucchini halves. Place in shallow baking dish. Add about ½-inch hot water to dish. Cover with foil and bake in a 350-degree oven until zucchini is tender when pierced with knife tip, about 30 minutes. Remove from oven and discard foil. Preheat broiler. Drain any water remaining in dish. Sprinkle halves with Parmesan cheese and put under broiler until cheese is light golden brown and bubbly.

Sharon Smith Bushey
(Mrs. Donald J.)

SWEET AND SOUR ZUCCHINI

Serves: 8

4 tablespoons margarine
2 tablespoons olive oil
10 small, young zucchini,
   thinly sliced

½ cup sugar
2 tablespoons vinegar
1 tablespoon chopped sweet basil
Salt and pepper, to taste

In large skillet melt margarine and add oil. Sauté zucchini, stirring it gently with a wooden spoon. Do not overcook. Transfer to a serving dish and keep warm. Add sugar to pan in which zucchini was cooked and stir. Add vinegar and bring to a boil for about 2 minutes. Add basil. Pour sauce over zucchini. Salt and pepper to taste. Serve at once.

Elizabeth Lincoln Preti
(Mrs. Robert F.)

BAKED VEGETABLE CASSEROLE
(LAHANA STÓ FOURNO)

Serves: 4 to 6

½ pound fresh string beans,
   trimmed
½ pound fresh sliced okra or
   peeled and cubed eggplant
   (optional)
1 large potato, peeled and cut
   into ½-inch slices
2 medium zucchini, cut into ½-
   inch slices
2 stalks celery, cut into 1-inch
   pieces
1 large onion, quartered

2 cloves garlic, finely minced
½ cup chopped parsley
1½ tablespoons chopped fresh
   dill or ½ tablespoon dried dill
2 teaspoons salt
½ teaspoon black pepper
½ pound tomatoes, fresh or
   canned
Approximately 2 cups boiling
   water
3½ tablespoons olive oil

Place all cut up vegetables, except tomatoes, in a large mixing bowl. Add garlic, parsley, dill, salt and pepper. If using fresh tomatoes, remove skin (dip tomatoes in boiling water for 10 seconds, then peel) and slice. If using canned tomatoes crush them well. Add tomatoes to the vegetables and toss gently. Arrange vegetables in a 4-quart baking dish or casserole, leaving some room at the top. Pour boiling water slowly over vegetables to nearly cover them. Pour olive oil on top. Cover and bake in preheated 450-degree oven for 15 minutes, then reduce heat to 350 degrees. Bake 1½ hours or until vegetables are tender and soft. Better reheated.

Sally Grindell Vamvakias
(Mrs. James G.)

YORKSHIRE PUDDING

Serves: 4 to 6

1 cup flour
1 teaspoon salt
1 cup milk, at room temperature

2 eggs, at room temperature
¼ cup roast beef drippings from
   roasting pan

Sift the flour and salt together. Beat the eggs and combine with the milk; add to the dry ingredients. One half hour before serving, pour the *hot* roast beef drippings into a heated 8-inch square pan. Pour batter into the drippings, do not stir. Bake in a preheated 400-degree oven for 30 minutes. Serve with standing rib or rolled rib roast.

Eileen A. Pugh
(Mrs. Richard F.)

BLENDER HOLLANDAISE SAUCE

Yield: 1 cup

3 egg yolks
2 tablespoons fresh lemon
  juice

Scant ¼ teaspoon salt
Dash cayenne pepper
⅔ cup butter, melted

Combine egg yolks, lemon juice, salt and cayenne in blender. Cover and blend on high speed for 3 seconds. With blender on high speed, very slowly pour hot melted butter into the egg mixture until combined. This may be made a day or two ahead and reheated very gently in a double-boiler. Only warm the sauce, do not cook it.

Patricia Pugh Britt
(Mrs. Michael E.)

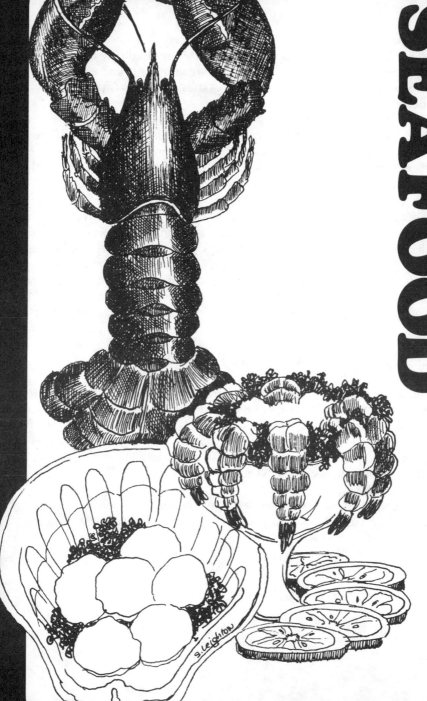

SEAFOOD

CAPE SHORE LOBSTER BAKE

Serves: 6 to 8

6 to 8 pounds clams
6 to 8 lobsters (1¼ pounds each)
6 to 8 ears of corn
1 pound hot dogs, optional
½ dozen eggs, optional

Seaweed
Butter, melted (for dunking
  lobster meat and clams)
Asbestos gloves (optional)

Prepare fireplace using cement blocks or rocks. A metal trash can with cover, lined with approximately two inches of stone, provides for a simple and convenient means of preparing a small, 6 to 8-person Downeast Bake. With an abundant supply of dry wood, start the fire and establish a good base of hot coals. Cover stones in bottom of container with salt water (sea water or salted fresh water). Cover with about 3 inches of fresh seaweed. Cover with fresh clams, which have been washed in cold water and wrapped in cheesecloth in individual portions. Allow 1 pound of clams per person. Cover with seaweed. Add 6 to 8 lobsters and cover with seaweed. Before adding corn, carefully pull back husk and remove silk! Fold back a couple of layers of husk. Add to bake and cover with seaweed. Hot dogs and eggs may be added if desired. Place cover on container, weight with rock if loose fitting. Place container over fire and cook for 50 minutes after steam starts coming out from under the cover. Have melted butter, lemon, salt, chips, beer and appetite ready when bake is opened up. A pair of asbestos gloves is handy at this point.

Comments: Do not pack any of the layers tightly as this will prevent the steam from circulating freely. For larger bakes a 3-foot to 4-foot square steel plate (⅜-inch to ½-inch thick) would be required. This is set on cement blocks and food added before starting the fire. Layering of food should be accomplished as described above, and then covered with a tarp or aluminum foil to contain the steam. Cooking time is, again, 50 minutes after steam is up.

Caution: If additional water is needed, pour in along side of container or directly onto the steel plate. Do not pour over top of bake as this will cause "cool down" and prevent or delay cooking.

Mr. & Mrs. Jack Smith

SHRIMP PENTAGON

Serves: 16

2 cups sliced green pepper
5 cups slivered onions
2 cups diced celery
1 cup chopped celery leaves
1 cup salad oil
1 cup chili sauce
1 cup seedless raisins

1 teaspoon each of thyme, curry,
  salt, pepper and cayenne
3 large bay leaves
½ cup chopped parsley
1⅔ cups almonds
2 (28-ounce) cans tomatoes
5 pounds shrimp, cooked

Cook green peppers, onions, celery and celery leaves in oil until onions are transparent, not brown. Add remaining ingredients and simmer gently, stirring occasionally. Add shrimp and put into 4-quart casserole dish. Heat just before serving. Serve over rice.

Candy MacDonald Gibbons
(Mrs. Albert E., Jr.)

SWEET AND PUNGENT SHRIMP

Serves: 4

¼ cup brown sugar
2 teaspoons cornstarch
½ teaspoon salt
¼ cup vinegar (cider)
1 teaspoon soy sauce
½ teaspoon ground ginger

1 (20-ounce) can pineapple
  chunks, drained (reserve
  syrup)
1 green pepper, cut into strips
1 medium onion, cut in rings
1 pound raw shrimp

Mix in saucepan the brown sugar, cornstarch and salt. Add vinegar, soy sauce, ginger and the pineapple juice. Cook this mixture until slightly thick, stirring constantly. Add green pepper strips, onion rings and pineapple chunks together with shrimp. Cook about 5 minutes, lifting and stirring once or twice until shrimp turn pink and curl up. (Avoid overcooking.) Serve with hot fluffy rice.

Hope Palmer Bramhall
(Mrs. Peter T. C.)

INDIAN FRIED SHRIMP

Serves: 6

2 pounds raw jumbo shrimp,
  shelled, deveined and
  butterflied
¼ cup lemon juice
½ teaspoon salt
¼ teaspoon ground ginger

1½ teaspoons curry
2 cups flour
1⅓ cups milk
2 teaspoons baking powder
Shaved coconut, toasted
Oil

Place shrimp in a marinade made of the next four ingredients. Leave shrimp in marinade overnight. Remove shrimp and combine marinade with flour, milk and baking powder to make a batter. Dredge the shrimp in flour and then dip in the batter. Roll in coconut. Fry 4 to 6 minutes at 375 degrees in hot oil. Serve with curry sauce.

Curry Sauce

1 medium onion, chopped
1 clove of garlic, chopped
1 stalk celery, chopped
1 tart apple, chopped
¼ pound ham, chopped
½ cup butter, melted
1 small bay leaf

1 tablespoon parsley
2 tablespoons flour
½ teaspoon ground mace
1 tablespoon curry
¼ teaspoon dry mustard
2½ cups chicken broth

Sauté the first eight ingredients gently for about 10 minutes. Add flour, mace, curry and mustard and cook 5 minutes longer. Remove bay leaf, add the chicken broth and simmer 1 hour. Strain. Reheat and serve.

The Committee

CLAM FRITTERS

Serves: 4

1 pint clams
2 eggs
⅓ cup milk
1⅓ cups flour

2 teaspoons baking powder
Salt
Pepper

Clean clams, drain from liquor and chop. Beat eggs until light, add milk and flour (mixed and sifted with baking powder). Add chopped clams and season lightly with salt and pepper. Drop by spoonfuls and fry in deep fat. Drain on paper towels.

The Committee

SHERRY SHRIMP

Serves: 4

4 tablespoons butter
6 garlic cloves, crushed
1½ pounds shrimp (shelled
and deveined)
¼ cup fresh lemon juice
¼ teaspoon pepper

1 cup sherry
2 teaspoons chopped parsley
2 teaspoons chopped chives
Salt, to taste
Lemon slices
Parsley

Melt butter in skillet over medium heat. Add garlic, shrimp, lemon juice and pepper. Cook, stirring until shrimp turns pink (approximately 5 minutes). Add sherry, parsley, chives and salt to taste. Bring to boil. Serve over rice. Garnish with lemon and parsley.

Lurana Marzilli

FISKEBOLLAR I SAUS
(NORWEGIAN FISH BALLS IN CREAM SAUCE)

Serves: 4

½ cup chopped onion
4 tablespoons margarine or
butter
4 tablespoons flour
¼ teaspoon nutmeg
½ teaspoon salt
¼ teaspoon pepper

½ teaspoon paprika
Liquid from fish balls plus light
cream to make 2 cups of liquid
1 can fish balls (available at
gourmet or specialty markets);
cut them in half if too big
½ pound cooked shrimp

Sauté onion in butter. Gradually add flour. Bubble for 1 or 2 minutes. Add seasonings. Gradually add liquid from fish balls and the cream. Bring to a boil, simmer gently, stirring constantly for 1 or 2 minutes. Add the fish balls and shrimp. Heat gently until heated through. (If preparing ahead of time do not heat through, just add the fish balls and shrimp and refrigerate until serving time.)

Elsie J. Andersen

"CROCKED" AND SHERRIED CRAB

Serves: 14 to 16

2 pounds crabmeat
9 tablespoons butter
¾ cup dry sherry
¾ cup light cream
3 eggs, beaten
3 (10-ounce) cans cream of
  mushroom soup

1½ teaspoons Worcestershire
  sauce
1 pound mushrooms, sliced
4 to 6 medium onions, chopped
Salt and pepper, to taste
¼ cup minute tapioca

Remove any cartilage or shell from crabmeat; break into pieces. Place in the bottom of slow cooker. Add all the remaining ingredients except tapioca. Stir gently. Cover and cook on high for 1 hour then on low for 4 to 6 hours. Add tapioca to thicken. Serve hot over toast points, rice or patty shells.

Patricia Pugh Britt
(Mrs. Michael E.)

BAKED CRAB

Serves: 6 to 8

1 pound fresh crabmeat
1 cup dry stuffing mix
Milk
1 cup mayonnaise
1 teaspoon Worcestershire sauce

1 teaspoon lemon juice
⅛ to ¼ teaspoon cayenne pepper
4 hard-boiled eggs, chopped
½ cup bread crumbs
2 tablespoons butter

Clean crabmeat. Put dry stuffing in measuring cup and pour milk over stuffing to make one cup. Mix all other ingredients together except bread crumbs and butter. Put into 2-quart casserole. Sprinkle with bread crumbs and dot with butter. Bake in a 350 degree oven for 20 to 30 minutes.

Sharon Staples Alexander
(Mrs. Alan R.)

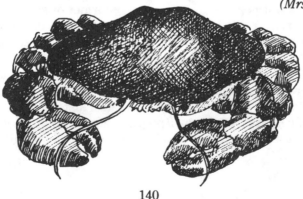

SCALLOPS WITH VERMOUTH

Serves: 4

½ cup flour
1 teaspoon salt
1 teaspoon pepper
1 teaspoon paprika

1½ pounds fresh scallops
¾ cup butter
6 to 8 tablespoons dry vermouth

Into a paper bag put flour, salt, pepper and paprika. Add scallops and shake until well coated. With slotted spoon remove scallops from bag. Using large fry pan, brown the scallops in melted butter. Add vermouth and simmer until tender.

Stephanie Coughlin Coney
(Mrs. John E., Jr.)

MARCE'S SCALLOPED OYSTERS

Serves: 4

½ pound soda crackers,
   crumbled
½ cup butter

1 pint oysters, drained
Salt and pepper, to taste
Milk—to cover casserole

Butter a 1½-quart covered casserole. Begin layering with soda crackers. Dot with butter, then oysters. Repeat layers. End with a layer of cracker crumbs. Pour enough milk in casserole to come to the top of the crackers. Cover and bake at 325 degrees 45 minutes. Remove cover and bake 15 minutes more.

Martha E. Britt
(Mrs. Edward T.)

BAKED HADDOCK

Serves: 6

2 pounds haddock
2 cups sour cream
½ cup mayonnaise
1 teaspoon celery salt
½ teaspoon pepper

¼ teaspoon thyme
½ teaspoon paprika
Dill weed or fresh dill
Lime wedges

Put haddock in greased shallow baking pan. Combine and pour over fish the sour cream, mayonnaise, celery salt, pepper, thyme, and paprika. Sprinkle with dill. Bake 40 minutes at 350 degrees. Serve with lime wedges.

Rho Francke Leavitt
(Mrs. William)

COQUILLE ST. JACQUES

Serves: 8

1 pound scallops
1 cup dry white wine
¾ teaspoon salt
4 peppercorns
1 tablespoon parsley
1 very small bay leaf
Scant ¼ teaspoon thyme
3 tablespoons finely chopped
   shallots
⅓ cup water

6 tablespoons butter
½ pound chopped mushrooms
3 tablespoons flour
½ cup milk
2 egg yolks
⅓ cup heavy cream
1 teaspoon lemon juice
Dash cayenne
½ cup shredded Swiss cheese

Combine first nine ingredients in saucepan. Bring to a boil; cover and simmer 5 minutes. Remove from heat and strain off liquids. There will be about 2 cups of liquid. Put liquid back on the heat and boil rapidly for 10 minutes or until liquid has reduced to 1 cup. Heat 2 tablespoons butter in skillet; add mushrooms; sauté for 8 minutes at low heat. Drain mushrooms and set aside. To make the sauce, melt 3 tablespoons butter in double boiler, blend in the flour; gradually add milk, stirring constantly until mixture is thick and smooth. Add reduced cooking liquid and cook for 1 minute. Beat egg yolks with cream in a bowl. Add hot sauce, a little at a time, beating after each addition. Put the sauce back in the pan and cook, stirring about 2 minutes until slightly thickened. Remove from heat and add lemon juice and cayenne. Refrigerate sauce, scallops and mushrooms separately. Before serving, bring scallops and mushrooms to room temperature. Heat sauce in double boiler. Add scallops and mushrooms to sauce in pan and heat. Spoon scallop mixture into 8 buttered shells. Sprinkle with Swiss cheese and dot with remaining butter. Broil 6 to 8 inches from heat for 3 minutes or just until lightly browned and bubbly.

Susan Hall Haynes
(Mrs. J. David)

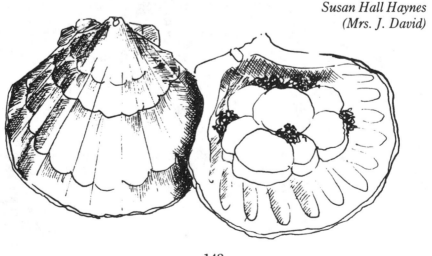

LEMONY BAKED STUFFED HALIBUT STEAKS

Serves: 8 to 10

2 large halibut steaks of equal size, cut ½-inch thick
½ teaspoon salt
⅛ teaspoon pepper

¼ cup melted butter or margarine
Juice of 1 lemon
Toothpicks

Preheat oven to 350 degrees. Sprinkle both sides of steaks with salt and pepper. Mix butter and lemon juice and brush lightly over both sides of steaks. Place 1 steak in a well-greased shallow baking pan (pan to fit size of steaks). Cover with stuffing and top with second steak. Fasten loosely with toothpicks. Brush with butter mixture and bake uncovered 30 to 40 minutes, brushing often with remaining butter until fish just flakes when touched with a fork. Remove toothpicks and serve with lemon butter.

Lemon Bread Stuffing

¼ cup chopped yellow onion
½ cup chopped celery
2 tablespoons butter or margarine
1¼ cups toasted bread crumbs
1½ teaspoons finely grated lemon rind

1 tablespoon lemon juice
1 tablespoon chopped parsley
¼ teaspoon salt
¼ teaspoon sage
⅛ teaspoon pepper
2 tablespoons milk

Sauté onion and celery in butter in a large skillet over moderate heat approximately 5 minutes, or until golden. Pour over bread crumbs. Add remaining ingredients and toss lightly to mix.

Deborah Spring Reed
(Mrs. Verner, III)

MAINE SEA BURGER

Serves: 4 to 6

2 cups finely chopped clams
1 cup corn flakes
1 egg, well-beaten
¼ cup milk

1 tablespoon minced onion
1 tablespoon minced celery
Salt and pepper, to taste
Shortening or oil for frying

Combine ingredients. Form into patties. Have hot shortening or oil about 1″ deep in skillet. Fry burgers until golden brown and serve piping hot.

Candice Carbone Thornton
(Mrs. Peter P.)

BAKED SWORDFISH AND MUSHROOMS

Yield: 4 to 6 servings

2 tablespoons chopped onion
¼ cup butter
1 pound mushrooms, sliced
Salt and pepper, to taste

Tarragon, to taste
2 swordfish steaks (1-inch thick)
½ cup white wine
¾ cup cream

Sauté onion in butter. Add the mushrooms and cook until tender. Season with salt, pepper, and tarragon. Place one steak in buttered baking dish and spread with ¾ mushroom mixture. Top with the other steak, salt, pepper and dot with 1 tablespoon of butter. Pour wine over all. Bake 25 minutes, basting occasionally, at 425 degrees. Transfer fish to serving platter. Add reserved mushroom mixture and cream to the baking dish. Cook until slightly thickened; pour over the fish on the serving platter.

Judith Adam
(Mrs. Robert L.)

FILET OF SOLE RIVE GAUCHE

Serves: 4

4 filets of sole
¼ cup flour
Salt and pepper
¼ cup butter, melted
¼ cup butter, melted
1 medium onion, diced

½ pound fresh mushrooms,
   sliced
1 tablespoon lemon juice
1 tablespoon chopped parsley
Salt and pepper

Coat the filets with flour seasoned with salt and pepper to taste. Melt the first ¼ cup butter and sauté the filets for 2 minutes per side or until golden brown. Remove filets from pan and keep warm in oven. Melt the second ¼ cup butter and sauté the onion until transparent. Add the mushrooms and cook for 2 minutes or until soft. Stir in the lemon juice and parsley, seasoned with salt and pepper to taste. Pour sauce over the fish and serve at once.

Patricia Pugh Britt
(Mrs. Michael E.)

VIENNESE FISH

Serves: 4

4 large potatoes, boiled in skin,
  then peeled and sliced
1 pound haddock
Salt and pepper, to taste
½ cup butter, melted
¾ cup sour cream

½ cup bread crumbs, seasoned
  or plain
½ teaspoon paprika
4 lemon slices
Salt and pepper, to taste

Butter 9 x 9-inch baking dish. Arrange boiled, sliced potatoes on all sides (*not* bottom) of dish. Place fish, cut into 4 portions, in bottom of pan and sprinkle with salt and pepper. Brush potatoes and fish generously with butter. Cover fish with sour cream and dust with bread crumbs and paprika. Bake in 350-degree oven for 25 to 30 minutes. Serve with lemon slices.

Karen Ker Day
(Mrs. Thomas)

FILET OF SOLE WITH CRABMEAT

Serves: 4

1½ to 2 pounds of sole (4 to 8
  sole filets of uniform size)
1½ tablespoons butter, melted
1 tablespoon flour
¼ teaspoon horseradish
⅛ teaspoon Worcestershire
  sauce
½ teaspoon lemon juice
2 dashes of hot pepper sauce
½ teaspoon salt

Pinch of onion salt
⅛ teaspoon MSG
Pepper, to taste
⅓ cup milk
1 cup crabmeat
2 tablespoons butter, melted
1½ teaspoons lemon juice
Paprika
Lemon wedges

Melt the 1½ tablespoons of butter; then add the flour and blend. Add horseradish, Worcestershire, lemon juice, hot pepper sauce, salt, onion salt, MSG and pepper, blending all together. Add milk and cook until quite thick, stirring constantly. Remove from heat and add crabmeat. At this point you can set aside and refrigerate or proceed as follows: Grease a 9 x 13 x 2-inch casserole and place one layer of filets in bottom of pan. Spread with crabmeat sauce, then top with another filet. Combine butter and lemon juice and pour over the top. Bake at 350 degrees for 30 minutes. Garnish with lemon wedges and sprinkle with paprika.

Deborah Lord Riley
(Mrs. William C.)

BAKED HADDOCK WITH CURRY SAUCE

Serves: 6

2 pounds haddock filet　　　　　1½ cups fine bread crumbs
½ cup evaporated milk

Rinse and dry haddock filets. Cut in serving size pieces. Dip pieces in evaporated milk then coat with bread crumbs. Place the fish in a flat 9 x 13 x 2-inch buttered baking dish. Bake 15 minutes in 350-degree oven. Remove dish from oven and spread curry sauce on fish, place under the broiler until bubbly and lightly brown. Serve immediately.

Curry Sauce

¾ cup mayonnaise　　　　　　　1 teaspoon curry powder
1 tablespoon lemon juice　　　　½ teaspoon prepared mustard
1 teaspoon basil

Combine all ingredients in the order given.

Elizabeth Lincoln Preti
(Mrs. Robert F.)

BAKED HADDOCK WITH CRABMEAT

Serves: 6 to 8

2½ pounds haddock filets　　　　¼ pound margarine, melted
2½ cups whole wheat bread,　　　½ cup water
　made into crumbs　　　　　　　½ cup mayonnaise
1 teaspoon salt　　　　　　　　　1 cup fresh crabmeat
¼ teaspoon ground peppercorns,　6 tablespoons margarine
　to taste　　　　　　　　　　　　½ cup shredded sharp cheese
½ cup chopped celery　　　　　　2 tablespoons white wine
1 cup chopped mushrooms　　　　½ cup slivered almonds
1 teaspoon parsley　　　　　　　　　(optional)
1 teaspoon chopped chives

Lay haddock filets in baking pan. Make stuffing with bread crumbs, salt, pepper, celery, mushrooms, parsley and chives. Moisten with ¼ pound of melted margarine, hot water and mayonnaise. Place stuffing over filets; cover with grated cheese. Bake 25 to 30 minutes in a 350-degree oven or until fish flakes when tested with fork. While fish is baking, sauté crabmeat in 6 tablespoons melted margarine. Stir in wine. Pour over baked fish. Sprinkle with slivered almonds and return to the oven and bake 5 minutes longer.

Lurana Marzilli

POULTRY

APPRICOT-GLAZED CHICKEN BREASTS

Serves: 10

10 whole chicken breasts, boned
   and skinned

18 ounces apricot preserves
1 package onion soup mix

Combine the preserves and the onion soup mix. "Paint" the inside of the chicken breasts with the apricot-onion mixture; roll tightly and place in a 9 x 13 x 2-inch glass casserole. Pour the remaining glaze over the chicken breasts. Cover with foil and bake at 350 degrees for 2 hours. Baste often during cooking. Can be prepared 1 day ahead and refrigerated. Remove from refrigerator 30 minutes before cooking.

Patricia Pugh Britt
(Mrs. Michael E.)

CHICKEN BREASTS AND MUSHROOMS
IN MADEIRA SAUCE

Serves: 6

2 tablespoons butter
3 whole chicken breasts, split
   and boned
1 teaspoon salt
¼ teaspoon pepper
¾ pound medium-sized
   mushrooms
2 teaspoons lemon juice

1 tablespoon butter
2 tablespoons chopped shallots
1 tablespoon flour
¾ cup Madeira wine
¾ cup heavy cream
¾ cup shredded Swiss cheese

Heat 2 tablespoons butter in large skillet. Add chicken and brown over medium high heat about 10 minutes on each side. Sprinkle both sides with salt and pepper. Transfer to a 12 x 8 x 2-inch baking dish. Trim mushrooms, toss with lemon juice, and set aside. Add 1 tablespoon butter to skillet; stir in shallots and sauté for 3 minutes. Add mushrooms and cook for 5 minutes or until slightly brown, stirring often. Blend in flour. Pour in wine; then add cream. Cook, stirring constantly, until thickened and bubbly. Mix in ½ cup of cheese. Spoon sauce over chicken. Sprinkle with remaining cheese. Bake at 400 degrees for 20 minutes or until chicken is bubbly and tender.

Susan Welky Corey
(Mrs. John B.)

CHICKEN CUTLETS IN VERMOUTH SAUCE

Serves: 4 to 6

3 whole chicken breasts,
skinned, boned, and split
to make 6 cutlets
Flour
3 eggs, beaten

Salt and pepper to taste
Garlic powder to taste
½ cup grated Parmesan cheese
3 tablespoons chopped parsley
Vegetable oil

Pound chicken to flatten and dip into flour to coat lightly. Combine the eggs, salt, pepper, garlic powder, Parmesan, and parsley. Dip floured cutlets into this egg mixture. Cook the coated cutlets in moderately hot oil until golden on both sides and cooked through. Can be made ahead up to this point or served immediately with the following sauce.

Vermouth Sauce

8 tablespoons butter, melted
4 tablespoons margarine, melted
2 or 3 cloves garlic, minced
½ package onion soup mix
2 tablespoons water

3 tablespoons soy sauce
½ cup minced parsley
Dash of pepper
½ cup sweet vermouth

Melt the butter and margarine together and sauté the garlic until lightly browned. Combine the onion soup mix with the water to form a paste and add to the sautéed garlic and butter. Add the remaining ingredients and bring to a boil; reduce heat, simmer for 15 minutes. The sauce can be made up to 1 week ahead of time and gently reheated. Serve hot sauce over the cutlets. To reheat cutlets, place in a preheated 350-degree oven for 10 or 15 minutes.

Priscilla Taggart Connard
(Mrs. G. Baer, Jr.)

CHICKEN 'N CORNED BEEF

Serves: 6

6 chicken breasts, boned
6 thin slices corned beef
6 slices bacon

1 (8-ounce) carton sour cream
1 (10¾-ounce) can cream of
mushroom soup

Place each breast on a slice of corned beef and wrap with a slice of bacon. Pour mixture of soup and sour cream over chicken. Cover tightly with foil and bake at 275 degrees for 3 hours.

Rebecca Bilbrey Sweeney
(Mrs. Eugene G., Jr.)

CHICKEN CURRY

Serves: 6

8 slices bacon
½ cup sliced celery
¼ cup chopped onion
1 clove garlic, minced
3 tablespoons flour
1 cup light cream

1¼ cups water
½ cup applesauce
3 tablespoons tomato paste
3 to 4 teaspoons curry powder
2 chicken bouillon cubes
3 to 4 cups cubed cooked chicken

Cook bacon until crisp. Drain, crumble, and set aside. Save 1 tablespoon of fat. Add celery, onion, and garlic. Sauté until tender. Blend in flour. Stir in cream, water, applesauce, tomato paste, curry powder and bouillon cubes. Cook and stir until thickened. Stir in chicken and bacon. Heat. Serve over cooked rice. Accompany with raisins, toasted coconut, chutney, and diced green peppers.

Sue Mahan Kimble
(Mrs. John D.)

BENGAL CHICKEN CURRY

Serves: 4 to 6

¼ cup olive oil
¼ cup butter
1 cup sliced onions
1 cup sliced fresh mushrooms
4 whole chicken breasts, boned,
    skinned and cut into 1½-inch
    pieces
¼ cup flour

1 teaspoon salt
¼ teaspoon pepper
1 teaspoon curry powder
1 teaspoon thyme
½ teaspoon tarragon
½ cup chicken broth
¼ cup white wine
1 cup heavy cream

In electric skillet melt together butter and olive oil and sauté onions and mushrooms. Dredge chicken in flour, salt and pepper. Add chicken to skillet and lightly brown. Add curry, thyme, and tarragon. Add broth, wine and cream. Stir, cover, and simmer 45 to 60 minutes until chicken is tender.

Susan Wilson Starbuck
(Mrs. Gary W.)

CHICKEN DIVAN

Serves: 12

5 whole chicken breasts, cooked,
   boned and diced
3 (10-ounce) packages frozen
   broccoli
1 (10¾-ounce) can cream of
   chicken soup
1 (10¾-ounce) can cream of
   mushroom soup

5 ounces sherry
½ (16-ounce) package herb
   seasoned stuffing mix
3 tablespoons butter
Mandarin orange sections,
   optional
Almonds, optional

Blanch the frozen broccoli for 2 minutes in boiling water. Drain well. Line the
bottom of a 9 x 13 x 2-inch casserole with the blanched broccoli; cover with the
diced chicken. Combine soups with the sherry and pour over the chicken and
vegetable. Melt the butter and sauté stuffing mix until all the butter is absorbed.
Sprinkle on top of casserole. Bake in a 325-degree oven for 35 minutes. Garnish
with mandarin oranges and almonds. This may be frozen before baking; if so,
defrost in refrigerator overnight. Remove from refrigerator 45 minutes before
baking and bake 45 minutes in a 325-degree oven.

Patricia Pugh Britt
(Mrs. Michael E.)

CHICKEN BOURSIN

Serves: 4

3 ounces Boursin cheese
1 (10-ounce) package frozen
   spinach or (8-ounce) can,
   finely chopped
¾ cup finely chopped almonds

4 small whole chicken breasts,
   boned and skinned
1½ cups ground bread crumbs
3 ounces Boursin cheese

Slowly melt 3 ounces Boursin over low heat, stirring constantly. Mix with
chopped spinach and add chopped almonds. Open chicken breasts and flatten.
Divide cheese mixture evenly between breasts. Roll up tightly (as jelly roll) and
close ends. Roll in fine bread crumbs. Bake at 350 degrees for about 35 minutes.
Time will vary depending on size and thickness of breasts. Melt remaining
cheese and pour evenly over chicken. Serve. This freezes well.

Kathleen Foshay Hanson
(Mrs. Robert)

CHICKEN CHABLIS

Serves: 4

4 large chicken breasts,
  boned and skinned
Salt
Nutmeg
2 tablespoons butter

½ cup sliced onions
½ cup sliced mushrooms
⅔ cup Chablis
1 teaspoon cornstarch
2 tablespoons Chablis

Sprinkle chicken on all sides with salt and nutmeg. In large skillet or electric fry pan, brown chicken in 2 tablespoons butter. Add onions, mushrooms and ⅔ cup Chablis. Boil, cover, reduce heat, and simmer 15 minutes. Remove chicken to warm serving platter. Bring pan juices to boil and cook, stirring until liquid is reduced. Stir in mixture of 1 teaspoon cornstarch and 2 tablespoons Chablis. Cook, stirring until thickened. Spoon sauce over chicken and serve.

Lurana Marzilli

CHICKEN BROCCOLI CASSEROLE

Serves: 4 to 6

2 (10-ounce) packages frozen
  broccoli
3 whole chicken breasts, boiled
2 (10¾-ounce) cans cream of
  chicken soup
1 cup mayonnaise

¼ cup lemon juice
1 teaspoon curry powder
2 cups buttered bread cubes
1 cup shredded Cheddar cheese

Cook, drain, and chop broccoli; place in bottom of 2-quart casserole. Remove chicken from bones and place bite-size pieces on top of broccoli. Mix soup, mayonnaise, lemon juice and curry powder. Pour on top of chicken. Top with bread cubes and cheese. Bake at 350 degrees uncovered for 45 minutes.

*Nickey Schmid Wilson
(Mrs. Donald W.)*

CHICKEN FLORENTINE

Serves: 6

2 pounds fresh spinach
1 tablespoon butter
1 clove garlic, crushed
Dash marjoram
Dash basil
1 tablespoon flour
⅓ cup light cream
1 (5-pound) chicken or 4 whole
  breasts, poached and sliced

3 tablespoons butter
3 tablespoons flour
¾ cup light cream
¾ cup chicken stock
Salt to taste
Pepper to taste
1 cup grated Parmesan cheese

Cook, drain, and chop spinach. Melt 1 tablespoon butter and add garlic, marjoram, and basil. Add 1 tablespoon flour and mix well. Add ⅓ cup cream and spinach and simmer for 5 minutes, stirring constantly. Put spinach mixture in bottom of 12 x 8 x 2-inch casserole. Cover with chicken. Melt 3 tablespoons butter and blend in 3 tablespoons flour. Add ¾ cup cream and ¾ cup chicken stock. Stir until thickened. Season with salt and pepper. Pour sauce over chicken. Cover with grated cheese. Bake at 400 degrees for 20 minutes or until cheese is slightly browned.

Merryl Gillespie Hodgson
(Mrs. Donald G.)

CHICKEN BREASTS VAUTIER

Serves: 10 to 12

6 chicken breasts, halved
  and skinned
Salt, to taste
1 pint sour cream
½ cup butter

2 medium onions, chopped
1 (16-ounce) package herb
  seasoned stuffing mix
½ cup hot water

Place the chicken breasts in a glass 9 x 13 x 2-inch casserole and salt according to taste. Spread sour cream evenly over the breasts. Melt the butter and sauté the onion; add the stuffing mix and water. Stir to combine thoroughly. Put the stuffing mix on top of the sour cream. Cover with foil and bake at 325 degrees for 90 minutes. Remove foil for the last 5 minutes of baking.

Patricia Pugh Britt
(Mrs. Michael E.)

CHICKEN MARSALA

Serves: 6 to 8

6 to 8 chicken breasts, boned,
  skinned (or veal cutlets)
1 cup grated Parmesan cheese
½ cup olive oil
¼ cup butter
1 pound mushrooms

1 (15-ounce) can tomato sauce
15 ounces sweet Marsala or
  cream sherry
Garlic salt, oregano, thyme
  to taste

Pound breasts until flattened, then dredge in Parmesan cheese. Brown in olive oil, drain, and set aside. Add butter to remaining olive oil and brown mushrooms. Remove mushrooms and set aside. In same skillet, add tomato sauce and wine. Sprinkle with garlic salt, oregano, and smaller amount of thyme. Simmer until sauce thickens. When ready to serve, add mushrooms and pour sauce over chicken and bake in 350-degree oven for 10 minutes.

Hope Palmer Bramhall
(Mrs. Peter)

CHICKEN IN PUFF PASTRY

Serves: 6

1 (10-ounce) package puff pastry
  shells, partially thawed
¼ cup corn oil
3 whole chicken breasts,
  skinned, boned and split
Salt

Freshly ground pepper
8-ounces whipped cream cheese
  with chives
6 to 8 ounces prosciutto ham,
  sliced

On lightly floured surface, roll out each pastry shell to a 7 to 9-inch circle, depending on size of the chicken breast. Set aside. Heat oil in skillet over medium to high heat. Season chicken with salt and pepper. Add to skillet and sauté on both sides until golden, 5 to 7 minutes. Drain well. Preheat oven to 450 degrees. Lightly grease baking sheet. Place a chicken breast on one half of each pastry circle. Spread 2 to 3 tablespoons of cream cheese over top of each piece. Place a slice of prosciutto ham over cream cheese. Fold remaining half of pastry over chicken, pressing edges to seal. Transfer to baking sheet and place seam side down. Reduce oven temperature to 400 degrees. Bake until pastry is puffed and golden, about 25 to 30 minutes. Serve hot.

Maryellen Turley Coles
(Mrs. Julian R.)

154

CHICKEN VEGETABLE PILAF

Serves: 6

3 whole chicken breasts,
  skinned, boned
¼ cup flour
1 teaspoon seasoned salt
2 tablespoons vegetable oil
1 cup uncooked long grain
  white rice
1 teaspoon salt
⅛ teaspoon pepper

2 cups water
1 medium onion, chopped
2 stalks celery, thinly sliced
2 chicken bouillon cubes
1 (10-ounce) package frozen
  Italian beans
2 medium tomatoes, cut into
  eighths
Seasoned salt

Cut chicken into bite-size pieces and toss in mixture of flour and seasoned salt. In large skillet, sauté chicken in oil until lightly browned. Add next 7 ingredients. Bring mixture to a boil and stir thoroughly. Reduce heat and place frozen beans on simmering mixture. Lay tomato wedges around edge. Sprinkle with seasoned salt. Cover and boil gently for 5 minutes. Separate beans with fork and continue to cook 10 minutes more until beans are tender and rice is cooked.

Becky Stevens
(Mrs. John)

CHICKEN GERALDINE

Serves: 4 to 6

1 (9-ounce) package frozen
  artichoke hearts
½ teaspoon salt
6 chicken breasts, boned,
  skinned, and cut into pieces
Pepper

8 lean slices bacon
4 tablespoons sweet vermouth
2 ripe tomatoes, peeled and
  chopped
½ cup shredded Cheddar cheese
½ teaspoon salt

Thaw artichokes completely and arrange to cover bottom of glass baking dish. Sprinkle ½ teaspoon salt over them. Place chicken over artichokes and sprinkle with pepper. Lay bacon on chicken; score edges to prevent curling. Pour vermouth over chicken. Roast, covered, at 350 degrees for 1 hour, spooning off excess fat from bacon. Combine tomatoes, cheese, and salt; spoon over chicken. Place under broiler to brown cheese. Serve immediately.

Susan Welky Corey
(Mrs. John B.)

PENNY'S CHICKEN BREASTS

Serves: 4

2 whole chicken breasts, boned
   and split
Salt to taste
Pepper to taste
¼ cup butter
¼ cup minced onion or shallots
1 clove garlic, minced

1 teaspoon paprika
1 bunch broccoli, cooked, hot
4 canned peach halves
1 cup sour cream or plain yogurt
¼ cup mayonnaise
¼ cup Parmesan cheese

Season chicken with salt and pepper. In small skillet, melt butter and sauté onions and garlic. Stir in paprika and turn chicken in mixture until well coated. Put into a shallow broiler-proof pan. Cover loosely with foil and bake at 375 degrees for 30 to 35 minutes. Arrange well-drained broccoli in pan beside chicken. Put peach halves next to broccoli. Mix sour cream and mayonnaise and spoon over all. Sprinkle with Parmesan cheese and broil 6 to 8 minutes.

*Sharon Smith Bushey
(Mrs. Donald J.)*

CITRUS CHICKEN

Serves: 6

3 chicken breasts, boned, halved,
   skinned and flattened
¼ cup melted butter
1 tablespoon orange liqueur
6 thin slices ham
Flour
2 eggs, slightly beaten
⅔ cup dry seasoned bread
   crumbs

¼ pound butter, cut in bits
2 cups fresh orange juice
1 tablespoon tarragon
1 teaspoon grated orange peel
½ teaspoon salt
6 (½-inch) thick orange slices
Grated orange peel
Minced parsley

Place chicken breast halves on a flat surface smooth side down. Brush with mixture of melted butter and liqueur. Place one slice of ham on each breast and roll up, securing with toothpicks. Roll in flour; shake off excess. Dip in egg and roll in bread crumbs. Arrange in a buttered shallow baking dish. Dot with butter bits. Bake at 400 degrees for 15 minutes, turning once. Mix together orange juice, tarragon, orange peel, and salt. Pour over chicken. Reduce oven temperature to 350 degrees. Cover chicken and bake 35 minutes longer, turning and basting occasionally. Remove toothpicks from chicken. Place each breast on an orange slice on a serving platter and spoon sauce over chicken. Garnish with grated orange peel and some finely minced parsley.

*Susan Welky Corey
(Mrs. John B.)*

CHICKEN L'INDIENNE

Serves: 4

2 tablespoons flour
½ teaspoon salt
½ teaspoon pepper
1 teaspoon paprika
1 teaspoon celery salt
1 teaspoon curry

1 teaspoon oregano
2 whole chicken breasts, boned
   and cut into pieces
2 tablespoons butter
¾ cup cream
½ cup sour cream

In paper bag combine first 7 ingredients. Drop chicken pieces into bag and shake to coat. In skillet, sauté chicken in butter until brown. Transfer to casserole and add cream. Cover and bake at 350 degrees for 35 minutes. Mix a little hot sauce from casserole with sour cream. Add to casserole and bake 10 minutes more.

Roselle Flynn Johnson
(Mrs. Steven M.)

CURRIED CHICKEN Á L' ORANGE

Serves: 4

2½ to 3-pound frying chicken,
   cut into pieces
1 to 2 teaspoons curry powder
½ cup orange juice

½ cup honey
½ cup prepared mustard
2 oranges, peeled and sliced
   into half cartwheels

Rinse and dry chicken. Sprinkle both sides with curry, rubbing into meat. Arrange in baking dish, skin side down. Combine orange juice, honey, and mustard in saucepan; simmer for 5 minutes. Pour sauce over chicken. Bake at 375 degrees for 30 minutes. Turn chicken and bake 20 to 30 minutes more until tender and brown. Place chicken on serving platter and garnish with orange cartwheels. Sauce may be poured over chicken or served in separate dish.

Barbara Troubh Epstein
(Mrs. Burton)

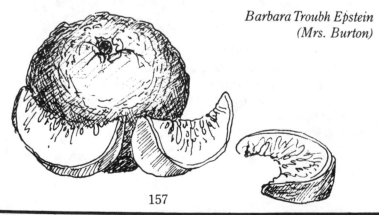

ITALIAN BONELESS CHICKEN

Serves: 8 to 10

6 eggs, beaten
2 cups grated Parmesan cheese
½ cup bread crumbs or wheat germ
4 cups finely chopped cooked chicken
3 tablespoons butter or margarine
½ cup chopped green pepper
½ cup chopped onion

1 tablespoon cooking oil
½ cup water
2 (15-ounce) cans tomato sauce
½ teaspoon Italian seasoning
¼ teaspoon crushed dried basil
¼ teaspoon garlic powder
⅛ teaspoon pepper
2 cups shredded mozzarella cheese

Combine eggs, cheese, and crumbs. Stir in chicken and mix well. With hands, shape into sixteen ¾-inch thick patties. In large skillet cook patties in butter over medium heat for 2 to 3 minutes on each side or until brown. Drain patties and arrange in two 10 x 6 x 2-inch baking dishes. Cook green pepper and onion in hot oil until tender. Remove from heat and add remaining ingredients except mozzarella. Spoon sauce over patties. Sprinkle with mozzarella. Bake casserole uncovered at 350 degrees for 25 minutes or until hot. Freezes well. Bake frozen casserole covered in 400-degree oven for 50 minutes. Then, uncover and bake 20 minutes more, or until heated through.

Sharon Smith Bushey
(Mrs. Donald J.)

CHICKEN DIJON

Serves: 4

4 chicken breasts, split, skinned and boned
3 tablespoons butter or margarine
2 tablespoons flour

1 cup chicken broth
½ cup light cream
2 tablespoons Dijon mustard
Tomato wedges
Parsley

In a large skillet cook chicken in butter or margarine until tender (about 20 minutes). Remove chicken to warm serving platter. Stir flour into skillet drippings. Add chicken broth and light cream. Cook and stir until mixture thickens and bubbles. Stir in mustard. Add chicken. Cover and heat 10 minutes. Garnish with tomato and parsley. Chicken can be browned and sauce made ahead. Combine and heat when guests arrive.

Katie Danoski Freilinger
(Mrs. James E.)

PIQUANT CHICKEN

Serves: 4

2 frying chickens, cut up
  or legs or breasts for 4
½ cup rosé or red wine
½ cup soy sauce
½ cup salad oil

4 tablespoons water
2 cloves garlic, sliced
2 teaspoons ground nutmeg
½ teaspoon oregano
2 tablespoons brown sugar

Remove skin and place chicken in casserole dish. Combine remaining ingredients, mix well and pour over chicken. Cover and bake at 350 degrees for 1 hour.

Elizabeth Mauney Blackwood
(Mrs. Robert S.)

ORIENTAL CHICKEN

Serves: 4 to 6

1½ pounds whole chicken
  breasts, skinned, split
  and boned
3 tablespoons soy sauce
2 teaspoons cornstarch
2 tablespoons dry sherry
1 teaspoon grated ginger root
1 teaspoon sugar
½ teaspoon salt

½ teaspoon crushed red pepper
2 tablespoons cooking oil
2 medium green peppers, cut into
  ¾-inch pieces
4 green onions, bias-sliced into
  1-inch lengths
1 cup walnut halves
Kumquats, to garnish

Cut chicken into 1-inch pieces. Set aside. In small bowl blend soy sauce into cornstarch; stir in dry sherry, ginger root, sugar, salt and red pepper. Set aside. Preheat a wok or large skillet over high heat; add cooking oil. Stir fry green peppers and green onions in hot oil 2 minutes or until crisp-tender. Remove from wok. Add walnuts to wok; stir fry 1 to 2 minutes or until just golden. Remove from wok. (Add more oil if necessary.) Add half of the chicken to hot wok or skillet; stir fry 2 minutes. Remove from wok. Stir fry remaining chicken 2 minutes. Return all chicken to wok or skillet. Stir soy mixture; stir into chicken. Cook and stir until thickened and bubbly. Stir in vegetables. Cover and cook, 1 minute more. Serve at once. Garnish with fresh kumquats and serve with hot cooked rice, if desired. Does not freeze well but can be prepared day before and baked at 325 degrees for 10 to 15 minutes.

Kathleen Foshay Hanson
(Mrs. Robert)

CHICKEN PIE FOIE GRAS

Serves: 4 to 6

6 tablespoons butter
2 medium onions, chopped
6 to 8 ounces mushrooms, sliced
4 tablespoons flour
2 cups chicken stock (preferably homemade)
1 (4¾-ounce) can liver paté

Salt and pepper, to taste
1 cup cooked, sliced, and drained carrots
1 cup cooked, sliced, and drained celery
3 cups diced cooked chicken
Pastry for 1 crust pie

Melt butter and sauté the onions until transparent. Add the mushrooms and cook until slightly soft. Blend in the flour and cook over medium heat for 3 minutes. Add the chicken stock and stir well to combine. Mash the liver paté and add to the above, stirring over medium heat until well combined. Season with salt and pepper to taste. Set aside at this point if desired. Reheat sauce before proceeding with recipe. Add the carrots, celery, and chicken to the sauce. Pour into a 2-quart casserole and top with pastry. Slash crust for steam to escape. Bake in a preheated 375-degree oven for 25 to 30 minutes or until crust is golden.

Patricia Pugh Britt
(Mrs. Michael E.)

BRUNSWICK STEW

Serves: 8 to 10

5 to 6-pound stewing chicken, cut up
8 cups water
1 teaspoon salt
1 (10-ounce) package frozen baby lima beans
1 (1 pound 13 ounce) can tomatoes

2 cups sliced onions
5 medium potatoes, diced
1 (1 pound) can sliced okra
2 (1 pound) cans whole kernel corn, drained
1 teaspoon salt
½ teaspoon pepper
1 tablespoon sugar

Place chicken in a large kettle; add the water and 1 teaspoon of salt. Cover and simmer gently for 2½ hours. Do not boil! Cool chicken in the broth. Remove meat from bones; skim fat from broth. Add all remaining ingredients to the broth (except the chicken); cover and simmer for 1 hour. Add the reserved chicken and adjust seasonings to suit taste. Serve piping hot.

Patricia Pugh Britt
(Mrs. Michael E.)

WHITE LASAGNA

Serves: 6

3 chicken breasts, halved
1¼ cups chicken broth
1 cup water
3 quarts water
1 tablespoon salt

¼ cup cooking oil
1 pound lasagna noodles
Sauce, see recipe below
¼ pound sliced prosciutto ham
Chopped fresh parsley

Cook chicken in large pan with broth and 1 cup water for ½ hour or until tender. Bone and cut into small pieces. Set aside. Reserve 1 cup broth for sauce. Bring 3 quarts water to boil. Add salt, oil and noodles. Cook until done. Drain and put on towel to dry. Prepare sauce. To assemble: Lightly butter 9 x 13-inch baking dish. Place a layer of noodles on bottom, then sauce, chicken and ham. Repeat this twice more. Then finish it off with a layer of noodles and sauce. Bake at 350 degrees for 20 to 25 minutes. Top with parsley.

Sauce

¾ cup butter
7½ tablespoons flour
2 cups milk
1½ cups heavy cream
1 cup reserved broth
½ teaspoon rosemary

½ teaspoon tarragon
½ teaspoon Beau Monde
½ teaspoon salt
1 dash nutmeg
1½ cups grated Parmesan
   cheese

In large saucepan melt butter. Blend in flour and cook, stirring constantly, over medium heat for 3 minutes. Add milk, cream and reserved broth, stirring constantly until mixture boils and begins to thicken. Add seasonings. Remove from heat and stir in cheese.

Judith Edison Irish
(Mrs. Rodney F.)

161

MEXICO CITY TAMALE PIE

Serves: 3 to 4

6 tamales
1 chicken breast, boiled
    (or leftover turkey)
1 (8-ounce) can tomato sauce
½ cup sweet chili sauce
1 cup canned or frozen
    whole-kernel corn

2 tablespoons sugar
2 tablespoons salad oil
½ cup seedless raisins
10 ripe olives, cut in strips
Salt to taste
Pepper to taste
1 cup grated Parmesan cheese

Remove husks from fresh or canned tamales and arrange in casserole. Slice and distribute chicken over top of tamales. Mix remaining ingredients, except Parmesan cheese, and pour over tamales and chicken. Sprinkle Parmesan cheese over this and bake at 375 degrees for 40 to 45 minutes.

India Horton Weatherill
(Mrs. Robert H.)

WILD DUCK WITH ORANGE SAUCE

Serves: 4

4 wild duck breasts
½ cup olive oil
¼ cup dry white wine
2 onions, thinly sliced

Few sprigs parsley
Salt
Freshly ground pepper
Butter

Combine the oil, wine, onions, parsley, salt and pepper. Marinate the duck breasts in the mixture for 1 hour. Drain, wipe the pieces dry with a paper towel and sauté gently in butter until tender, 20 to 30 minutes. Meat will be medium rare. Arrange duck breasts on hot platter. Pour hot sauce over it. Garnish with orange slices and sprigs of lemon verbena.

Orange Sauce

1 cup orange juice
1 tablespoon grated orange rind
1 tablespoon cornstarch

3 tablespoons sugar
2 tablespoons orange liqueur

Mix cornstarch to a paste with a little of the orange juice. Combine in a saucepan with the rest of the juice and sugar. Cook until thick and clear, stirring as it cooks. Add the orange rind and the liqueur and serve hot.

Linda Ryman Frinsko
(Mrs. F. Paul)

MURGH MASALLAM
(INDIAN CHICKEN WITH RICE)

Serves: 8

1 large roasting chicken

Marinade

2 cloves garlic, minced
¼ teaspoon ground ginger
½ teaspoon ground red pepper
½ teaspoon ground turmeric

1 teaspoon salt
½ pint (or more) plain yogurt
¼ cup oil
6 large onions, chopped

Masala

2 cloves garlic, minced
1 tablespoon shredded,
   unsweetened coconut
¼ teaspoon ginger
¼ teaspoon pepper
½ teaspoon cloves
½ teaspoon cumin
1 pinch mace
1 teaspoon cinnamon
1 teaspoon cardamon

1 teaspoon salt
¼ teaspoon cayenne
⅛ teaspoon nutmeg
⅛ teaspoon saffron
1 teaspoon coriander
1 tablespoon slivered almonds
2 cups uncooked rice
2 teaspoons salt
4¼ cups water

Clean chicken and pat dry. Poke holes in breast, legs, etc. with ice pick or cut small slits with knife. Rub marinade over and inside chicken and refrigerate at least 2 hours. (May do overnight). Sauté onions in oil in a large skillet until limp but *not* brown. Add garlic and coconut and stir on low heat. Add remaining masala ingredients and stir to mix. Put chicken in roasting pan with a lid. Add 2 cups rice, 2 teaspoons salt, and 4¼ cups water to roasting pan, making sure rice is all in water. Pour masala over chicken and rice. Cover and bake at 375 degrees for 1 hour. Reduce heat to 325 degrees and bake 2 hours more. If you have a pretty roasting pan, use it for this. It is difficult to transfer and will probably fall apart if you attempt it. For an authentic Indian dinner, serve Kela Ka Rayta for dessert.

Sue Bernard Ewing
(Mrs. Robert M.)

VEGETABLE STUFFING

Serves: Will stuff 6 pound chicken

½ cup butter
3 large carrots, pared and
    chopped
1 cup chopped celery
2 cups sliced mushrooms
1 cup chopped onion

1 cup chopped green pepper
¼ cup sliced apples
1 teaspoon salt
½ teaspoon dried thyme
Dash pepper
2 cups fresh bread crumbs

In hot butter using 6-quart Dutch oven, over medium heat, sauté carrots, celery, mushrooms, onions and green peppers for 5 minutes. Add apples, salt, thyme, pepper and bread crumbs. Toss lightly until mixed. Stuff chicken or capon.

Lurana Marzilli

DANISH STUFFING
(FOR CHICKEN OR TURKEY)

Serves: Will stuff a 4 to 6 pound bird

1½ cups chopped apples
3½ cups soft bread crumbs
½ cup seedless raisins
2 tablespoons butter
1 teaspoon lemon juice
2 stalks celery, chopped

¼ teaspoon cinnamon
½ teaspoon salt
1 medium onion, chopped
¼ cup chopped nuts
¼ cup bouillon or water

Combine all ingredients gently until well blended. Stuff bird or bake stuffing separately in greased loaf pan at 375 degrees for 30 minutes. Stuffing may be prepared ahead and frozen.

Mary Morse Reevy
(Mrs. John)

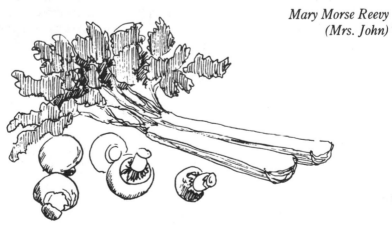

MEATS

FOOLPROOF ROAST BEEF

Flour	Pepper
Salt	Standing Rib Roast

Sprinkle the roast with flour, salt and pepper to coat all surfaces. Place in a shallow roasting pan, fat side up. Place meat in a preheated 500 degree oven as follows:

    2 Ribs (4½ to 5 pounds) 25 to 30 minutes
    3 Ribs (8 to 9 pounds) 40 to 45 minutes
    4 Ribs (11 to 12 pounds) 55 to 60 minutes

After the specified cooking time, turn oven off and leave meat in the oven for 2½ hours after cooking. *Do not open the oven door at any time* until ready to serve. The meat will be medium rare and perfect every time.

The Committee

RUTH HOWARD'S BOEUF BOURGUIGNON

Serves: 6

2½ pounds lean beef cut into cubes
3 tablespoons butter
1 tablespoon vegetable oil
¼ cup brandy, warmed
2 teaspoons tomato paste
1 teaspoon meat glaze
4 teaspoons potato flour
2 cups beef broth
½ cup burgundy wine
¼ cup port wine

¼ cup dry sherry
Pepper, freshly ground
1 small bay leaf
2 teaspoons butter
6 ounces fresh mushrooms
1 teaspoon lemon juice
2 teaspoons butter
1 (16-ounce) bag of small frozen onions
1 teaspoon granulated sugar

Melt butter in 5 quart Dutch oven. Add oil and brown meat a few pieces at a time on all sides. Remove meat as it browns. When all pieces are browned, return meat to pan and flame with ¼ cup warmed brandy. Remove meat to another pan. Remove pan from heat, add tomato paste, meat glaze, flour, beef broth, burgundy, port, sherry, and freshly ground black pepper. Stir over heat until contents boil, then add beef and bay leaf. Cover Dutch oven with waxed paper and then lid. Cook 2½ to 3 hours at 325 degrees. Melt butter, add mushrooms, sprinkle with lemon juice and cook briskly 2 minutes. Set aside. Melt butter, add onions and brown until golden. Sprinkle with sugar and shake pan to glaze. Set aside. Add mushrooms and onions ½ hour before serving. May be prepared 1 to 2 days ahead or frozen.

Dale R. Bryant

BEEF ROULADEN

Serves: 8 to 10

3 pounds top round steak, sliced
   ¼-inch thick
Dijon style mustard
Salt and pepper to taste
8 to 10 slices bacon
2 or 3 dill pickles, sliced
   lengthwise into 4 pieces each

2 tomatoes, sliced thin
2 large onions, sliced thin
Toothpicks
8 tablespoons butter
1 bay leaf
1 small onion
Flour

Pound meat slices to about ⅛-inch thickness. Lay slices of meat on piece of wax paper. Spread each slice with mustard, salt and pepper. Place one slice of bacon, dill pickle and tomato on each piece of beef; then add several thin slices of onion to each piece of beef. Roll each slice of beef, holding ingredients in. Secure ends and center with toothpicks. Place beef rolls in large skillet with melted butter and sear them slightly. After rolls are seared (very dark brown) add water to the skillet so there is approximately 1 to 1½-inches of liquid in the skillet, also add 1 crushed bay leaf and one small onion, sliced. Cover and simmer for approximately 1½ hours. Make gravy by mixing flour and water to make a paste, then adding to liquid in the skillet.

Mildred Foge Taggart
(Mrs. James E.)

COLD FILET OF BEEF WITH SOUR CREAM FILLING

Serves: 4 to 6

2 to 3 pounds beef filet
1 carrot, onion and celery stalk,
   finely chopped
4 tablespoons butter, divided
½ cup water
½ pound slab bacon, cut into
   ¼-inch cubes

1 tablespoon oil
1 garlic clove
1 cup sour cream
Salt and pepper

In bottom of broiler pan sauté carrot, celery and onion in 2 tablespoons butter. Add ½ cup water to pan. Place filet on rack of pan and roast for 25 minutes at 450 degrees. Let cool 20 minutes. Transfer filet to platter. Save drippings and vegetable pieces. Sauté bacon in oil and garlic until crisp. Combine sour cream with pan drippings, bacon, salt and pepper. Cut wedge in filet 1½-inch wide by 1-inch deep. Fill cavity. Cut filet wedge in ¾-inch slices and reassemble on top of filling.

Roselle Flynn Johnson
(Mrs. Steven M.)

CONTREFILET

Serves: 8 to 10

2 tablespoons butter
1 tablespoon prepared mustard
1 tablespoon Worcestershire
  sauce
½ teaspoon garlic salt
1 teaspoon salt
Dash of pepper

1 tablespoon gravy browning
  sauce
1 teaspoon monosodium
  glutamate
4 to 5 pounds whole beef
  tenderloin

Combine all the ingredients except the meat to form a marinade. Rub the marinade into the meat thoroughly. Cover and refrigerate several hours. Bring meat to room temperature. Place tenderloin in a shallow baking pan, tucking the thin end under. Bake at 400 degrees for 45 minutes for rare and 50 minutes for medium rare. Baste meat during cooking adding water to pan juices when necessary. This is foolproof and needs no additional seasoning.

Patricia Pugh Britt
(Mrs. Michael E.)

TERIYAKI STEAK

Serves: 6 to 8

2 flank steaks, or sirloin
3 tablespoons honey
2 tablespoons vinegar
1½ teaspoons garlic powder
  or garlic salt

1½ teaspoons ginger
¾ cup salad oil
¼ cup soy sauce

Mix all ingredients in blender or food processor, except flank steaks. Blend well. Add 2 additional tablespoons of honey if oil separates from sauce. Pour mixture over steak and turn and cover with foil. Refrigerate overnight, being sure to turn at least once. Charcoal or oven broil for 5 to 6 minutes each side. Slice in ½-inch to ¾-inch long strips.

Susan Welky Corey
(Mrs. John B.)

HOBO STEAK

Serves: 4 to 6

2½ pounds sirloin steak,
  2½-inches thick
1 teaspoon seasoned salt
2 tablespoons garlic spread

1 teaspoon seasoned pepper
2 tablespoons salad oil
1 cup Italian bread crumbs

Remove fat from steak. Make paste of seasonings and spread over meat. Cover with crumbs. Place in brown paper bag and secure tightly. Place on cookie sheet and bake at 375 degrees for 30 minutes, then at 425 degrees for 15 minutes. Remove any paste on bag and spread on sliced meat. May be done ahead.

Nancy Bokron Curran
(Mrs. Richard E., Jr.)

CHINESE CURRIED BEEF

Serves: 4

1 pound beef (top round, flank
  steak or shaved steak)
1 medium onion, sliced

3 tablespoons cooking oil,
  divided
3 cups fresh broccoli, cut in
  ½-inch pieces

Thinly slice beef across the grain into bite size strips. Prepare vegetables. Heat wok or large skillet over high heat. Add 2 tablespoons of oil. Stir fry onion and broccoli for 4 minutes. Remove vegetables. Add remaining 1 tablespoon of oil to wok along with ½ of the meat. Stir fry for 2 minutes. Remove the meat and repeat with remaining meat. Push meat away from the center of wok. Add about ½ to ¾ cup of Chinese cooking sauce (see recipe below) to wok. Cook and stir until thickened and bubbly. Return all meat and vegetables to wok. Cook 1 minute more, or until heated through. Do not overcook. Serve with rice.

Chinese Cooking Sauce

3 tablespoons soy sauce
2 teaspoons curry powder
3 tablespoons cornstarch

1 to 3 teaspoons salt, to taste
1 (10¾-ounce) can beef broth

Combine all ingredients in a jar. Shake until blended.

Lee Morse Edwards
(Mrs. Dwight H.)

NEW ENGLAND BOILED DINNER

Serves: 4 to 6

5 or 6 pounds beef brisket,
   corned
Cold water
1 sprig thyme
1 sprig parsley
1 onion stuck with cloves
2 onions
Pepper

1 whole carrot
1½ pounds carrots, peeled and
   quartered
Small potatoes, peeled
Turnip, peeled and sliced
Small beets, unpeeled
1 head cabbage, quartered

Put brisket in a large pot and cover with cold water. Add thyme, parsley, onions, pepper and carrot. Bring to a slow boil with lid off. Skim as necessary. Cover and simmer gently for 3 hours. One half hour before finishing, add additional carrots, potatoes, turnip; 15 minutes later add the cabbage. Cook beets and peel. Serve with mustard, horseradish sauce and pickles. A jar of pickled beets may be substituted if fresh ones are not available; cook separately.

Method To Corn Beef

8 cups water
1 cup salt
3 tablespoons sugar
1 bay leaf
6 peppercorns

1 clove garlic, minced
2 teaspoons mixed pickling
   spices
5 or 6 pounds beef brisket

Combine all ingredients except beef, stirring well. Add beef brisket. Cover it with a plate and place a heavy weight on it. Leave the meat in the brine for 36 hours, turning occasionally. Use for New England Boiled Dinner.

Deborah Spring Reed
(Mrs. Verner Z.)

BEEF IN SOUR CREAM

Serves: 4 to 6

4 slices bacon, diced
2 pounds beef, cut in 1-inch
  cubes
4 onions, chopped
1 clove garlic, minced
2 teaspoons salt
¼ teaspoon pepper

½ teaspoon marjoram
⅔ cup dry white wine
1 pint sour cream
Chopped parsley
Paprika

Cook bacon in kettle until browned. Remove bacon and set aside. Add beef to fat remaining in kettle and brown on all sides. Add onion and garlic and cook a few minutes. Stir in bacon and next four ingredients. Bring to a boil, cover and simmer 1½ hours or until meat is tender. Add a little broth or water if necessary. Stir in sour cream and heat gently. Sprinkle with parsley and paprika. May be done ahead excluding sour cream. When reheating, add sour cream.

Barbara Gee Chellis
(Mrs. Thomas D.)

POT ROAST AUTRICHIENNE

Serves: 6

5 to 6 pound pot roast (round,
  rump or eye of chuck)
2 teaspoons salt
¼ teaspoon pepper
2 tablespoons oil
1 large onion, chopped
1½ tablespoons paprika

½ cup water
1 (10½-ounce) can beef bouillon
1 bay leaf
1 teaspoon caraway seeds
½ cup water
3 tablespoons flour
1 cup sour cream

Sprinkle salt and pepper on meat, brown meat in the vegetable oil. Remove the meat and add the onion to the oil and sauté until golden. Sprinkle the paprika on the onions and cook for 1 minute. Return meat to pan and add ½ cup water, the bouillon, bay leaf, and caraway seeds. Cover, bring to a boil, reduce heat and simmer for 4 hours. Remove meat to a heated platter, discard bay leaf, and skim fat. Blend ½ cup water with the flour and add to the pan juices. Cook until thick. Lower heat, add the sour cream, and heat through. Pour sauce over meat and serve.

Patricia Pugh Britt
(Mrs. Michael E.)

171

POT ROAST INDIENNE

Serves: 8

4 pounds lean beef (chuck
  or round)
1 teaspoon salt
2 tablespoons lemon juice
3 slices bacon
⅔ cup chopped onion
¼ cup chopped parsley (or less)

4 whole cloves
½ teaspoon cinnamon
½ bay leaf
1 cup canned tomatoes
1 teaspoon sugar
1 cup orange juice

Season meat with salt and lemon juice. Cook bacon until crisp; remove from pan. Add meat to bacon drippings. Brown on all sides. Combine parsley, onion, cloves, cinnamon, bay leaf, tomatoes and sugar. Add to beef. Crumble bacon over meat. Bring to boil; reduce heat and cover; simmer 10 minutes. Add orange juice and simmer, covered, about 3 hours or until tender. If necessary, add water to keep moist.

Barbara Gee Chellis
(Mrs. Thomas D.)

PERKED POT ROAST

Serves: 6 to 8

3 to 5-pound round steak roast
Fresh garlic, slivered
Onion, slivered
1 cup wine vinegar

Oil
2 cups strong coffee
2 cups water
Salt and pepper, to taste

Cut slits in roast about 2 inches deep. Insert slivers of garlic and onion into slits. Place beef in a bowl and pour vinegar over it. Make sure some vinegar gets into slits. Refrigerate for 24 to 48 hours. Discard vinegar and place meat in a Dutch oven. Brown in oil on all sides. Pour coffee over roast and add water. Cover. Cook slowly for 6 hours on top of the stove. Before serving, add salt and pepper. Thicken gravy. May add more water if necessary.

Carol Such Bouton
(Mrs. Dale C., Jr.)

BEEF BIRDS

Serves: 4 to 6

1½ pounds round steak, sliced
  very thin
1 pound sausage meat flavored
  with marjoram and thyme
1 onion, chopped
Flour
2 tablespoons butter

Olive oil
1 cup red wine
1 (10¾-ounce) can bouillon,
  diluted
½ pound mushrooms
Salt, pepper

Pound beef slices very thin between waxed paper. Cook sausage. Drain off fat. Sauté onion and add to sausage. Spread a spoonful on each slice of beef and roll up. Secure with twine or toothpicks. Dredge in flour. Beginning with seam side down, brown on all sides in butter and oil. Place in shallow casserole, pouring wine and bouillon on. Simmer until tender, 1 hour, in oven at 325 degrees. Remove birds to platter, reduce sauce and add mushrooms. Correct seasonings and pour over birds.

Roselle Flynn Johnson
(Mrs. Steven M.)

CHINESE BEEF AND RADISHES

Serves: 6

1½ pounds thinly sliced beef
2 tablespoons cornstarch
4 tablespoons soy sauce
8 tablespoons water
6 tablespoons oil

⅔ cup white vinegar
1 cup sugar
2 cups red radishes, thinly sliced
1 cup chopped scallions
White rice

Marinate beef in cornstarch, soy sauce and water. Heat 6 tablespoons oil in frying pan. Add vinegar and sugar and heat to boiling point. Lower heat and add radishes. When radishes are almost transparent, add scallions. Add beef and stir until just cooked. Serve over rice.

Jane (Ba) Davidson Kopp
(Mrs. Donald A.)

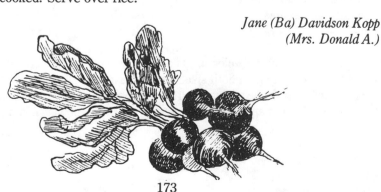

LASAGNA ALLA CAROLA

Serves: 6 to 8

½ cup chopped onion
3 tablespoons olive oil
2 cloves garlic, chopped
½ teaspoon oregano
1 bay leaf
2 (32-ounce) jars marinara sauce
6 Italian sausages, skinned
¾ pound chuck *and*
¼ pound pork, ground together

¼ teaspoon oregano
⅛ teaspoon basil
1 clove garlic, chopped
1 (16-ounce) box lasagna noodles
16 ounces ricotta cheese
16 ounces mozzarella cheese
½ cup Parmesan cheese, freshly
grated

To make tomato sauce, sauté onion in olive oil. Add garlic, oregano and bay leaf. Stir in marinara sauce. Cook over low heat until everything else is ready. Brown sausage meat in frying pan and set aside. Brown ground meat in another frying pan and sprinkle with spices while cooking and stirring. In large pot, boil lasagna as directed. Drain immediately and add some olive oil to prevent sticking. Cover large rectangular baking pan with thin layer of sauce. Place layer of lasagna over sauce. Add thin layer of sauce. Add cooked sausage meat. Place layer of lasagna. Add thin layer of sauce. Cover with ricotta. Place layer of lasagna. Add thin layer of sauce. Cover with chopped meat. Place layer of lasagna. Add thin layer of sauce. Cover with mozzarella. Place layer of lasagna. Add thin layer of sauce. Sprinkle with grated Parmesan. Cook at 350 degrees for 45 minutes, or until bubbly.

Nancy Montgomery Beebe
(Mrs. Michael)

GRANDMOTHER MUSKIE'S POLISH MEATLOAF

Serves: 4 or 5

2 pounds ground chuck
2 cups bread cubes
1 egg

½ cup milk
1 medium onion, chopped
Salt and pepper, to taste

In large bowl, mix all ingredients. Make two large patties and brown in hot skillet. When very brown on both sides, lower heat; add 1-inch water to pan and simmer for 1 hour. Keep adding small amount of water while cooking; make your favorite gravy with pan liquid. Pour gravy over meat and serve immediately.

Jane G. Muskie
(Mrs. Edmund S.)

LAYERED MEAT LOAF

Serves: 6 to 8

2 pounds ground beef
2 cups soft stale bread crumbs
¾ cup milk
2 eggs, slightly beaten
⅓ cup chopped onion
½ cup chopped green pepper
2 tablespoons horseradish

2 teaspoons salt
1 tablespoon prepared mustard
Approximately ¾ pound thinly
 sliced Cheddar cheese
⅓ cup parsley
Paprika

Mix meat, crumbs, milk, eggs, onion, green pepper, horseradish, salt and mustard. Put ⅓ of mixture in 9 x 5 x 3-inch loaf pan. Layer ⅓ of cheese, sprinkle with half the parsley. Cover with second third of meat mixture and cheese, add remaining parsley, then remaining meat. Bake at 375 degrees for about 1 hour. Cover with remaining cheese and place in oven until cheese melts. Sprinkle with paprika. Remove meat from pan with wide spatula.

Merryl Hodgson
(Mrs. Donald C.)

MATCHLESS MEAT LOAF

Serves: 6

3 tablespoons light molasses
3 tablespoons prepared mustard
3 tablespoons vinegar
4 tablespoons catsup
1 cup milk
2 eggs
1 envelope of dehydrated onion
 soup mix

3 cups soft bread crumbs
1 teaspoon monosodium
 glutamate
½ teaspoon oregano
¼ cup chopped parsley
3 pounds ground beef

Mix in order, mashing bread crumbs. Mix well. Pack in loaf pan or mold in shallow pan. Bake at 350 degrees for 1½ hours.

Joyce Sarat White
(Mrs. David W.)

CHEESE MEAT LOAF

Serves: 4 to 6

2 pounds ground beef
4 eggs
½ package herbed seasoned
   stuffing mixture

1 green pepper
1 pound Swiss cheese
6 ounces fresh mushrooms
A little milk

Chop the green pepper and cut the Swiss cheese into small pieces. Slice the mushrooms. Combine ground beef, eggs, stuffing mix, green pepper, Swiss cheese and mushrooms. Add a little milk. Mix and pour into loaf pan. Bake at 350 degrees for 50 to 60 minutes.

Nancy Beaulieu White
(Mrs. Jeffrey M.)

ITALIAN MEAT PIE

Serves: 4 to 6

1 pound ground beef
⅔ cup quick or old fashioned
   oats, uncooked
½ cup catsup
½ cup chopped onion

1 egg
¾ teaspoon salt
⅛ teaspoon pepper
⅛ teaspoon garlic powder

For meat pie shell, combine all ingredients and mix well. Press into bottom and sides of 9-inch pie plate. Partially bake in preheated 350-degree oven for 8 minutes. Drain.

Filling

2 medium sized zucchini, sliced
   ¼-inch thick *or* 1 (9-ounce)
   package frozen Italian cut
   green beans, cooked and
   drained
1 cup shredded Mozzarella
   cheese (4-ounces)

½ cup catsup
½ cup ripe olive slices
½ teaspoon oregano leaves,
   crushed
½ teaspoon basil leaves, crushed
2 tablespoons grated Parmesan
   cheese

Combine zucchini, ½ cup Mozzarella, catsup, olives and seasonings. Spoon into meat pie shell. Top with remaining Mozzarella cheese; sprinkle with Parmesan and continue baking in 350 degree oven for 15 to 18 minutes. Cut into wedges and serve.

Jean Winn Swan
(Mrs. Robert M.)

"JOE'S" YUMMY SPECIAL

Serves: 6 to 8

2 (10-ounce) packages frozen
  spinach, cooked
2 medium-sized onions, chopped
4 tablespoons olive oil
2 pounds ground round steak

2 teaspoons salt
1 teaspoon pepper
Garlic powder (optional)
4 eggs

Drain cooked spinach thoroughly, pressing out as much water as possible. Sauté onions in oil; add meat and seasonings and cook until browned. Add spinach, mix well. Reduce heat. Add eggs, stirring mixture with fork until well combined (about 4 minutes).

Barbara Morris Goodbody
(Mrs. James B.)

NASTY NACHO CASSEROLE

Serves: 8

1 pound ground beef
1 (1¼-ounce) package taco
  seasoning mix
1 (10½-ounce) can enchilada dip
1 (10-ounce) package nacho
  chips, divided in half

1 (16-ounce) can cream-style
  corn
12 ounces Monterey Jack
  cheese, shredded
1 (8-ounce) bottle taco sauce

Brown meat, add taco seasoning according to package directions. Add enchilada dip and heat through. Set aside. Grease a 2½-quart casserole and place half of the crushed nacho chips in the bottom. Place half of the meat mixture on top of the crushed chips. Continue layering with half the creamed corn, half the cheese and half the taco sauce. Repeat all layers. Bake at 350 degrees for 40 minutes. Cover last 15 minutes. May be frozen, defrosted completely, and then cooked as above.

Candice Carbone Thornton
(Mrs. Peter P.)

CHILI

Serves: 12

3 garlic cloves, minced
2 tablespoons vegetable oil
4 pounds round steak, ground
6 large onions
4 large green peppers
3 (1-pound) cans tomatoes
4 (1-pound) cans red kidney
   beans, drained

2 (6-ounce) cans tomato paste
¼ cup chili powder
1 teaspoon white vinegar
3 dashes cayenne pepper
3 whole cloves
1 bay leaf
Salt and pepper, to taste

Cook garlic in oil until golden. Crumble ground round and cook 10 minutes, breaking up to brown evenly. Pour off some of the oil and drippings into another skillet and cook sliced onions and green pepper until tender. Add to cooked ground round with tomatoes, kidney beans, tomato paste, chili powder, vinegar, cayenne pepper, cloves, bay leaf, salt and pepper. Cover, cook over low heat for 1 hour. Better prepared ahead, freezes well.

Lorraine Petrio-Gorski Shuman
(Mrs. Michael)

LOUISIANA BEEF STEW

Serves: 6 to 8

3 tablespoons flour
½ teaspoon celery salt
1 teaspoon salt
Pepper
3 pounds chuck steak, cut up
2 tablespoons oil
1 (28-ounce) can of tomatoes

3 medium onions, sliced
⅓ cup red wine vinegar
½ cup molasses
½ cup water
½ cup raisins
1 pound carrots, thinly sliced

Shake meat in bag with first four ingredients, then brown in oil. Put next 5 ingredients in heavy pot with meat. Bring to a boil, then simmer for 2 hours. Add raisins and carrots. Simmer 30 minutes more. Thicken with cornstarch and water mixture if desired. Serve on noodles or rice. May be prepared ahead. May be frozen.

Martha White Nichols
(Mrs. Christopher)

PORK TENDERLOIN FOR TWO

Serves: 2

1 to 2 ounces melted butter
(not margarine)
3 to 4 pork tenderloins
1 small onion, sliced
Juice of ½ lemon plus some
of the pulp
4 ounces dry white wine
Freshly cracked pepper
Rosemary, a sprinkle

Garlic powder, a sprinkle
1 tablespoon flour
White wine
5 to 6 ounces strong chicken
broth
8 large mushrooms, sliced
2 to 3 tablespoons butter
Fresh parsley
2½ ounces sour cream

Melt butter and wait until foam starts disappearing. Dry the meat, add to butter and brown on both sides. Add onion, lemon juice, wine and seasonings. Cook slowly for 15 minutes. Remove meat and keep hot. Mix flour with a little white wine. Add and stir. Add broth, blending all the time. Simmer for 3 to 5 minutes. In another small pan, sauté the mushrooms in butter until they are barely cooked. Add these to sauce on other burner. Let everything simmer for 4 minutes. Cut the meat into very thin slices. Chop a little parsley and add to the sour cream. Blend this into sauce until it is very hot but do not let it boil. Stir in the meat and serve at once. Sprinkle parsley over the top.

Mallory Marshall Hambley
(Mrs. Clarke)

INEBRIATED PORK

Serves: 10 to 12

6 to 8 pounds fresh ham, boned
   and tied
2 to 3 cloves garlic, crushed
1 onion, thinly sliced
1 bay leaf
½ teaspoon ground clove
¼ teaspoon ground ginger

¼ teaspoon ground nutmeg
1 tablespoon salt
1 teaspoon crushed rosemary
Dry red wine
½ cup raisins
½ cup pine nuts
Hot pepper sauce

Place ham in a large, deep nonmetallic container with the garlic, onion, season-ings and enough red wine to cover. Turn it once and let stand 3 to 4 days in refrigerator turning every day. To roast, let stand at room temperature for sev-eral hours. Turn 2 to 3 times. Place on rack in shallow roasting pan. Roast 25 minutes per pound at 325 degrees. Baste frequently with strained and heated marinade. Skim fat from pan juices. Bring to a boil. Thicken if you wish with *buerre manie* (see recipe below). Add raisins, pine nuts and a good dash of hot pepper sauce to the gravy.

Buerre Manie

Mix together equal amounts of softened butter and flour. When you want to thicken a gravy, just add.

Carol Such Bouton
(Mrs. Dale C., Jr.)

POLYNESIAN PORK

Serves: 4 to 6

1 whole loin of pork,
   boned and tied
Salt
Pepper
Rosemary
½ cup soy sauce

½ cup catsup
¼ cup honey
2 large garlic cloves, crushed
Preserved kumquats
Watercress

Put meat on rack in a shallow roasting pan and sprinkle with salt, freshly ground pepper and a little rosemary. Roast pork in a moderate oven, 350 degrees, for 2 to 2½ hours or until tender when tested with a fork. Baste frequently with the mixture of soy sauce, catsup, honey and crushed garlic. To serve, transfer pork to a heated platter and garnish with preserved kumquats and sprigs of watercress.

Hope Palmer Bramhall
(Mrs. Peter)

PORK CHOPS WITH ORANGE SAUCE

Serves: 4

4 center-cut pork chops   Paprika
Salt   4 tablespoons or more water
Pepper

Salt and pepper chops. Sprinkle with paprika. Brown in skillet for 15 to 20
minutes. When browned, lower heat, add water and cook for 45 to 60 minutes.
Make sure that water does not boil off and add more if necessary. Spoon sauce
over chops.

Orange Sauce

5 tablespoon sugar   10 whole cloves
1½ teaspoons cornstarch   2 teaspoons grated orange rind
¼ teaspoon salt   ½ cup fresh orange juice
¼ teaspoon cinnamon   Orange slices, skin removed

In saucepan, mix sugar, cornstarch, salt, cinnamon, cloves, orange rind and
juice. Cook, stirring until thickened and clear. Add orange slices. Cover and
remove from heat.

Merryl Hodgson
(Mrs. Donald G.)

SWEET IRENE'S HAM LOAF

Serves: 4 to 6

1 pound ham   1 egg
½ pound pork   ½ cup milk
½ pound veal   ½ to 1 teaspoon pepper
3½ slices stale bread

Have butcher grind the meat together. Dampen bread in water, squeeze dry,
and crumble finely. Combine meat, bread crumbs, egg, milk and pepper. Form
into 2 loaves. Pour the following sauce over the loaves.

Sauce

1 cup light brown sugar   ¾ cup vinegar
1 teaspoon dry mustard

Simply combine the sugar, mustard, and vinegar. Pour over the loaves and baste
frequently during baking. Bake for 2 hours at 300 degrees.

Eileen A. Pugh
(Mrs. Richard F.)

RATATOUILLE WITH SAUSAGE

Serves: 12

Olive oil
2 large eggplants, peeled, cut
    into strips
8 medium zucchini, cut into
    ½-inch slices
5 large onions, sliced
6 garlic cloves, minced
6 green peppers, seeded and
    diced
8 large tomatoes, peeled, cut
    into strips

1 cup finely chopped parsley
2 teaspoons thyme
2 teaspoons oregano
2 teaspoons basil
Salt
Pepper
1 dozen sweet or mild Italian
    sausages

Heat oil in a large heavy pan. Briefly sauté zucchini and eggplant in batches over medium heat, about 5 minutes. Remove and drain on paper towel. Sauté garlic, onion and green pepper in same oil until soft. Add more oil if needed. Preheat oven to 350 degrees. Layer sautéed vegetables, tomatoes, parsley and seasonings in a 6-quart casserole. Stir gently to mix. Bake, covered, 35 minutes. Meanwhile, brown the sausages. Drain, cool and slice ¼-inch thick. Return to pan and sauté 2 to 3 minutes on each side. After the vegetables have baked 35 minutes, add the sliced sausage, pushing most of the slices down into the vegetable mixture. Reserve some for the top. Return to oven and bake, uncovered, for 20 minutes. Can all be done ahead of time. The ratatouille should be put together ahead. Bring to room temperature before heating.

Judy Bishop Condren
(Mrs. Arthur)

VEAL AND MUSHROOMS WITH MADEIRA SAUCE

Serves: 4

1 pound veal, pounded thin
Flour—enough to coat veal
3 tablespoons butter, use more if
    necessary
Salt and pepper to taste

½ pound mushrooms, sliced
3 tablespoons butter
½ cup beef bouillon
½ cup Madeira
¼ cup sherry

Sauté veal that has been coated with flour in 3 tablespoons melted butter, adding salt and pepper. Cook quickly turning once. Remove from skillet and keep warm. Melt 3 tablespoons butter, add mushrooms and stir and cook 2 to 3 minutes. Add broth, Madeira and sherry. Stir and cook. Add veal and cook 5 to 10 minutes covered.

Dodo Martineau Stevens
(Mrs. Paul S.)

VEAL RAGOUT

Serves: 4 to 6

1 to 1½ pounds stewing veal
¼ to ½ cup salad or olive oil
Salt, pepper and garlic powder
  to taste
1 large onion, sliced in half rings
2 medium green peppers, sliced
  in half rings

2 celery stalks, sliced
2 large carrots, sliced in circles
½ pound fresh mushrooms,
  sliced
2 to 2½ cups marinara sauce
¼ to ½ cup Marsala or sherry
  (optional)

Season veal well. Heat skillet or frying pan to 375 degrees and sauté veal in oil until browned. Stir as necessary. Remove veal and drain. Remove oil. Pour ½ of marinara sauce into casserole dish. Add veal, vegetables and then remaining sauce. Mix all ingredients. Cook for 1 hour in 350-degree oven in covered casserole. Veal should be tender. Add wine and cook an additional 5 to 10 minutes. Freezes well.

Barbara Troubh Epstein
(Mrs. Burton R.)

VEAL SCALOPPINE WITH CHEESE

Serves: 4

2 pounds veal, cut into thin, even
  slices
½ cup butter, divided
3 tablespoons Marsala wine
1 tablespoon flour
½ cup milk
½ cup water

1 bouillon cube
Dash nutmeg
Freshly ground black pepper,
  to taste
½ pound Swiss or Gruyere
  cheese, sliced thin

Pound veal lightly until very thin. Heat 6 tablespoons butter in skillet, add veal and wine and cook a few seconds on each side. Remove from heat. For sauce melt remaining butter in saucepan, add flour and stir with wire whisk until blended. Meanwhile, bring water and milk to a boil and dissolve bouillon cube in the mixture. Add, all at once, to the butter-flour mixture, stirring vigorously with whisk until sauce is thickened and smooth. Season with nutmeg and pepper. Arrange veal in a single layer in a shallow baking dish. Scrape loose the brown particles from skillet and pour the drippings over the meat. Top with sauce and arrange the cheese over all. Can make ahead and refrigerate at this point. Heat in a preheated oven, 425 degrees until cheese melts and turns brown, about 20 minutes.

Sandra Edson Tuttle
(Mrs. Richard)

VEAL CUTLETS FOYOT

Serves: 4

1½ pounds of veal cutlets
Salt and pepper
3 tablespoons butter
½ cup chopped onion

½ cup bread crumbs
½ cup shredded Swiss cheese
½ cup dry white wine
3 tablespoons melted butter

Place cutlets in baking dish in a single layer. Season with salt and pepper. Sauté onion in butter until golden. Combine crumbs and cheese. Spread onions over cutlets. Top with crumb mixture and press to be sure mixture adheres. Cover with wine and melted butter. Bake 30 minutes at 325 degrees. Can be assembled ahead of time. Allow extra baking time if taking from refrigerator.

Judi Adam
(Mrs. Robert L.)

MOUSSAKA

Serves: 6

1½ pounds eggplant, sliced
  ½-inch thick
2 eggs, beaten
1 cup matzo meal
¼ cup oil
1½ pounds lean ground lamb
16 ounces spaghetti sauce
½ teaspoon oregano
¼ teaspoon cinnamon

Garlic powder, to taste
1 package onion soup mix
1 pint sour cream
1 tablespoon flour
2 eggs, beaten
¾ cup grated Parmesan cheese
10 ounces shredded mozzarella
  cheese

Soak the eggplant in salted water for 20 minutes. Drain well on paper towels. Dip eggplant slices in egg, then into matzo meal. Brown both sides in hot oil until golden. Blot on paper towels to absorb excess oil. Sauté the lamb. Add the spaghetti sauce, oregano, cinnamon, and garlic powder. Simmer 10 to 15 minutes. Set aside. Mix the onion soup mix, sour cream, and the flour thoroughly; stir in the 2 remaining eggs and beat until smooth. In the bottom of a 2½-quart casserole, place ⅓ of the eggplant, top with ½ of the meat mixture, sprinkle with both cheeses. Spread ½ of the sour cream mixture over this. Begin layering again with ⅓ of the eggplant, remaining half of meat mixture, sprinkle with both cheeses, last ⅓ of the eggplant, remainder of sour cream. Sprinkle both cheeses on top and bake 30 to 40 minutes at 375 degrees. Remove from oven 10 minutes before cutting to serve. This may be prepared ahead of time and refrigerated. Bring to room temperature before baking.

Patricia Pugh Britt
(Mrs. Michael E.)

LAMB CURRY

Serves: 4

¼ cup butter
1 large onion, chopped
1 clove garlic, minced
1 tart apple, peeled, cored,
  and chopped
1 green pepper, cut into
  ⅛-inch strips
2 teaspoons curry

1½ teaspoons flour
3 fresh or 8 ounces canned
  tomatoes, chopped
2 cups chicken broth
3 cups cooked lamb, cubed
Salt and pepper, to taste
Lime juice, to taste

Melt the butter and sauté the onion, garlic, apple, and green pepper until soft but not brown. Stir in the curry. Stir in the flour and cook over medium heat until golden brown, about 3 minutes. Add the tomatoes and chicken stock and continue cooking until thick and smooth. Stir often. Add the lamb, salt and pepper and heat through. Serve with rice. Sprinkle with lime juice.

The Committee

ATHENIAN LAMB

Serves: 6 to 8

5 pound boned leg of lamb
4 to 5 cloves fresh garlic, slivered
1 cup fresh mint leaves
1½ to 2 tablespoons oregano

Salt and pepper, to taste
Olive oil
Fresh lemon juice—from
  3 lemons

Make slits in lamb and insert garlic, mint leaves, and oregano at regular intervals. Pour olive oil and lemon juice over meat. Then rub entire meat surface with additional mint, oregano, salt and pepper. Cover and marinate 24 hours, turning meat several times. Preheat oven to 500 degrees, place meat on a rack with water in bottom of pan and sear meat for 20 minutes. Reduce heat to 425 degrees and cook, basting often (adding more water to pan juices when necessary). Cook about 2 hours and 20 minutes or until meat thermometer reads 172 degrees. Use a deep roaster but do not cover—water depth should not touch meat. Water helps to cut down on spattering.

Helen Patrinos Gianfrancesca
(Mrs. Anthony)

LAMB SHANKS IN RED WINE

Serves: 6

6 lamb shanks
Flour
Salt
Pepper
Oregano
3 tablespoons butter
1 tablespoon olive oil
1 garlic clove, crushed
2 tablespoons brandy

3 cups dry red wine
3 cups water
½ cup diced celery
½ cup diced carrots
1 cup chopped onion
1 bay leaf
Pinch of thyme
1 teaspoon meat extract
    or *glace de viande*

Roll lamb shanks in flour. Sprinkle with salt, pepper, and oregano. Brown in heavy kettle in butter, olive oil and garlic. When completely browned, pour warmed brandy over lamb and ignite. When flame dies, transfer contents of kettle to a heavy casserole. Add wine, water, celery, carrots, onion, bay leaf and thyme. Cover casserole and bake in moderate oven at 350 degrees for 2 hours. Remove fat from sauce and thicken with *buerre manie* (see recipe below). Stir in 1 teaspoon *glace de viande* or meat extract. Correct seasoning with salt, pepper and a little lemon juice.

Buerre Manie

1 tablespoon flour mixed to a
    paste with 1 tablespoon butter.

Hope Palmer Bramhall
(Mrs. Peter T. C.)

APRICOT SAUCE FOR LAMB

Yield: 2 cups

1 (16-ounce) can of apricots,
with juice
2 tablespoons wine vinegar
1 tablespoon brown sugar

2 tablespoons butter
Pinch nutmeg
Pinch cinnamon

Purée apricots. Turn into a saucepan and add remaining ingredients. Simmer gently for 10 minutes. Serve hot.

Anne Reevy Neiman
(Mrs. G. W.)

HOT CRANBERRY-RAISIN SAUCE

Yield: 4 cups

1 (12-ounce) package cranberries
1 cup dark seedless raisins
12 ounces cherry preserves

¼ cup sugar
1 tablespoon grated orange peel
½ teaspoon salt

In blender, blend half the cranberries and raisins with ½ cup water until berries are finely chopped. Pour into 4-quart pan. Repeat with remaining ingredients and ½ cup water. Heat mixture to boiling, reduce heat and simmer for 5 minutes, stirring. Cover and refrigerate. Can be served cold or reheated. Serve within a week. Delicious on baked ham.

Anne Reevy Neiman
(Mrs. G. W.)

MARINADE FOR BEEF

Yield: 1½ cups

2 ounces bleu cheese
1 tablespoon butter
1 small onion
Dash hot pepper sauce
¼ cup lemon juice
½ cup sherry

¼ cup corn oil
Ground pepper, to taste
1 teaspoon celery salt
Dash ground cloves
Dash garlic powder

Combine above ingredients and blend well. Marinate meat for 8 to 48 hours, turning occasionally. Broil meat on both sides, then roast until done.

Anne Reevy Neiman
(Mrs. G. W.)

BLENDER BÉRNAISE SAUCE

Yield: Approximately 1 cup

2 tablespoons white wine
1 tablespoon tarragon vinegar
2 teaspoons chopped shallots
   or scallions

1 to 2 teaspoons dried tarragon
¼ teaspoon black pepper

Combine all the above ingredients in a saucepan and cook over high heat until almost all the liquid has evaporated. Set this purée aside.

3 egg yolks
2 tablespoons fresh lemon juice
Scant ¼ teaspoon salt

Dash cayenne pepper
⅔ cup butter, melted

Combine yolks, lemon juice, salt and cayenne in blender. Cover and blend on high speed for 3 seconds. With blender on high speed, very slowly pour melted butter into egg mixture. Pour reserved purée into the above sauce and blend on high speed for 4 seconds. This may be made 2 days ahead and reheated very gently in double boiler. Reheat carefully, only to warm the sauce. Do not cook it or sauce will separate.

Patricia Pugh Britt
(Mrs. Michael E.)

CUMBERLAND SAUCE

Yield: 2½ cups

2 cups ruby port wine
⅓ cup slivered orange peel
⅔ cup orange juice

2 tablespoons lemon juice
1 (10-ounce) jar red currant jelly
Dash cayenne

In medium saucepan, combine port and orange peels. Cook over medium heat until reduced to 1⅓ cups. (Approximately 10 to 15 minutes). Stir in orange juice, lemon juice, currant jelly, and cayenne until well blended. Bring to boil, reduce heat and simmer uncovered for 10 minutes, or until jelly is melted. Serve hot or cold with ham or chicken.

Clarabell Connard
(Mrs. G. Baer, Sr.)

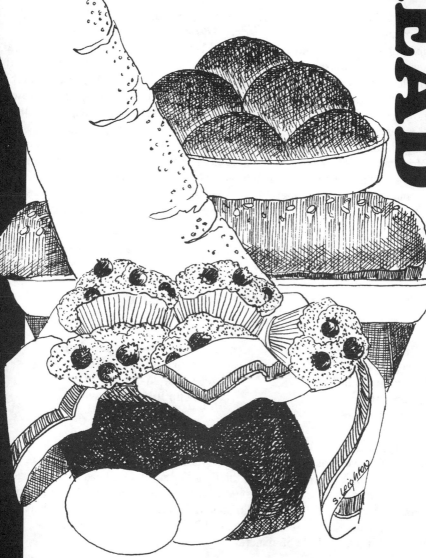

BREAD

REFRIGERATOR-RISE OATMEAL BREAD

Yield: 2 loaves

½ cup warm water
2 packages yeast
1¾ cups warm milk
¼ cup brown sugar
1 tablespoon salt

3 tablespoons margarine
5 to 6 cups flour
1 cup rolled oats
Oil

Measure the warm water into a large bowl. Stir in the yeast until dissolved. Add warm milk, sugar, salt and margarine. Add 2 cups of the flour and beat with a mixer until smooth (about 1 minute). Add 1 more cup of flour and the oats. Beat vigorously with a wooden spoon. Add enough additional flour to make a smooth dough. Turn out onto a lightly floured board and knead 8 to 10 minutes until the dough is smooth and elastic. Cover the dough with plastic wrap and then a towel and let it rest for 20 minutes. Divide the dough in half. Roll each half into a 12 x 8-inch rectangle. Roll up into loaves. Place each loaf into a greased 8 x 4 x 2-inch loaf pan. Brush loaves with oil. Cover loosely with plastic wrap and refrigerate for 2 to 24 hours. When ready to bake, remove the dough from the refrigerator and uncover the dough carefully. Let the dough stand uncovered for 10 minutes at room temperature. Puncture any gas bubbles with a greased toothpick or metal skewer. Bake the loaves in a 400-degree oven for 30 to 40 minutes.

Lorraine Petrio-Gorski Shuman
(Mrs. Michael)

SHREDDED WHEAT BREAD

Yield: 2 loaves

2 shredded wheat biscuits
  (regular size), crushed
1 teaspoon salt
⅓ cup sugar
⅓ cup molasses

3 tablespoons shortening
2 cups boiling water
1 yeast cake
½ cup lukewarm water
7 to 8 cups flour

Dissolve shredded wheat, salt, sugar, molasses and shortening in the boiling water. Dissolve yeast in the ½ cup lukewarm water. Add to first mixture. Add 6½ cups flour. Mix and add rest of the flour, ½ cup at a time, as needed. Knead until elastic and not sticky. (If using dough hook on mixer, knead about 10 minutes.) Let rise until doubled in bulk, about 2 hours in a warm place. Punch down and make into 2 loaves. Place in greased 9 x 5 x 3-inch pans and let rise. Bake at 350 degrees for 30 to 35 minutes.

Jane (Ba) Davidson Kopp
(Mrs. Donald A.)

NO-FAIL WHOLE WHEAT BREAD (AND VARIATIONS)

Yield: 3 large loaves

3 packages yeast
3 cups warm water
½ cup vegetable oil
½ cup honey, molasses or brown
  sugar

1 tablespoon salt
7 to 9 cups flour, using at least 2
  to 4 cups of whole wheat flour
½ cup powdered milk (optional)
1 egg, slightly beaten (optional)

Preheat large mixing bowl with hot tap water while assembling the ingredients. Empty bowl and measure warm water into it. Add honey, molasses or brown sugar. Sprinkle yeast over water-sugar mixture. Let stand until dissolves (mixture will become foamy—do not let it become too foamy). Stir in oil and salt. Add powdered milk and egg if you are using them. Stir in 2 cups of white flour, then stir in the 2 to 4 cups of whole wheat flour. Continue adding flour until dough becomes too stiff to stir. Turn out onto a floured board and knead enough of the remaining flour into the dough to make it firm but pliable. Knead for about 8 minutes until dough is smooth, elastic and not sticky. Place dough in a large greased bowl. Turn dough to grease top. Let rise until doubled. Punch down. Let rise again in the bowl or shape it into loaves at this point. Divide the dough into 3 pieces. With your hands, shape each piece into a 10 x 16-inch rectangle, roll up like a jelly roll, starting with the 10-inch side. Put into three 9 x 5 x 3-inch greased loaf pans. Let rise until almost double (45 to 60 minutes). Bake in a 375-degree oven for 15 minutes. Reduce heat to 350 degrees and continue baking for 20 to 25 minutes more until golden. Remove from pans and cool on racks. Very moist bread. Can be varied infinitely by substituting different kinds of flour, or substituting 1 to 2 cups oatmeal, or varying the sweetener. When substituting flours, add where the whole wheat flour is added.

Lee Morse Edwards
(Mrs. Dwight H.)

BULGUR YEAST BREAD

Yield: 2 loaves

½ cup bulgur (cracked wheat)
1 cup warm water
1 package dry yeast
¼ cup warm water
2 cups milk

2 tablespoons sugar
2 tablespoons soft shortening
2 teaspoons salt
6 to 6¼ cups flour

Soak the bulgur in 1 cup warm water for at least 30 minutes. Dissolve yeast in ¼ cup warm water in a large mixing bowl. Combine milk, sugar, shortening and salt in a saucepan and heat to lukewarm. Add to the yeast mixture. Stir in 2 cups flour and beat well. Add soaked bulgur and enough more flour to make a stiff dough. Turn out onto a floured surface and knead until smooth. Return to bowl and cover. Let rise until doubled in bulk. Divide into 2 balls, roll out and form bread loaves. Place in lightly greased 9 x 5 x 3-inch bread pans and let rise until doubled. Bake in a 400-degree oven for 25 to 30 minutes. Bread should sound hollow when tapped.

Elizabeth Baird

ANADAMA BREAD

Yield: 2 loaves

2 cups water
1 teaspoon salt
½ cup stone ground corn meal
½ cup molasses

2 tablespoons shortening
1 cake yeast
½ cup lukewarm water
5 cups flour

Bring the 2 cups of water to boiling point. Just before it boils add salt and corn meal. Cook for 5 minutes. Add the molasses and shortening. Cool. Soak the yeast in ½ cup of lukewarm water for 10 minutes. Add to the cooled corn meal mixture. Add the flour gradually, beating well. Turn the dough onto a floured board and knead for 10 minutes. If the dough is too sticky, use up to an additional cup of flour. Place the dough in a greased bowl. Cover and set in a warm place to rise until doubled. Punch down and form 2 loaves. Put into greased 9 x 5 x 3-inch loaf pans and let rise until doubled. Bake in a 375-degree oven for 30 to 40 minutes. Brush the crust with melted butter.

Hope Palmer Bramhall
(Mrs. Peter T. C.)

RUSSIAN BLACK BREAD

Yield: 2 round loaves

4 cups rye flour
3 cups unbleached white flour
1 teaspoon sugar
2 teaspoons salt
2 cups bran cereal
2 tablespoons crushed caraway
  seeds
2 teaspoons instant coffee (dry)
2 teaspoons onion powder

½ teaspoon crushed fennel seed
2 packages active dry yeast
2½ cups water
¼ cup vinegar
¼ cup dark molasses
1 ounce unsweetened chocolate
¼ cup margarine
1 teaspoon cornstarch
½ cup cold water

Combine the flours. In a large bowl mix 2½ cups of the flour mixture with the sugar, salt, cereal, caraway seeds, instant coffee, onion powder, fennel seeds, and the undissolved dry yeast. Combine 2½ cups water with the vinegar, molasses, chocolate and margarine in a saucepan and heat on low until the liquids are very warm. The margarine and the chocolate need not totally melt. Gradually add this to the dry ingredients and beat at medium speed of an electric mixer, scraping the bowl occasionally. Add ½ cup of the flour mixture. Beat for 2 minutes, scraping the bowl often. Stir in enough more flour to make a soft dough. Turn out onto a lightly floured board. Cover and let rest for 15 minutes, then knead until smooth and elastic—about 10 minutes. Dough may be sticky. Place in a greased bowl, turning to grease the top. Cover and let rise in a warm place until doubled. Punch down the dough and turn out onto a floured board. Divide in half and shape each half into a ball about 5 inches in diameter. Place each ball in the center of an 8-inch round pie pan or cake pan. Cover and let rise in a warm place until doubled. Bake in a 350-degree oven for 45 to 50 minutes. Meanwhile combine the cornstarch and cold water in a small saucepan and cook over medium heat until the mixture starts to boil, then cook for 1 minute stirring constantly. As soon as the bread is baked brush the cornstarch mixture over the top of the loaves. Return the bread to the oven for 2 to 3 minutes until the glaze is set. Turn the loaves out of the pans and cool on racks.

Patricia Pugh Britt
(Mrs. Michael E.)

MAINE POTATO BREAD
(A WHITE BREAD)

Yield: 3 loaves

9 cups flour
¼ cup vegetable shortening
1 small Maine potato, cooked
2 cups potato water (water you
   cooked the potato in)

5 tablespoons sugar, divided
2 packages dry yeast
⅓ cup instant nonfat dry milk
¾ cup warm water
1 tablespoon salt

Mix 3 cups of the flour with the vegetable shortening. Set aside. Boil the potato in enough water to leave you with 2 cups of potato water after the potato is cooked. Measure the water. Let the potato and the 2 cups of water cool to lukewarm, then pour into your blender and purée for 1 minute. Pour this into a large bowl and add 2½ tablespoons of sugar and the yeast. Stir, then let stand for 5 minutes. Blend in 3 cups of flour. Mix well, cover with a towel and let this batter rise until doubled. Meanwhile, mix the nonfat dry milk with the ¾ cup of warm water. Stir down the batter and add the milk mixture, the other 2½ tablespoons sugar and the salt. Now, add the flour-shortening mixture and stir in the remaining 3 cups of flour. Turn the dough out onto a floured board and let rest for 5 minutes while you wash and butter the bowl. Knead the dough until smooth and elastic (about 10 minutes). Put the dough in the greased bowl, turn the dough to grease the top, cover with a piece of buttered waxed paper and a towel and let rise until doubled. Punch down and shape into 3 loaves. Place the loaves into 3 greased 8 x 4-inch loaf pans, cover with a towel, and let rise until doubled. Bake in a 375-degree oven for 40 minutes. Remove from the pans and cool on racks. This bread makes excellent sandwiches and even better French toast.

The Commiteee

OATMEAL-SESAME BREAD

Yield: 2 loaves

1 cup rolled oats
2 cups boiling water
½ cup sesame seeds
1 package dry yeast
½ cup warm water
¼ cup dark molasses

¼ cup dark corn syrup
1½ teaspoons salt
3 tablespoons melted butter or
   margarine, divided
4½ to 5 cups unbleached white
   flour

Stir together the rolled oats and boiling water in the top of a double boiler; cover and cook over simmering water until water in the top pan is absorbed. Transfer the oats to a large bowl and let cool. In a dry frying pan over medium heat, stir the sesame seeds until browned. Dissolve the yeast in the ½ cup warm water and let sit for 5 minutes. Add it to the cooled oats. Stir in the molasses, corn syrup, salt, 2 tablespoons of the melted butter, and sesame seeds. Beat in about 4 cups of the flour to make a stiff dough. Turn the dough out onto a floured board. Let it rest for 2 to 3 minutes while you wash and grease the bowl. Knead the dough until it is smooth and elastic (10 to 20 minutes), adding additional flour as needed to prevent sticking. Form dough into a ball, then turn the dough in the greased bowl to coat the top. Cover and let rise in a warm place for about two hours (or overnight in a cool kitchen). Punch the dough down, knead it again briefly and shape into two loaves. Place each loaf in a greased (on the bottom only) 8½ x 4½-inch loaf pan. Cover and let rise until doubled. Brush tops with the remaining 1 tablespoon melted butter. Bake in a 400-degree oven for about 40 minutes. Turn out onto racks to cool.

The Committee

ANGEL BISCUITS

Yield: 6 dozen

5 cups self-rising flour
⅓ cup sugar
1 teaspoon baking soda
1 cup shortening

2 tablespoons dry yeast
¼ cup lukewarm water
2 cups buttermilk

Combine flour, sugar and baking soda; then cut in shortening. Add yeast which has been dissolved in the water. Then add buttermilk. Let dough rise until doubled. Roll out on a floured board and cut into biscuits with a cutter. Gently fold rolls in half. Bake in a 450-degree oven for 10 to 12 minutes. Dough may be covered and stored in refrigerator for up to one week.

Carol Potter Day
(Mrs. Richard B.)

ELLEN'S HERBERT HOTEL ROLLS

Yield: 18 to 20 rolls

Hot Rolls

1 cup milk	¼ cup warm water
¾ cup vegetable shortening	1 package yeast
¼ cup sugar	4 to 5 cups flour
½ teaspoon salt	2 eggs

Scald the milk, shortening, sugar and salt. Cool to lukewarm. Place ¼ cup warm water in a bowl, add the yeast and stir to dissolve. Add the lukewarm milk mixture and two cups of the flour. Beat well and add the eggs. Beat well again and add more flour to make a soft dough. Cover the dough and let it rise until doubled. Shape into rolls or make into the cinnamon rolls (recipe below). Let rise until double before baking in a 400-degree oven for 10 to 12 minutes.

Cinnamon Rolls

Hot roll dough as above	1 cup granulated sugar
½ cup butter or margarine	1 teaspoon cinnamon
1 cup brown sugar	Handful of chopped pecans

Divide dough in half. Roll out each half into a 24 x 12-inch rectangle. Mix together the butter, sugars, cinnamon and pecans. Spread both pieces of dough with this mixture. Roll up jelly-roll fashion, starting with the 24-inch side. Pinch to seal the edges. Cut into 1½-inch slices and place on greased cookie sheets. Flatten each roll. Let rise in a warm place until doubled. Bake in a 400-degree oven for 10 to 12 minutes. Remove immediately from the cookie sheets and cool on racks.

These freeze well. To serve from the freezer, take out as many as you need and put on a cookie sheet. Put into a 400-degree oven, turn the oven off, and let the rolls warm for 5 to 8 minutes.

Bonnie Bonjean Dowling
(Mrs. Patrick A.)

KINGFIELD WHOLE WHEAT ROLLS

Yield: One 9 x 13 pan full

¾ cup milk
3 tablespoons sugar
4 teaspoons salt
⅓ cup butter or margarine
⅓ cup molasses

1½ cups warm water
2 packages dry yeast
4½ cups whole wheat flour
2¾ cups flour

Scald milk; stir in sugar, salt, butter and molasses. Put the yeast in warm water, stir to dissolve. Stir into the lukewarm mixture 2 cups whole wheat flour and 2 cups white flour. Beat until smooth. Add enough of the remaining flour to make a soft dough. Knead until smooth (10 minutes). Let rise in warm place until doubled. Punch down and shape into rolls and place in a buttered 9 x 13-inch glass pan. Cover and let rise until doubled. Bake in a 400-degree oven for 25 to 30 minutes.

Bonnie Bonjean Dowling
(Mrs. Patrick A.)

CORN BREAD

Yield: One 8-inch cake

¾ cup corn meal
1¼ cups flour
1 cup sugar
½ teaspoon salt
3 teaspoons baking powder

4 tablespoons powdered milk
1 large egg
¾ cup warm water
¼ cup butter, melted

Mix together the corn meal, flour, sugar, salt, baking powder and powdered milk. (This mixture may be stored in a screw-top jar until needed.) Beat the egg until thick, then add the warm water and the melted butter. Mix the dry and the wet ingredients and pour into a greased 8-inch pan. Bake in a 425-degree oven for 25 minutes. It has a sweet taste and does not crumble.

Martha White Nichols
(Mrs. Christopher)

SPIDER CORN CAKE

Yield: One 8-inch cake

1 tablespoon butter
1⅔ cups corn meal
⅓ cup flour
2 eggs
1 cup sour milk or
1 cup milk with 1 tablespoon
  vinegar added

1 teaspoon baking soda
¼ cup sugar
½ teaspoon salt
1 cup sweet milk

Melt the butter in a hot spider pan. Mix all ingredients except the sweet milk together. Turn mixture into spider and add the cup of milk. *Do not stir.* Bake spider in a 375-degree oven for 25 to 30 minutes. Spider cake has a line of creamy custard through the center. Slice as a pie and top with a generous pat of butter for the Flavor of Maine!

India Horton Weatherill
(Mrs. Robert H.)

APRICOT BREAD

Yield: 1 large loaf

1½ cups chopped dried apricots
Water
1 large egg
½ cup sugar
2 tablespoons melted butter,
  margarine or oil
2½ cups flour

5 teaspoons baking powder
¼ teaspoon baking soda
½ teaspoon salt
1 cup milk
½ cup chopped walnuts

Cover apricots with water and boil for 5 minutes. Drain well. Let drain while making the batter. Beat the egg; add the sugar and butter. Sift together the flour, baking powder, soda and salt and add alternately with the milk to the egg mixture. Gently fold in the apricots and the nuts. Pour into a 9 x 5 x 3-inch loaf pan and bake in a 350-degree oven for about 50 minutes. Test center with a tooth-pick to check doneness.

Barbara Gee Chellis
(Mrs. Thomas D.)

PUMPKIN BREAD

Yield: 2 large loaves

3 cups sugar
1 cup salad oil
4 large eggs, beaten
1 (16-ounce) can pumpkin or 2
   cups cooked, mashed pumpkin
3½ cups flour
1 teaspoon baking powder
2 teaspoons salt

2 teaspoons baking soda
½ teaspoon ground cloves
1 teaspoon cinnamon
1 teaspoon allspice
⅔ cup water
1 to 1½ cups chopped pecans
   (optional)

Using an electric mixer, combine sugar, oil and eggs. Beat until light and fluffy. Stir in the pumpkin. Combine the dry ingredients and stir into the pumpkin mixture. Add the water and the nuts, mixing well. Spoon the batter into 2 well-greased 9 x 5 x 3-inch loaf pans. Bake in a 350-degree oven for 65 to 75 minutes.

For extra-special occasions, try this frosted with an orange-cream cheese frosting. Scrumptious!

Orange Cream Cheese Frosting

1 (8-ounce) package cream
   cheese, softened
¼ cup butter, softened

2 cups powdered sugar
1½ teaspoons vanilla extract
1 tablespoon grated orange rind

Combine cheese and butter in a large mixing bowl. Beat until light and fluffy (an electric mixer on medium is suggested). Add the sugar and beat until well blended. Add the vanilla and the orange rind.

Sharon Staples Alexander
(Mrs. Alan R.)

ZUCCHINI BREAD

Serves: 10 to 12

2 cups flour
2 teaspoons baking soda
1 teaspoon salt
¼ teaspoon baking powder
3 teaspoons ground cinnamon
3 eggs

1 cup vegetable oil
1½ cups sugar
2 medium zucchini, grated
1 teaspoon vanilla
1 cup raisins
1 cup chopped walnuts

In a small bowl sift the flour, soda, salt, baking powder and cinnamon. In a large bowl mix the eggs, oil, sugar, zucchini and vanilla. Beat until well mixed. Stir in the flour mixture. Mix until smooth. Stir in the raisins and nuts. Pour the mixture into a greased 13 x 9 x 2-inch pan. Bake in a 350-degree oven for 40 minutes.

Shirley Thompson Leighton
(Mrs. Thomas M.)

CARROT BREAD

Yield: 2 loaves

1½ cups salad oil
2 cups sugar
3 large eggs
2 cups fresh grated carrots
1 (8¼-ounce) can crushed
  pineapple

1 cup chopped nuts
3 teaspoons vanilla
3 cups flour
1 teaspoon salt
1 teaspoon baking soda
3 teaspoons cinnamon

Mix the oil, sugar and eggs together. Add the grated carrots and the pineapple, then the nuts and the vanilla. Add the dry ingredients, stirring until smooth. Bake in 2 greased and floured 9 x 5 x 3-inch loaf pans in a 325-degree oven for 55 to 60 minutes. Remove from pans and cool on a rack.

Pamela Merkel Whipple
(Mrs. James C.)

GRAM'S DATE AND NUT BREAD

Yield: 2 small loaves

1½ cups boiling water
1 (8-ounce) package dates,
  chopped
1½ cups sugar
2 tablespoons butter or
  margarine, melted

1 egg
2 teaspoons baking soda
3 cups flour
¼ teaspoon salt
1 teaspoon vanilla
1 cup chopped walnuts

Pour water over dates and let cool. Cream sugar and butter. Add egg and mix. Dissolve baking soda with dates and water. Add flour, salt, vanilla and date mixture and mix. Stir in nuts. Bake in a 350-degree oven for 60 minutes.

Carol Potter Day
(Mrs. Richard B.)

STRAWBERRY NUT BREAD

Yield: 4 small loaves

1 cup butter
1½ cups sugar
1½ teaspoons vanilla
¼ teaspoon lemon extract
4 eggs
3 cups flour

1 teaspoon salt
1 teaspoon cream of tartar
½ teaspoon baking soda
1 cup strawberry jam
½ cup sour cream
1 cup chopped walnuts

Cream butter, sugar, vanilla and lemon extract until fluffy. Add the eggs, one at a time, beating well after each addition. Sift together the flour, salt, cream of tartar and soda. Combine jam and sour cream. Add the jam mixture alternately with the dry ingredients to the creamed mixture, beating until well combined. Stir in the nuts. Divide the batter among 4 greased and floured 4½ x 2¾ x 2¼-inch loaf pans. Bake in a 350-degree oven for approximately 50 to 55 minutes until done. Cool 10 minutes in pans; remove and cool completely on wire racks.

Sue Mahan Kimble
(Mrs. John D.)

POPPY SEED TEA BREAD

Yield: 2 loaves

3 cups flour
2½ cups sugar
1½ teaspoons salt
1½ teaspoons baking powder
3 eggs
1½ cups milk

1 cup plus 2 tablespoons oil
2 tablespoons poppy seed
1½ teaspoons vanilla extract
1½ teaspoons almond extract
1½ teaspoons butter flavoring

Preheat oven to 325 degrees. In a large bowl of electric mixer, blend all ingredients until well mixed (about 2 minutes). Pour into greased and floured 9 x 5 x 3-inch loaf pans. Bake 60 minutes or until cake tester is clean. Cool 10 minutes in pan.

Glaze

¼ cup orange juice
¾ cup sugar
½ teaspoon vanilla

½ teaspoon almond extract
½ teaspoon oil

In a medium pan, heat all ingredients until sugar melts. Prick cake with fork and pour glaze over cake while warm.

*Jean Potter Benton
(Mrs. Don C., III)*

FRUITED EGGNOG BREAD

Yield: One large loaf

2¾ cups flour
¾ cup sugar
1 tablespoon baking powder
1 teaspoon salt
½ teaspoon mace
1½ cups eggnog

¼ cup margarine, melted
1 egg, beaten
1 tablespoon rum
¾ cup walnuts or pecans
¾ cup mixed candied fruit

In a large bowl, mix the first five ingredients. Stir in the eggnog, margarine, egg and rum just until the flour is moistened. The batter will be lumpy. Fold in the nuts and fruits. Spread the mixture in a greased 9 x 5-inch loaf pan and bake for 1 hour in a 350-degree oven. Cool the bread in the pan for 10 minutes. Remove from pan and cool on a wire rack.

*Sharon Smith Bushey
(Mrs. Donald J.)*

LEMON TEA CAKE

Yield: 1 large loaf

½ cup butter
1 cup sugar
2 eggs
Grated rind of one lemon

1½ cups flour
1 teaspoon baking powder
½ teaspoon salt
½ cup milk

Topping

Juice of one lemon   ½ cup sugar

Cream the butter and sugar. Add the eggs and lemon rind and beat well. Add sifted dry ingredients alternately with the milk. Pour the batter into a well-greased 9 x 5 x 3-inch loaf pan and bake in a 350-degree oven for 1 hour. Add lemon juice to ½ cup sugar and spoon this over hot cake as soon as it is taken from the oven. Remove the cake from the pan and cool on a rack.

Leslie MacDougall Webber
(Mrs. Walter E.)

RHUBARB COFFEE CAKE

Yield: One 13 x 9 x 2-inch cake

2 cups flour
1¼ cups sugar
1 teaspoon baking soda
1 teaspoon salt
1 teaspoon cinnamon
¼ teaspoon cloves
¼ teaspoon allspice

2 large eggs
½ cup salad oil
⅓ cup milk
2 cups fresh rhubarb (can use
    frozen rhubarb in a pinch),
    unpeeled and cut into small
    pieces

Sift dry ingredients. Mix eggs and oil in another bowl. Add egg-oil mixture to dry ingredients. Blend in milk. Fold in the rhubarb. Pour into a greased 9 x 13 x 2-inch pan. Spread topping over the unbaked cake. Bake in a 350-degree oven for about 50 minutes.

Topping

4 tablespoons butter
⅔ cup flour
½ cup light brown sugar

¾ cup coconut
¼ cup chopped nuts

Blend together the butter, flour and brown sugar. Add coconut and nuts.

Martha White Nichols
(Mrs. Christopher)

CHRISTMAS CRANBERRY CAKE

Serves: 8

1 cup sugar	1 teaspoon baking powder
2 tablespoons butter	1 cup milk
2 cups flour	2 cups cranberries

Mix above ingredients and spread in greased 8-inch round pan. Bake at 350 degrees for 1 hour.

Sauce

1 cup butter	1 tablespoon vanilla
1 cup heavy cream	1 tablespoon cornstarch
1 cup sugar	

Melt butter in saucepan. Add cream and sugar and boil until blended. Add vanilla and cornstarch. Mix well and serve warm over cold cake.

Cake can be made several days ahead and sauce added at last moment.

Shirley Thompson Leighton
(Mrs. Thomas M.)

DANISH COFFEE CAKE

Yield: 1 large tube cake

½ cup shortening	1 teaspoon vanilla
1 cup sugar	2 cups flour
2 large eggs	1 teaspoon baking powder
1 cup sour cream or milk with	1 teaspoon baking soda
1 tablespoon vinegar added	¼ teaspoon salt

Topping

½ cup chopped nuts	½ cup brown sugar
1 teaspoon cinnamon	

Cream shortening and sugar. Add eggs, sour cream and vanilla. Sift flour, baking powder, soda and salt. Add to the egg mixture. Pour half of the batter into a greased tube pan. Add half the topping. Top with remaining batter and then remaining topping. Bake in a 350-degree oven for 45 minutes. For a slightly darker cake, put the topping right in with the batter. This prevents the nuts and sugar from falling off when you remove the cake from the pan!

Mildred A. Muir

POPOVERS

Yield: 6 to 8 popovers

3 large eggs
1 cup milk
1 cup flour

3 tablespoons melted butter
   or margarine
¼ teaspoon salt

In a blender combine eggs, milk, flour, butter and salt. Cover and blend 30 seconds or until combined. Fill 6 to 8 well-greased custard cups or popover tins half full. Bake in a 400-degree oven for 40 minutes. Remove from cups. Serve hot with butter. For crispy popovers, prick tops with a fork to let steam escape before removing from the oven.

Sharon Smith Bushey
(Mrs. Donald J.)

PORTLAND COUNTRY CLUB'S BLUEBERRY CAKE

Yield: One 9 x 9-inch cake

¾ cup sugar
½ cup butter
1 egg
½ cup milk

2 cups flour
½ teaspoon salt
2 teaspoons baking powder
2 cups blueberries

Cream sugar and butter together. Mix egg and milk. Sift dry ingredients together and add alternately to cream mixture with the liquid. Fold in blueberries. Pour batter into a greased 9 x 9-inch pan. Spread topping over cake batter and bake in a 375 degree oven for 30 to 40 minutes.

Topping

½ cup sugar
⅓ cup flour

¼ cup butter, softened
1 teaspoon cinnamon

Sift dry ingredients and cut in the butter until it forms lumps the size of peas.

SPECIAL BLUEBERRY MUFFINS

Yield: 12 muffins

½ cup vegetable shortening
1¼ cups sugar
2 large eggs
½ cup milk
2 cups flour

2 teaspoons baking powder
½ teaspoon salt
1½ cups Maine blueberries, fresh
  or frozen

Cream vegetable shortening with the sugar. Add the eggs and mix well. Add the milk and mix well again. Sift into the first mixture, the flour, baking powder and salt. Mix by hand. Fold in the blueberries very gently. Fill muffin tins to the top. Sprinkle each muffin with sugar. Bake in a 375-degree oven for about 30 minutes until golden brown.

Try to find the tiny Maine wild blueberries for these. The taste is worth the effort!

Jane (Ba) Davidson Kopp
(Mrs. Donald A.)

DATE BRAN MUFFINS

Yield: Muffins and more muffins

2 cups bran buds
4 regular size shredded
  wheat biscuits
½ cup boiling water
1 cup oil
3 eggs
½ teaspoon salt

3 cups sugar
5 cups flour
4½ teaspoons baking soda
½ teaspoon baking powder
1 quart buttermilk
1 cup dates
1 cup raisins

Mix all the ingredients together. This makes 3 quarts of batter. Bake in muffin tins filled ¾ full in a 350-degree oven for about 25 minutes.

The batter keeps in the refrigerator for 3 to 4 weeks. Just pour out what you need and store the rest.

Sally Grindell Vamvakias
(Mrs. James G.)

FRENCH DOUGHNUT MUFFINS

Yield: 12 muffins

1 large egg, beaten
½ cup milk
⅓ cup melted butter
1½ cups plus 2 tablespoons flour

¾ cup sugar
2 teaspoons baking powder
¼ teaspoon salt
¼ teaspoon nutmeg

Topping

⅓ cup melted butter
1 teaspoon cinnamon

½ cup sugar
½ teaspoon vanilla

Beat egg; add milk and ⅓ cup melted butter. Combine flour, sugar, baking powder, salt and nutmeg. Blend well with the egg mixture. Fill greased muffin tins half full and bake in a 400-degree oven for 15 minutes or until browned. Immediately remove muffins from the pan and dip in the remaining ⅓ cup melted butter. Roll in cinnamon, sugar, vanilla mixture. Serve warm.

Rho Francke Leavitt
(Mrs. William)

CINNAMON CRESCENTS

Yield: 4 dozen

1 (8-ounce) package cream
    cheese
½ pound butter or margarine
2 cups flour
Cinnamon

Sugar
Apricot jam
Walnuts (optional)

Let cream cheese and butter come to room temperature, then blend cream cheese and butter with the flour. Form into a ball, put in a covered bowl and refrigerate overnight. When ready to make crescents, cut ball into quarters. Knead each section lightly in flour. Roll each section into a circle in cinnamon-sugar mixture. Spread with apricot jam, sprinkle on the optional walnuts. Cut each circle into 12 pie-shaped pieces. Roll up starting with the wide end and shape into crescents. Sprinkle cinnamon-sugar on top. Bake on greased cookie sheets in a 325-degree oven for 25 minutes until brown.

Susan Welky Corey
(Mrs. John B.)

WILLA ALLEN DOWLING'S CINNAMON TWISTS

Yield: 2 batches of 12 twists each

1 cup flour
1 tablespoon salt
½ cup sugar
⅔ cup vegetable shortening
2 cups boiling water
2 packages yeast
¼ cup warm water

2 large eggs
5 cups flour
½ cup butter or margarine,
    melted
1½ cups sugar
3 or 4 tablespoons cinnamon

To make up the dough: Put 1 cup flour, salt, ½ cup sugar and ⅔ cup vegetable shortening in a large bowl. Pour over this 2 cups boiling water. Stir well and let cool to lukewarm. When batter is cool, dissolve 2 packages of dry yeast in ¼ cup warm water. Add the yeast mixture to the batter, then stir in 2 eggs. Add, cup by cup, 5 cups of flour. This will be a firm dough. Cover with a piece of waxed paper and a plate and refrigerate for at least 2 hours or up to 1 week. This dough makes up into 2 batches of Cinnamon Twists.

To make up the twists: Take half of the dough from the refrigerator and roll out on a floured cloth into a 6 x 18-inch rectangle. Cut into 1½-inch strips across. You will end up with about twelve 6 x 1½-inch strips. Melt ½ cup butter or margarine in a pie plate. In another pie plate (or any flat pan) mix 1½ cups sugar and the cinnamon—you want a rich, nut-brown color. Then take a strip of dough, roll first in the melted butter, then in the cinnamon sugar, twisting as you go. Lay finished strips in a greased 13 x 9 x 2-inch glass baking pan. Cover with waxed paper and a towel and let rise for at least 2 hours or overnight. In the morning (or after 2 hours) remove the paper and the towel. Put rolls in oven, turn oven on to 425 degrees and bake for 20 minutes. Immediately turn out of the pan onto a wire rack to cool. Proceed with the second half of the dough when you want more rolls.

Bonnie Bonjean Dowling
(Mrs. Patrick A.)

COOKIES

BEACON HILL COOKIES

Yield: 36

1 (6-ounce) package semi-sweet
   chocolate chips
2 egg whites
Dash of salt

½ cup sugar
½ teaspoon vanilla
½ teaspoon vinegar
¾ cup chopped walnuts

Melt chocolate chips in double-boiler. In separate bowl, beat egg whites and salt until foamy. Gradually add sugar until stiff peaks form. Add vanilla and vinegar. Fold in melted chocolate and nuts. Drop by teaspoonfuls onto greased cookie sheet. Bake in preheated 350-degree oven for 8 to 10 minutes.

Cathy Leach

BLUEBERRY DROP COOKIES

Yield: 4 dozen

½ cup shortening
1 cup sugar
1 egg, well-beaten
2½ cups flour
2½ teaspoons baking powder

¼ teaspoon salt
¼ teaspoon nutmeg
¼ teaspoon cinnamon
½ cup milk
1½ cups fresh blueberries

Cream shortening and sugar. Add egg and mix well. Add sifted dry ingredients alternately with milk. Stir in berries. Drop by teaspoonfuls onto greased cookie sheets. Bake at 375 degrees for 10 to 12 minutes.

Leslie MacDougall Webber
(Mrs. Walter)

CHOCOLATE COCONUT COOKIES

Yield: 2 dozen 2-inch cookies

2 egg whites
¼ teaspoon cream of tartar
½ cup sugar
½ teaspoon vanilla

1½ cups coconut
1 (6-ounce) package semi-sweet
   chocolate chips, melted

Beat egg whites until foamy. Add cream of tartar and beat until stiff but not dry. Add sugar gradually. Fold in vanilla, coconut and melted chocolate. Drop onto greased cookie sheet. Bake at 375 degrees for 12 minutes.

Susan Hall Haynes
(Mrs. J. David)

CRUNCHY CHIP COOKIES

Yield: 2½ or 3 dozen

½ cup butter or margarine
¼ cup sugar
¾ cup brown sugar
1 egg
¾ teaspoon vanilla
1 cup flour

½ teaspoon baking soda
¼ teaspoon salt
1 cup rolled oats
1 (6-ounce) package butter
   brickle chips
1 cup broken chow mein noodles

Cream butter and sugars until fluffy. Beat in egg and vanilla. Sift together flour, soda and salt and add to creamed mixture, mixing well. Stir in oats, chips and noodles. Drop by teaspoonfuls onto lightly greased cookie sheets, 2-inches apart; flatten a bit with hand or fork. Bake at 350 degrees for 12 to 15 minutes or until golden brown. Cool on wire racks.

M. J. Bailey Larned
(Mrs. F. Stephen)

COCONUT CRISPS

Yield: 6 dozen plus

¾ pound butter
1½ cups sugar
1½ cups brown sugar
3 eggs
1½ teaspoons vanilla
3 cups flour

1½ teaspoons baking powder
¼ teaspoon salt
4 cups cornflakes
2 cups coconut
1 cup chopped walnuts or
   macadamia nuts

Cream sugar and butter; add eggs, one at a time, beating well after each addition. Add vanilla. Sift flour, baking powder, and salt and add to the batter. Mix cornflakes, coconut, and nuts. Gently fold this mixture into the batter. Drop by teaspoonfuls onto a greased baking sheet and bake at 325 degrees for 15 minutes or until golden.

Suzanne Falk Figuers
(Mrs. Horace H.)

GRETCHEN'S SOFT GINGER COFFEE COOKIES

Yield: 100 small or 80 large cookies

½ cup butter
½ cup vegetable shortening
1 cup sugar
½ cup molasses
3 large eggs

1 teaspoon baking soda
1¼ teaspoons ground ginger
1 teaspoon cinnamon
3 cups unbleached flour or
    enough for a soft dough

Cream together the butter, shortening and sugar. Add the rest of the ingredients. Drop by teaspoonfuls onto greased cookie sheets and bake in a 350-degree oven for 8 minutes or until soft but firm. Frost the cooled cookies with the coffee frosting (see recipe below).

Frosting

3 tablespoons strong coffee
¼ cup butter or margarine
Pinch of salt

¼ teaspoon vanilla extract
1½ to 2 cups powdered sugar

Cream all ingredients together.

Bonnie Bonjean Dowling
(Mrs. Patrick A.)

HOLIDAY BILLY GOATS

Yield: 7 to 8 dozen

1 cup butter
1½ cups sugar
3 egg yolks
1 teaspoon vanilla
2½ cups flour
1 teaspoon baking soda

⅛ teaspoon salt
1 teaspoon cinnamon
¼ teaspoon cloves
2 tablespoons sour milk
4 cups chopped walnuts
1 pound dates, chopped

Cream butter and sugar well. Add egg yolks and vanilla and beat with electric mixer for 2 to 3 minutes at medium speed until light and fluffy. Sift together flour, baking soda, salt and spices. Add dry ingredients to egg mixture. Add sour milk and blend well. Add dates and nuts and mix. Drop by teaspoonfuls 1 inch apart onto a greased cookie sheet. Bake in a preheated 325-degree oven for 20 minutes.

Antoinette Figuers Pierce
(Mrs. Thomas M.)

LEMON-ZUCCHINI COOKIES

Yield: 72 to 84

2 cups flour
1 teaspoon baking powder
½ teaspoon salt
¾ cup butter or margarine
¾ cup sugar

1 egg, beaten
1 teaspoon (or more) grated
  lemon peel
1 cup shredded unpeeled
  zucchini
1 cup chopped walnuts

Stir together flour, baking powder, salt and set aside. In large bowl, cream butter and sugar until light. Beat in egg and lemon peel until fluffy. At low speed, stir in flour mixture until dough is smooth. Stir in zucchini and walnuts. Drop by rounded teaspoonfuls onto greased cookie sheets. Bake at 375 degrees for 15 to 20 minutes or until lightly browned. While warm, drizzle lightly with lemon frosting.

Lemon Frosting

1 cup powdered sugar

1½ tablespoons lemon juice

Mix well.

Dorothy Ryan
(Mrs. Donald J.)

McGINTY COOKIES

Yield: 1½ dozen

½ cup shortening
1 cup brown sugar
1 egg, lightly beaten
1 cup flour
¾ teaspoon salt

¼ teaspoon baking powder
½ teaspoon baking soda
2 tablespoons milk
½ cup raisins

Thoroughly cream shortening and sugar. Add egg and beat well. Sift dry ingredients and add alternately with milk. Mix well after each addition. Stir in raisins. Drop by teaspoonfuls onto greased cookie sheet. Bake at 325 degrees for 15 minutes or until edges start to brown. Cookie should be chewy.

Linda Treworgy Faatz

MERINGUE COOKIES

Yield: 36 to 40 cookies

2 egg whites
⅛ teaspoon salt
⅛ teaspoon cream of tartar
1 teaspoon vanilla

¾ cup sugar
1 (6-ounce) package semi-sweet
  chocolate chips
¼ cup chopped walnuts

Beat together egg whites, salt and cream of tartar until soft peaks form. Add vanilla. Gradually add sugar and beat until stiff. Fold in chocolate chips and chopped walnuts. Line cookie sheets with brown paper; drop batter onto brown paper and bake at 300 degrees for 25 minutes.

Patricia Pugh Britt
(Mrs. Michael E.)

OATMEAL COOKIES

Yield: Approximately 3 dozen

½ cup sugar
½ cup brown sugar
½ cup shortening
1 egg
½ teaspoon grated lemon rind
1½ tablespoons molasses

½ teaspoon vanilla
⅞ cup (¾ cup plus 2 tablespoons)
  flour
½ teaspoon baking soda
½ teaspoon salt
1½ cups rolled oats

Mix sugar, shortening, egg and flavorings. Add flour, soda, salt and rolled oats. Form into a roll and refrigerate before slicing and baking. Bake any quantity; remainder will keep in refrigerator. Bake at 325 degrees for about 12 minutes or until lightly browned.

Elizabeth Mauney Blackwood
(Mrs. Robert)

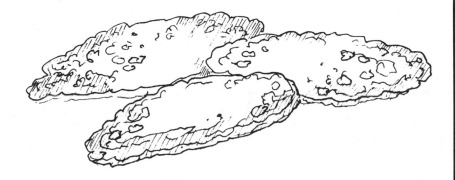

PUMPKIN COOKIES

Yield: 48 cookies

1½ cups pumpkin
½ cup butter
1¼ cups sugar
2 eggs
2 cups flour
½ cup wheat germ
2 teaspoons baking powder

1 teaspoon baking soda
1 teaspoon cinnamon
½ teaspoon salt
½ cup raisins (optional)
½ cup chopped walnuts
 (optional)

Cut a pumpkin in half. Bake halves shell side up in a baking pan at 325 degrees for 1 hour, or until pumpkin meat is soft. Remove from oven and cool. Measure 1½ cups for cookies. The rest may be frozen. Mix all ingredients together. Drop batter by teaspoonfuls onto greased cookie sheets. Bake at 400 degrees for 15 minutes or until lightly browned.

Gretchen Harris Ramsay
(Mrs. Scott W.)

PEANUT BUTTER ROUNDUPS

Yield: 4 dozen

1 cup margarine
1 cup sugar
1 cup light brown sugar
2 eggs
1 cup peanut butter

2 cups flour
2 teaspoons baking soda
½ teaspoon salt
1 cup rolled oats
1 teaspoon vanilla

Beat shortening and sugars together. Add eggs and beat well. Add peanut butter and beat again. Sift flour, soda and salt and add to creamed mixture. Stir in oats. Add vanilla. Roll small amounts of dough in hands to size of walnuts. Place on ungreased cookie sheet. Press down with fork. Bake at 350 degrees for 12 minutes.

Elizabeth Lincoln Preti
(Mrs. Robert)

PECAN CRISPS

Yield: 65

1½ cups flour
1 cup sugar
¾ teaspoon salt
½ cup soft butter

1 egg, separated
3 tablespoons milk
1 teaspoon vanilla
1 cup finely chopped pecans

Mix together flour, sugar and salt. Add butter, egg yolk and milk. Mix with fingertips or fork. Add vanilla and pecans. Form into small balls and place on ungreased cookie sheet. Press to ⅛-inch thick with bottom of buttered glass dipped in sugar. (One greasing does all, but dip into sugar after each pressing.) Brush with slightly beaten egg white. Bake at 350 degrees for 8 to 10 minutes, until medium brown. Do not overbake. Remove cookies from sheets at once

Eileen A. Pugh
(Mrs. Richard F.)

THUMB COOKIES

Yield: 4 dozen

1 cup butter
¾ cup powdered sugar
2 cups flour
¼ teaspoon salt

¼ teaspoon baking powder
1 teaspoon vanilla
Jelly (plum or apricot or favorite preserve)

Cream butter and sugar. Sift dry ingredients 3 times and add to creamed mixture. Add vanilla. Shape into ¾-inch balls. Place 1 inch apart on greased cookie sheet. Press down center of each with thumb. Bake at 350 degrees for 9 to 14 minutes. Fill with jelly.

Marjorie Brown Hampton
(Mrs. Colin C.)

LEMON BONBON COOKIES

Yield: 2½ dozen

1 cup butter
⅓ cup powdered sugar, sifted
¾ cup cornstarch

1¼ cups flour
½ cup finely chopped pecans

Cream butter and sugar until light and fluffy. Add cornstarch and flour; mix well. Chill until dough is easy to handle. Shape dough into 1-inch balls. Scatter nuts on waxed paper or foil and place dough balls on top. Flatten with bottom of a tumbler, or with hand, dipped in flour. Using a spatula, place cookies on cookie sheet nut side down. Bake at 350 degrees for 12 to 15 minutes. Cool and frost with Bonbon Frosting.

Bonbon Frosting

1 cup powdered sugar, sifted
1 teaspoon butter

2 tablespoons lemon juice

Joan Rooney Barnes
(Mrs. Charles P., II)

ROCKS

Yield: 3 dozen

1 cup sugar
⅔ cup butter
1½ cups flour
1 teaspoon cinnamon
¼ teaspoon ground cloves

1 cup chopped walnuts
¾ cup chopped dates
¾ cup raisins
1 teaspoon baking soda dissolved
    in 2 tablespoons hot water

Cream butter and sugar. Add flour, spices, walnuts, dates and raisins. Add baking soda mixture. Drop by heaping teaspoonfuls onto greased cookie sheet. Bake at 375 degrees for 10 to 12 minutes.

Carol Potter Day
(Mrs. Richard B.)

CHINESE ALMOND COOKIES

Yield: A lot

6 cups flour
2 teaspoons baking powder
2½ cups sugar
1 pound shortening
2 eggs, slightly beaten

1 teaspoon almond extract
1 teaspoon vanilla
1 egg, slightly beaten
Almonds, halved

Combine first 7 ingredients. Shape into balls and flatten with base of a glass. Brush tops with another slightly beaten egg. Place ½ almond on each cookie. Bake at 350 to 375 degrees for 15 minutes.

Julianne Radkowski Opperman
(Mrs. John R.)

SOUTHERN SPICE COOKIES

¾ cup shortening
1 cup sugar
¼ cup molasses
1 egg, beaten
2 cups flour
¼ teaspoon salt

2 teaspoons baking soda
1 teaspoon cinnamon
1 teaspoon cloves
1 teaspoon ginger
½ cup sugar

Cream shortening and sugar. Add molasses and egg, beat well. Add flour and next 5 ingredients; blend well. Roll into small balls (size of walnuts), dip in sugar and place 2-inches apart on greased cookie sheet. Bake in 375-degree oven for 8 minutes. When baked they will have a cracked effect.

Margo Greep

COCONUT BUTTER BALLS

Yield: 3 dozen

½ cup butter
2 tablespoons powdered sugar
½ teaspoon vanilla

1 cup flour
¾ cup shredded coconut
Powdered sugar, sifted

Cream butter. Add sugar and vanilla and cream together until light and fluffy. Add flour all at once and blend well. Add coconut, mixing well. Shape into small balls and place on ungreased baking sheet. Chill 15 minutes. Preheat oven to 350 degrees. Bake 15 minutes or until lightly browned. Roll in sifted powdered sugar while still warm. May use chopped walnuts or pecans in place of coconut.

Lisabeth Lepoff

FROSTED ALMOND COOKIES

Yield: 3 to 4 dozen

1 cup butter
1 egg
1¼ cups sugar

2½ cups flour
1 tablespoon almond extract

Combine all ingredients and chill. Roll and cut into desired shapes. Bake at 375 degrees for 10 to 12 minutes. Frost when cooled.

Frosting

1 cup powdered sugar
1 teaspoon almond extract

Milk (enough to moisten)
Food coloring, if desired

Roselle Flynn Johnson
(Mrs. Steven)

FRENCH GINGER MOLASSES COOKIES

Yield: 4 to 5 dozen

1 cup shortening
⅔ cup molasses
⅓ cup brown sugar
2 teaspoons baking soda

2 teaspoons ginger
1 teaspoon salt
3 cups flour

Blend shortening, molasses and sugar. Sift together dry ingredients and add to molasses mixture. Mix and knead on floured board. Roll into a roll, 1½-inches in diameter. Roll in waxed paper and store in refrigerator. Cut into very thin slices and bake on greased cookie sheet 375 degrees for 8 to 10 minutes.

Elizabeth Oldham Sawyer
(Mrs. Stewart)

FINNISH SOUR CREAM RINGS

Yield: 6 dozen

1 cup butter or margarine
1 cup sugar
½ cup sour cream
¼ teaspoon salt

1 teaspoon almond extract
3 cups flour
Sugar for dipping

Cream butter and add sugar, then other ingredients. Chill well in refrigerator. Roll by hand into pencil-thin rolls (approximately 4-inches long). Bring together as a wreath and dip in sugar (red-optional). Bake on greased sheet at 400 degrees for 8 to 10 minutes.

Dee Dee Dana Bradford
(Mrs. John)

WHOOPIE PIES

Yield: 12 large or 24 small whole whoopie pies

½ cup shortening
1 cup sugar
2 egg yolks
1 teaspoon vanilla
2 cups flour

1 teaspoon baking powder
1 teaspoon baking soda
½ teaspoon salt
4 tablespoons cocoa
1 cup sour milk

Cream shortening and sugar. Add egg yolks and vanilla. Add sifted dry ingredients alternately with sour milk. Place by tablespoonfuls onto greased cookie sheet. Bake at 400 degrees for 10 minutes. Cool cookies before filling.

Filling

2 egg whites
¾ cup shortening
2 cups powdered sugar

1 teaspoon vanilla
Salt

Beat egg whites until light and fluffy. Cream shortening and sugar until smooth and add to beaten egg whites. Add vanilla and a pinch of salt. Fill between 2 cookies, sandwich-fashion.

Ruth E. Harris
(Mrs. Philip)

APRICOT BARS

Yield: 2½ dozen

1½ cups flour
1 teaspoon baking powder
¼ teaspoon salt
1½ cups quick cooking rolled
   oats

1 cup brown sugar
¾ cup butter
¾ cup apricot preserves

Sift together dry ingredients. Stir in oats and brown sugar. Cut in butter until crumbly. Pat ⅔ of crumbs in 11 x 7 x 1½-inch pan. Spread preserves. Top with remaining crumbs. Bake at 375 degrees for 35 minutes. Cool.

Mrs. Madelyn Busker Cohen

BLUE RIBBON BROWNIES

Yield: 1 dozen

2 (1-ounce) squares unsweetened
   chocolate
½ cup butter or margarine
2 eggs
1 cup sugar

½ teaspoon vanilla
½ cup flour
⅛ teaspoon salt
1 cup walnuts

Melt chocolate with butter. Beat eggs until foamy; beat in sugar gradually until fluffy thick. Stir in vanilla and chocolate mixture; then fold in flour, salt and walnuts. Spread in greased 8 x 8-inch pan. Bake at 350 degrees for 30 minutes or until cake tester comes out clean. Cool on wire rack. To double recipe, use 9 x 13-inch pan. Do not overbake.

Nancy Armbruster Cragin
(Mrs. Charles L., III)

TOLLHOUSE BROWNIES

Yield: 2 dozen

2 (16-ounce) packages chocolate
  chip cookie dough, softened
  (found in dairy section)
1 (8-ounce) package cream
  cheese, at room temperature

2 eggs
½ cup sugar
1 teaspoon vanilla

Grease well a 9 x 13-inch pan; spread one softened package cookie dough in bottom of pan. Mix cream cheese, eggs, sugar and vanilla well and pour over dough. Drop pieces of dough from second package over filling. Bake at 350 degrees for 35 minutes. If top is not brown enough, place under broiler for desired browning. Watch carefully. Refrigerate when cooled. Can also be frozen and eaten as an ice cream-type sandwich.

Nancy Armbruster Cragin
(Mrs. Charles L.,III)

LEMON LOVENOTES

Yield: 24 small bars

1 cup butter
2 cups flour

½ cup powdered sugar

Mix and press into 9 x 13-inch pan. Bake at 325 degrees for 15 minutes.

Filling

4 eggs
2 cups sugar
4 tablespoons flour
1 teaspoon baking powder

4 tablespoons lemon juice
4 teaspoons grated lemon rind *or*
  1 teaspoon lemon extract

Mix all ingredients and pour over baked mixture. Bake at 350 degrees for 25 minutes. Frost with:

Frosting

¾ cup powdered sugar
1 tablespoon butter

1 teaspoon vanilla
½ teaspoon milk

Mix well.

Roselle Flynn Johnson
(Mrs. Steven)

CHEESE CAKE BARS

Yield: 4 dozen

Crust

⅔ cup butter
⅔ cup brown sugar

2 cups flour
1 cup chopped walnuts

Combine ingredients with a fork. Reserve 1 cup for topping. Press into greased 9 x 13-inch pan and bake at 350 degrees for 10 minutes.

Filling

2 (8-ounce) packages cream
  cheese
½ cup sugar
2 eggs

4 tablespoons milk
2 tablespoons lemon juice
2 teaspoons vanilla

Beat cream cheese. Add sugar and beat. Add eggs and beat. Add remaining ingredients and beat. Pour onto baked crust. Add reserved crumbs to the top. Bake at 350 degrees for 25 minutes. Chill well before serving.

Elizabeth King Cimino
(Mrs. Santo)

HENRY BARS

Yield: 24 (2-inch) squares

Base

⅔ cup margarine
1 cup brown sugar
4 cups quick oats

½ cup corn syrup
2 teaspoons vanilla

Cream margarine and sugar. Add oats, syrup and vanilla. Press firmly into ungreased 13 x 9-inch pan. Bake at 350 degrees for 15 minutes. Cool and spread with topping. Refrigerate.

Topping

1 (6-ounce) package chocolate
  chips

⅔ cup chunky peanut butter

Melt and spread on cooled base. Then refrigerate. Cut into bars after about an hour.

Susan Hall Haynes
(Mrs. J. David)

FROSTED COFFEE BARS

Yield: 60 small squares

½ cup shortening
½ teaspoon salt
1 teaspoon vanilla
1 cup brown sugar
1 egg
½ cup hot coffee

1½ cups flour
½ teaspoon baking powder
½ teaspoon soda
½ teaspoon cinnamon
½ cup chopped raisins
¼ cup chopped nuts

Cream shortening. Add salt and vanilla. Gradually add brown sugar to above. Add egg and mix until light and creamy. Add hot coffee. Sift flour; measure, then sift together with the other dry ingredients. Add to creamed mixture. Add raisins and nuts. Pour into greased 15½ x 10½-inch jelly roll pan. Bake at 350 degrees for 20 minutes. Place on rack to cool. Frost while still hot.

Frosting

1 cup powdered sugar
¼ teaspoon salt
1 tablespoon butter

1 teaspoon vanilla
Hot coffee

Combine first 4 ingredients and add enough hot coffee to make a thin frosting. Spread on hot bars.

Patricia Pugh Britt
(Mrs. Michael E.)

HOPE'S APPLE SQUARES

Yield: 1½ dozen

3 eggs
1¾ cups sugar
2 cups flour
1 teaspoon baking powder
1 teaspoon cinnamon

½ teaspoon salt
1 cup oil
1 teaspoon vanilla
1 cup chopped walnuts
2 cups thinly sliced apples

Preheat oven to 350 degrees. Beat eggs. Add sugar gradually, beating until light and fluffy. Sift together dry ingredients and add to eggs and sugar. Add oil and vanilla. Fold in nuts and apples. Bake in greased 9 x 13-inch dish for 40 to 45 minutes.

Barbara Morris Goodbody
(Mrs. James)

SPIKED CHOCOLATE SQUARES

Yield: 24

1¼ cups flour
¾ teaspoon baking powder
½ teaspoon salt
½ cup soft butter or margarine
¾ cup brown sugar
1 large egg
¼ cup coffee liqueur

1 (6-ounce) package semi-sweet
   chocolate chips
½ cup chopped walnuts
1 tablespoon coffee liqueur
   (for tops of bars)
Walnut halves (optional)

Sift flour with baking powder and salt; set aside. Cream butter, sugar and egg. Stir in coffee liqueur, then flour mixture, blending well. Fold in chocolate chips and walnuts. Turn into greased 7 x 11 x 1½-inch baking pan and spread level. Bake at 350 degrees about 30 minutes, until top springs back when touched lightly in center. Remove from oven and cool in pan 15 minutes. Then brush top with remaining coffee liqueur. When cold, spread with Brown Butter Icing. Let stand until icing is set; then cut into bars making 4 lengthwise strips and cutting into sixths across the pan. Top each bar with a walnut half.

Brown Butter Icing

2 tablespoons butter
1 tablespoon coffee liqueur

2 teaspoons milk or light cream
1½ cups powdered sugar, sifted

Place butter in saucepan over low heat; heat until butter is lightly browned. Remove and add coffee liqueur, milk or cream and sugar. Beat until smooth. Spread on cold bars.

Jean Potter Benton
(Mrs. Don Carlos, III)

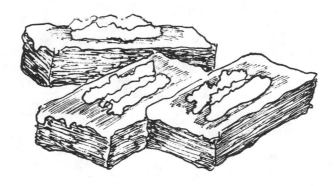

225

GERMAN CHOCOLATE BARS

Yield: 4 dozen

2 cups flour
2 cups sugar
1 cup water
2 tablespoons cocoa
½ cup butter or margarine
½ cup solid shortening

2 eggs, well-beaten
1 teaspoon vanilla
½ cup buttermilk, mixed with
 1 teaspoon baking soda
1 teaspoon cinnamon

Mix flour and sugar in large bowl; set aside. Blend water, cocoa, butter and shortening in pan and bring to a boil. After mixture boils, add to flour and sugar. Then add eggs, vanilla, buttermilk-soda mixture, and cinnamon. Bake in greased and floured jelly roll pan at 400 degrees for 20 minutes. Frost immediately.

Frosting

½ cup butter or margarine
6 tablespoons milk
2 tablespoons cocoa

1 teaspoon vanilla
1 pound powdered sugar
1 cup pecans

While cake is baking, melt margarine, milk, cocoa and vanilla, stirring while melting. When creamy, add powdered sugar and pecans. Frost cake. When cool, cut into bars.

Susan Welky Corey
(Mrs. John)

CATHEDRAL WINDOWS

Yield: 4 to 6 dozen

1 (6-ounce) package semi-sweet
   chocolate chips
4 tablespoons margarine
2 eggs, slightly beaten
1 cup crushed vanilla wafers

1 cup ground nuts
1 cup powdered sugar
1 (10½-ounce) package colored
   mini-marshmallows
Coconut

Melt chocolate chips and margarine in double boiler. Cool. Mix next 4 ingredients and add to the cooled chocolate mixture. Add marshmallows. Divide into 4 balls; place each on a sheet of waxed paper spread with coconut. Roll into logs. Wrap in waxed paper and refrigerate. Slice as needed.

Sandra Edson Tuttle
(Mrs. Richard)

FROSTED PRALINE BARS

Yield: 24 bars

Bars

4 eggs
1 cup sugar
1 cup brown sugar
1¾ cups flour
1¼ teaspoons baking powder

1 teaspoon cinnamon
¼ teaspoon allspice
¼ teaspoon nutmeg
1 cup coarsely chopped pecans

Preheat oven to 350 degrees. Grease 13 x 9 x 2-inch pan. Beat eggs until thick and lemon colored. Add sugars, a little at a time, beating well after each addition. Sift dry ingredients together; fold into egg mixture. Stir in pecans. Spread in greased pan. Bake 35 to 40 minutes. Cool slightly and frost.

Frosting

1 cup brown sugar
¼ cup butter or margarine
1 (7-ounce) bottle lemon-lime
   carbonated beverage

¼ teaspoon vanilla
¾ cup coarsely chopped pecans

Combine sugar, butter and beverage in a saucepan. Cook over medium heat, stirring until sugar is dissolved. Cook gently without stirring until mixture reaches 236 degrees (soft-ball stage). Cool to 110 degrees (until hand can be placed comfortably on bottom of saucepan). Add vanilla; beat until frosting loses its gloss. Add pecans. Spread frosting over praline bars.

Brian R. Edwards

CRUNCHY FUDGE "SINWICHES"

Yield: 25 (1½-inch) squares

1 (6-ounce) package butterscotch
 chips

½ cup chunky peanut butter
4 cups rice cereal

In large saucepan, combine butterscotch chips and peanut butter; heat until chips melt and mixture is smooth. Add rice cereal; stir until coated with butterscotch mixture. Press one-half of mixture into buttered 8 x 8-inch pan. Chill in refrigerator while preparing fudge mixture.

Fudge

1 (6-ounce) package semi-sweet
 chocolate chips
½ cup sifted powdered sugar

2 tablespoons butter or
 margarine
1 tablespoon water

In double boiler over hot water, melt chocolate chips mixed with sugar, butter and water. When smooth pour over cooled cereal mixture, covering all. Spread remaining cereal mixture evenly over chocolate and gently press into chocolate mixture. Refrigerate 1 hour; then cut into squares. To double recipe, use greased 9 x 13-inch pan.

Nancy Armbruster Cragin
(Mrs. Charles L.,III)

SIR WALTER RALEIGHS

Yield: 48 bars

1 to 1½ cups unsalted slivered
 almonds
1 cup margarine
½ cup brown sugar
½ cup sugar
1 egg yolk

1 teaspoon vanilla
1¾ cups presifted all-purpose
 flour
1 (12-ounce) package semi-sweet
 chocolate chips

Place the almonds in a small pan and toast in a 350-degree oven for 10 minutes, stirring after the first 5 minutes. Set aside. Cream the butter and sugar until light and fluffy. Add the egg yolk and vanilla and beat well. Gradually add the flour and mix. Spread the dough in a greased 9 x 13 x 2-inch pan and bake for 20 minutes at 350 degrees. Remove from oven and immediately spread chocolate chips over the hot cookie crust. As the chocolate melts, spread evenly over the cookie crust. While chocolate is still warm, sprinkle the toasted nuts on top and press lightly with fingers so nuts will stick to the chocolate as it hardens. Cut into squares while still slightly warm, but cool completely before removing from pan.

The Committee

DESSERTS

PEANUT BUTTER PIE

Serves: 6 to 8

Pastry for one 9-inch pie
1 cup light corn syrup
½ cup sugar
3 eggs, beaten
¼ teaspoon salt

1 tablespoon butter, melted
1 teaspoon vanilla
½ cup peanut butter, smooth
  or chunky
Whipped cream

Line pie pan with pastry. Combine corn syrup and sugar. Add eggs, salt, butter and vanilla. Stir in peanut butter until filling is smooth. Pour into pie shell. Bake at 400 degrees for 15 minutes, then reduce heat to 350 degrees and continue baking an additional 30 to 35 minutes. (Filling center will appear soft when pie is removed from oven.) Chill. Top pie with whipped cream at serving time.

India Horton Weatherill
(Mrs. Robert H.)

HARVEST APPLE PIE

Serves: 8

Pie Shell

½ cup grated Cheddar cheese
⅓ cup vegetable shortening
1 cup flour

½ teaspoon salt
3 to 4 tablespoons ice water

Filling

½ cup sugar
½ cup dark brown sugar
¼ cup flour
½ teaspoon cinnamon
¼ teaspoon nutmeg
⅛ teaspoon salt

¼ cup butter
6 cups peeled and thinly sliced
  apples
2 teaspoons lemon juice
¼ cup heavy cream

Make pie shell by cutting cheese and shortening into flour. Add salt. Moisten with water. Form ball and roll, to make 9-inch pie shell. For filling, mix first 6 ingredients of filling. Cut in butter until mixture is crumbly. Put apples in large bowl and sprinkle with lemon juice. Add 1 cup of filling mixture and mix gently. Arrange apples in pie shell and cover with remaining filling mix. Press down well. Cover with foil and place on cookie sheet. Bake 30 minutes in preheated 400-degree oven. Uncover and bake 20 to 25 minutes more, until apples are tender. Pour cream over and bake 10 minutes longer. Serve with vanilla ice cream.

Jane (Ba) Davidson Kopp
(Mrs. Donald A.)

SOUR CREAM CUSTARD APPLE PIE

Serves: 8

9-inch unbaked pie crust
2 tablespoons flour
¼ teaspoon salt
1 egg

1 cup sour cream
¾ cup sugar
1 teaspoon vanilla
3 cups diced apples

Beat together flour, salt, egg, sour cream, sugar and vanilla. Stir in apples and pour into shell. Bake at 400 degrees for 25 minutes.

Topping

1 cup chopped walnuts
½ cup flour
½ cup butter, softened
⅓ cup sugar

⅓ cup brown sugar
1 tablespoon cinnamon
Pinch of salt

Mix all topping ingredients and sprinkle on top of baked pie. Bake an additional 15 to 20 minutes at 375 degrees.

Merryl Gillespie Hodgson
(Mrs. Donald G.)

KEY LIME PIE

Serves: 8

3 eggs, separated
⅓ cup lime juice, fresh
1 (15-ounce) can sweetened
  condensed milk

Coconut pie crust, baked
Whipped cream for garnish
2 tablespoons flaked coconut,
  toasted

Beat egg yolks. Add lime juice to beaten yolks and beat until blended. Add condensed milk. Fold in stiffly beaten egg whites. Fill baked pie shell. Freeze and serve frozen, with whipped cream garnish and coconut sprinkled on top.

Coconut Pie Crust

2 tablespoons butter, softened   1½ cups flaked coconut

Spread butter evenly on bottom and sides of 9-inch pie plate. Sprinkle with coconut and press evenly into butter. Bake at 300 degrees until golden brown, approximately 15 to 20 minutes.

Priscilla Taggart Connard
(Mrs. G. Baer, Jr.)

MACADAMIA NUT PIE

Serves: 8

3 extra large eggs
⅔ cup sugar
1 cup light corn syrup
¼ cup butter, melted
4 teaspoons dark rum
1 teaspoon vanilla

1 cup chopped macadamia nuts
Unbaked 9-inch pie shell
1 cup heavy cream
1 teaspoon sugar
½ teaspoon vanilla

Beat together eggs, ⅔ cup sugar, corn syrup, butter, rum and 1 teaspoon vanilla until thoroughly mixed. Stir in nuts. Turn into pie shell. Bake at 375 degrees for 45 minutes. Cool on wire rack. Whip cream with sugar and vanilla until stiff. Spread on cooled pie.

Judith Edison Irish
(Mrs. Rodney F.)

FRESH STRAWBERRY PIE

Serves: 8

9-inch pie shell
1½ quarts fresh strawberries
1 cup sugar
3 tablespoons cornstarch

2 tablespoons lemon juice
Heavy cream, whipped and
  sweetened

Prepare and bake pie shell. Cool. Wash and hull strawberries. Reserve half. Mash the rest in a saucepan. Mix sugar and cornstarch and add to mashed berries. Cook 5 minutes, stirring constantly, until thick and clear. Stir in lemon juice. Cool. Add remaining berries, saving 4 or 5 for garnish. Pour into baked pastry shell. Chill. Before serving, top with whipped cream and garnish with strawberries.

India Horton Weatherill
(Mrs. Robert H.)

CRÈME DE MENTHE PIE

Serves: 8

20 butter crackers, crushed
1 teaspoon baking powder
1 teaspoon vanilla
1 cup chopped pecans

3 egg whites
1 cup sugar
½ gallon vanilla ice cream
Crème de menthe

Combine first 4 ingredients. Beat egg whites until stiff. Gradually add sugar and beat well until very stiff peaks form. Fold into cracker mixture. Put into greased 9-inch pie pan. Bake at 350 degrees for 30 minutes. Put in freezer for 1 hour. Top with ice cream. Sprinkle with crème de menthe.

Carol Ann Such Bouton
(Mrs. Dale C.)

FUDGE RIBBON PIE

Serves: 8

9-inch pie shell, baked and
   cooled

1 quart peppermint ice cream

Sauce

2 tablespoons butter
2 ounces unsweetened chocolate
1 cup sugar

⅔ cup evaporated milk
1 teaspoon vanilla

Combine the butter, chocolate, sugar, and milk in a saucepan. Cook over medium heat until thick and bubbly. Remove from heat and stir in vanilla. Cool completely. Spread ½ of the ice cream on pie shell and then layer ½ of the fudge sauce over the ice cream. Freeze until hard. Spread remainder of ice cream over frozen layers. Top with last of the fudge sauce. Freeze overnight.

Meringue

3 egg whites
½ teaspoon vanilla
¼ teaspoon cream of tartar

6 tablespoons sugar
3 tablespoons peppermint candy,
   crushed

Combine the egg whites, vanilla, and cream of tartar, beat until soft peaks form. Gradually add the sugar, beating until sugar is dissolved. Gently fold in the crushed peppermint candy. Spread meringue over the frozen pie sealing to the edge of crust. Place pie on a wooden board and bake in a 475-degree oven for 5 to 6 minutes, or until meringue is golden. Serve immediately.

The Committee

FROZEN CHOCOLATE WALNUT PIE

Serves: 6 to 8

Crust

2 cups toasted walnuts, finely
  chopped
5 tablespoons plus 1 teaspoon
  brown sugar

5 tablespoons butter, chilled and
  cut into small pieces
2 teaspoons dark rum

Blend all ingredients for crust until mixture holds together. Press into bottom and sides of a 10-inch pie plate. Freeze for at least 1 hour.

Filling

6 ounces semi-sweet chocolate
½ teaspoon instant coffee
  powder
4 eggs, room temperature
1 tablespoon dark rum

1 teaspoon vanilla
2 cups heavy cream
2 ounces semi-sweet chocolate,
  shaved

Melt chocolate with coffee in top of double-boiler over hot water. Remove from heat and whisk in eggs, rum and vanilla until mixture is smooth. Let cool 5 minutes. Whip the cream until stiff and gently fold into chocolate mixture. Blend completely. Pour into crust and freeze. One hour before serving, remove to refrigerator. Sprinkle with shaved chocolate.

Martha White Nichols
(Mrs. Christopher)

FROZEN PUMPKIN PIE

Serves: 6 to 8

1 pint vanilla ice cream
2 to 3 tablespoons candied
  ginger, finely chopped
9-inch graham cracker crust
1 cup canned pumpkin
1 cup sugar

½ teaspoon salt
½ teaspoon ginger
½ teaspoon nutmeg
1½ cups miniature
  marshmallows
1 cup heavy cream, whipped

Stir ice cream until softened. Quickly fold in chopped ginger. Spread over graham cracker crust. Freeze until firm. Combine pumpkin with next 5 ingredients. Fold in whipped cream. Spoon over ice cream layer and freeze.

Judith Topham Flaker
(Mrs. James R.)

CRANBERRY SURPRISE PIE

Serves: 8

2 cups fresh cranberries   1 cup sugar
½ cup sugar   1 cup flour
½ cup chopped walnuts   ½ cup butter, melted
2 eggs   ½ cup shortening, melted

Wash cranberries and spread over bottom of well-greased 10-inch pie pan. Sprinkle sugar and walnuts over the top. Beat eggs well and add sugar gradually. Beat until thoroughly mixed. Add flour and melted butter and shortening (which have been melted together). Mix and beat well. Pour batter over top of cranberries and nuts. Bake at 325 degrees for 1 hour or until crust is golden brown. Serve with ice cream or whipped cream.

Susan Hall Haynes
(Mrs. J. David)

FRENCH COCONUT PIE

Yield: Two 8-inch pies or 28 (3-inch) tarts

5 large eggs   1 cup flaked coconut
8 tablespoons margarine, melted   2 unbaked 8-inch pie shells
¾ cup buttermilk

In blender or food processor, mix eggs, margarine, buttermilk and coconut. Pour into unbaked shells. Bake at 350 degrees for 35 to 40 minutes for pies or 25 to 30 minutes for tarts or until a knife inserted in custard comes out clean.

Jean Potter Benton
(Mrs. Don C., III)

BAKIE'S PECAN PIE

Serves: 6 to 8

3 eggs   4 tablespoons butter, melted
½ cup sugar   ½ teaspoon vanilla
¾ cup light corn syrup   1 cup broken pecans
Pinch of salt   9-inch unbaked pie shell

Preheat oven to 400 degrees. Mix egg, sugar, corn syrup and salt together. Add melted butter and vanilla. Stir pecans (save a few whole ones to sprinkle on top). Pour into pie shell. Bake at 400 degrees for 10 minutes. Reduce heat to 350 degrees. Bake until set, approximately 35 to 40 minutes.

Marguerite Saylor Bouton
(Mrs. Dale, Sr.)

MUD PIE

Serves: 8

8 ounces chocolate wafers
¼ cup butter or margarine,
   melted
1 quart coffee ice cream

1½ cups chocolate fudge sauce
½ cup whipped cream
¼ cup walnuts

Crush wafers. Add butter and mix well. Press into 9-inch pie pan. Cover with softened ice cream. Cover with foil and place in freezer until ice cream is firm. Remove from freezer and top with fudge sauce. Return to freezer for 10 hours. Before serving, top pie with whipped cream and walnuts.

Maryellen Turley Coles
(Mrs. Julian R.)

SOUR CREAM-CHOCOLATE CHIP CAKE

Serves: 12

6 tablespoons butter
1 cup sugar
2 eggs
1⅓ cups flour
1½ teaspoons baking powder

1 teaspoon baking soda
1 cup sour cream
1 (6-ounce) package semi-sweet
   chocolate chips
1 tablespoon sugar

Cream butter and 1 cup sugar together. Add eggs and other ingredients, alternating dry ingredients and sour cream. Spread batter in a greased 9 x 13-inch pan. Sprinkle chocolate chips and 1 tablespoon sugar on top. Bake at 350 degrees for 35 minutes.

Mrs. Nancy Evans Wolff

OLD FASHIONED BLUEBERRY CAKE

Serves: 8 to 10

1 cup sugar
¼ cup butter
1 egg
1½ cups flour
1 teaspoon cream of tartar

½ cup milk
½ teaspoon baking soda
1 cup blueberries
½ teaspoon salt

Cream sugar and butter. Add egg and beat well. Add flour, salt, cream of tartar, milk and baking soda. Fold in blueberries. Bake in a greased 9 x 13 x 2-inch pan at 375 degrees for 30 minutes. This is an old Maine recipe. Especially good served with crabmeat or lobster salad.

Elizabeth Mauney Blackwood
(Mrs. Robert S.)

CASSATA TORTE

Serves: 6 to 8

4 tablespoons golden raisins
4 tablespoons brandy
1 (3 x 9-inch) frozen pound cake, thawed
16 ounces ricotta cheese
2 tablespoons heavy cream

¼ cup sugar
¼ cup chopped nuts
2 ounces semi-sweet chocolate, coarsely chopped
2 tablespoons almond paste (optional)

Soak raisins in liqueur for 1 hour prior to preparing filling. Cut cake horizontally in 3 equal slices. Place ricotta in bowl and beat with electric beater until smooth. While continuing to beat, add cream, sugar, and liqueur drained from raisins. With spatula fold in raisins, nuts, chocolate and almond paste. Place bottom slice of cake on serving platter and spread with ½ ricotta mixture. Carefully place another slice of cake on top. Spread remainder of ricotta on this layer. Cover with the third slice of cake. Gently press loaf together. Chill covered for 2 to 3 hours or until firm. After chilled, frost with the following frosting.

Frosting

9 ounces semi-sweet chocolate, cut in small pieces
½ cup plus 1 tablespoon very strong black coffee

¾ cup unsalted butter, cut in ½-inch pieces, chilled

Melt chocolate and coffee in top of double boiler over simmering water, stirring until chocolate has melted. Remove from heat and beat in butter 1 piece at a time. Continue beating until smooth. Chill to thicken consistency for spreading. With spatula spread frosting over top and ends of cake. Refrigerate.

Priscilla Taggart Connard
(Mrs. G. Baer, Jr.)

McLELLAN CAKE

Serves: 8

1 (18.5-ounce) package yellow cake mix
1 (3¾-ounce) package instant vanilla pudding

4 eggs
¾ cup dry sherry
¾ cup vegetable shortening
1 tablespoon fresh grated nutmeg

Mix above ingredients well, then beat for 5 minutes. Bake in greased 10-cup tube pan at 350 degrees for 45 minutes. Cool in pan before inverting onto plate.

Miss Charlotte McLellan

STRUDEL

2 cups flour
1 cup margarine
½ cup ice cold club soda
Apricot preserves
Raisins

Coconut
Chopped nuts
Cinnamon and sugar, mixed
Powdered sugar

Blend the flour and the margarine together. Add the club soda and mix well with your hands. Make into 3 circles, like flat pancakes, wrap in foil and chill overnight or longer. Remove from the refrigerator and roll out as thin as possible on a pastry cloth generously dusted with powdered sugar. Spread with the preserves, raisins, coconut and chopped nuts. Sprinkle with cinnamon sugar and roll up. Do not split the roll. Bake in a 350-degree oven for 40 minutes. Use teflon cookie sheets. Wrap whole rolls in foil until ready to serve.

Mrs. Freda Klayman Shapiro

RHUBARB TORTE

Serves: 9

1 cup sugar
3 tablespoons cornstarch
4 cups sliced rhubarb
½ cup water
Few drops red food coloring
1 recipe Graham Cracker Crust

½ cup whipping cream
1½ cups miniature
  marshmallows
1 (3¾-ounce) package vanilla
  instant pudding mix

Combine sugar and cornstarch; stir in rhubarb and water. Cook and stir until thickened. Reduce heat to low and cook an additional 2 to 3 minutes. Add food coloring. Spread on cooled graham cracker crust. Cool. Meanwhile, whip cream. Fold in marshmallows. Spoon on cooled rhubarb mixture. Prepare pudding according to package directions; spread over all. Sprinkle with 2 tablespoons of reserved crust crumbs. Chill.

Graham Cracker Crust

1 cup graham cracker crumbs
2 tablespoons sugar

4 tablespoons butter or
  margarine, melted

Combine crumbs, sugar and butter. Reserve 2 tablespoons. Put remainder in a 9-inch square pan. Bake in 350-degree oven for 10 minutes. Cool.

Lee Morse Edwards
(Mrs. Dwight H.)

CHOCOLATE HUNGARIAN TORTE

Serves: 8

Torte

6 large eggs, separated
¼ teaspoon salt
1 cup powdered sugar, sifted
¼ cup cocoa, sifted

1 teaspoon vanilla extract
1½ cups whipped heavy cream,
  sweetened

Separate eggs. Beat whites with salt until stiff but not dry. Beat in powdered sugar, 1 tablespoon at a time; then fold in cocoa. Beat egg yolks until thick and lemon-colored and fold into cocoa mixture. Add vanilla. Spread in 15 x 10 x 1-inch pan lined with foil and greased with shortening. Bake at 350 degrees for 20 minutes. Turn out onto towel sprinkled with powdered sugar. Gently peel off foil, using spatula to separate cake from foil. Cool and cut crosswise into quarters. Assemble layers together, spreading whipped cream on each layer except top. Refrigerate.

Glaze

1 tablespoon butter
1 (1-ounce) square unsweetened
  chocolate
½ cup powdered sugar, sifted

2 tablespoons boiling water
Dash of salt
½ teaspoon vanilla
Sliced almonds

Melt butter and chocolate in double boiler over boiling water. Remove from heat. Add powdered sugar, water, salt, and vanilla and beat until smooth and glossy. Spread only top of torte with glaze. Decorate with sliced almonds. Chill well and slice.

Susan Welky Corey
(Mrs. John B.)

MARIE'S OATMEAL CAKE

Serves: 8

10 tablespoons butter
1½ cups quick oats
2 cups boiling water
½ cup sugar
1 cup brown sugar

1½ teaspoons baking soda
2 cups flour (preferably 1 cup
   white and 1 cup whole wheat)
1½ teaspoons cinnamon
3 eggs, beaten

Cut butter into small pieces; combine with oats and boiling water. Cover and let stand 15 minutes. Mix together sugars, soda, flour and cinnamon. Stir oat mixture into flour mixture. Add beaten eggs and stir well. Pour into greased and floured 9 x 13-inch baking pan. Bake at 350 degrees for 40 minutes.

Frosting

¼ cup brown sugar
½ cup sugar
¼ cup milk
4 tablespoons butter

1 teaspoon vanilla
1 cup chopped walnuts or pecans
1 cup shredded coconut

Heat sugars, milk and butter to boiling. Boil 45 seconds, stirring constantly. Remove from heat and add remaining ingredients. Spread on hot cake.

Mary Beth Christman Sweeney
(Mrs. John J.)

APPLE KNOBBY CAKE

Yield: 8 servings

1 cup sugar
1 tablespoon shortening
1 teaspoon vanilla
1 egg, slightly beaten
3 cups diced and peeled apples
½ cup chopped nuts
1 cup flour

1 teaspoon cinnamon
1 teaspoon salt
1 teaspoon soda
1 teaspoon nutmeg
Sweetened whipped cream,
   optional

Preheat oven to 350 degrees. Cream together sugar, shortening and vanilla. Stir in egg, apple and nuts. Sift together dry ingredients and stir into apple mixture. Pour into 8-inch square glass pan. Bake for 1 hour until cake tester is clean. Top with sweetened whipped cream.

Della Parker
Dock Fore

REINE DE SABA

Serves: 8 to 10

Cake

⅔ cup semi-sweet chocolate
  chips
1 tablespoon coffee dissolved in
  2 tablespoons boiling water
½ cup unsalted butter
⅔ cup sugar
3 egg yolks

3 egg whites
¼ teaspoon cream of tartar
2 tablespoons sugar
⅓ cup pulverized almonds
¼ teaspoon almond extract
¾ cup cake flour

Mix chocolate chips and coffee. Set aside. Cream butter and sugar together until light and fluffy. Beat in egg yolks. In separate bowl, beat egg whites with cream of tartar. Beat in 2 tablespoons sugar. Set aside. Add melted chocolate to creamed mixture. Stir in almonds, extract and flour. Stir in ¼ of the egg whites. Rapidly fold in the remaining egg whites. Turn the batter into a buttered and floured 8-inch round cake pan. Bake at 350 degrees for 20 to 25 minutes. Cool 10 minutes and invert on a rack. When completely cooled, glaze.

Chocolate Glaze

4 ounces German sweet
  chocolate
2 ounces semi-sweet chocolate
¼ cup sugar

½ cup milk
¼ cup unsalted butter
¼ cup slivered almonds

Boil together first 4 ingredients. Cover and let stand for 15 minutes. Whisk in butter. Allow to cool slightly and ladle over cake. Decorate with almonds.

Judith Bishop Condron
(Mrs. Arthur)

SERENDIPITY CAKE

Serves: 12

½ cup butter
½ cup shortening
2 cups sugar
5 egg yolks
2 cups flour
1 teaspoon baking soda

1 cup buttermilk
1½ teaspoons vanilla
4 ounces coconut
1 cup chopped pecans
5 egg whites, stiffly beaten

Cream butter and shortening. Add sugar and beat until smooth. Add egg yolks and beat well. Combine flour and soda and add to creamed mixture, alternating with buttermilk. Add vanilla, coconut, and pecans. Fold in egg whites. Pour into 3 greased and floured 8-inch pans. Bake in 350-degree oven for 25 to 30 minutes.

Frosting

1 (8-ounce) package cream
  cheese
1 cup butter

1 pound powdered sugar
1 teaspoon vanilla

Beat cheese and butter until smooth. Add sugar and mix well. Add vanilla. Be sure cake is completely cooled before frosting.

Rebecca Bilbrey Sweeney
(Mrs. Eugene G., Jr.)

BLUEBERRY SOUR CREAM CAKE

Serves: 8 to 10

1½ cups flour
½ cup sugar
½ cup butter, at room
  temperature
1½ teaspoons baking powder
1 egg
1½ teaspoons vanilla

1 quart fresh or frozen
  blueberries, thawed
2 cups sour cream
2 egg yolks
½ cup sugar
1 teaspoon vanilla

Position rack in center of oven and preheat to 350 degrees. Generously butter a 9 or 10-inch spring-form pan. Combine first 6 ingredients in large bowl and mix thoroughly. Turn into prepared pan and sprinkle evenly with blueberries. Combine sour cream, egg yolks, sugar and vanilla; blend well. Pour over blueberries. Bake for 1 hour or until edges of custard are lightly browned.

Carla Marcus

CARROT CAKE

Yield: 12 servings

2 cups flour	1½ cups salad oil
1 teaspoon baking powder	2 cups sugar
1 teaspoon baking soda	4 eggs
1 teaspoon cinnamon	2 cups grated carrots
¼ teaspoon salt	1 cup chopped nuts

Preheat oven to 350 degrees. Sift flour, baking soda, baking powder, cinnamon and salt. Set aside. Combine oil, sugar, and eggs in a large mixing bowl. Mix well. Add flour mixture and stir until moistened. Stir in carrots and nuts. Pour into greased and floured tube pan. Bake at 350 degrees for 50 to 60 minutes. Cool. Frost with cream cheese frosting.

Cream Cheese Frosting

½ cup butter or margarine	1 (16-ounce) box powdered sugar
1 (8-ounce) package cream	1 teaspoon vanilla
cheese, softened	Chopped nuts (optional)

Mix butter, cream cheese, powdered sugar and vanilla together until smooth. Spread on cooled cake. Sprinkle with chopped nuts.

Judith Bishop Condren
(Mrs. Arthur)

APRICOT BRANDY POUNDCAKE

Serves: 10 to 12

3 cups sugar	½ teaspoon rum flavoring
1 cup butter	1 teaspoon orange extract
6 eggs, beaten	¼ teaspoon almond extract
3 cups flour	½ teaspoon lemon extract
¼ teaspoon baking soda	1 teaspoon vanilla extract
1 cup sour cream	½ cup apricot brandy

Grease and lightly flour large tube pan. Preheat oven to 325 degrees. Cream sugar and butter. Add beaten eggs. Sift together flour and soda. Combine sour cream, flavorings and brandy. Add flour and sour cream mixtures, alternately, to sugar mixture. Mix until just blended. Turn into pan and bake at 325 degrees for 70 minutes.

Mrs. Dale K. Bryant

CHOCOLATE APPLE WALNUT CAKE

Serves: 12

½ cup butter or margarine
1 cup sugar
1 egg
1½ cups chopped walnuts
1⅔ cups flour
½ teaspon salt

1 teaspoon baking soda
1 teaspoon cinnamon
½ teaspoon allspice
4 tablespoons cocoa (not instant)
2 cups applesauce, heated
1 teaspoon vanilla

Cream butter. Slowly add sugar and cream until fluffy. Add egg and beat well. Sift a little flour over the walnuts and mix. Sift together remaining flour, salt, baking soda, spices and cocoa. Add flour mixture alternately with heated apple-sauce to creamed mixture. Stir in vanilla. Fold in nuts. Spoon into greased and floured 10-inch tube or bundt pan. Bake at 350 degrees for 45 to 60 minutes, or until cake tester comes out clean. Cool in pan 10 minutes. Remove to rack to finish cooling.

Frosting

3 squares unsweetened baking
   chocolate, melted over hot
   water
¼ cup milk

1 egg
1 tablespoon butter
½ teaspoon vanilla
1 cup sifted powdered sugar

Place ingredients in glass container of blender and cover. Blend 15 to 20 seconds. Do not add more sugar because frosting thickens as it sets. Frost top of cake and let frosting drip down sides of the cake.

Janet Knowles Hawkes
(Mrs. H. Theodore)

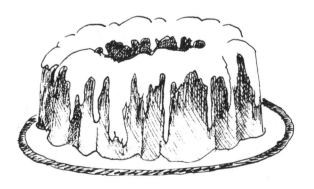

CHOCOLATE ZUCCHINI CAKE

Yield: 13 x 9 x 2-inch Cake

8 tablespoons margarine
½ cup vegetable oil
1¾ cups sugar
2 large eggs
1 teaspoon vanilla
½ cup buttermilk
2½ cups flour
1 teaspoon baking soda
½ teaspoon baking powder

½ teaspoon salt
4 tablespoons cocoa
1 teaspoon cinnamon
2 cups grated raw zucchini,
  unpeeled
1 (6-ounce) package semi-sweet
  chocolate chips
½ cup chopped walnuts

Cream margarine and oil with sugar. Add eggs one at a time, beating well after each addition. Blend in vanilla and buttermilk. Sift dry ingredients and add to creamed mixture. Stir in zucchini. Pour into greased and floured 9 x 13 x 2-inch pan. Sprinkle with chocolate chips and nuts. Bake at 325 degrees approximately 45 minutes.

Carol Potter Day
(Mrs. Richard B.)

HUNDRED DOLLAR CHOCOLATE CAKE

Serves: 8 to 10

2 cups flour
4 tablespoons cocoa
2 teaspoons baking soda
½ teaspoon salt
1 cup sugar

1 cup salad dressing
  (not mayonnaise)
1 cup cold water
2 teaspoons vanilla

Sift flour, cocoa, soda and salt together. Blend sugar, salad dressing and water in separate bowl. Add flour mixture and vanilla. Pour into greased 13 x 9 x 2-inch baking pan. Bake at 350 degrees for 20 to 30 minutes, until done.

Fudge Frosting

¼ cup water
3 squares unsweetened chocolate
2 tablespoons margarine
12 large marshmallows, cut up

⅛ teaspoon salt
2 cups powdered sugar, sifted
1 teaspoon vanilla

Over low heat, heat and stir first five ingredients until soft and well blended. Add powdered sugar and vanilla. If too stiff, add a few drops of hot water.

Audrey Freeman Gough
(Mrs. Joseph T., Jr.)

ORANGE RING CAKE

Serves: 8 to 10

1 cup butter
3 egg yolks
1 cup sugar
Grated rind of 1 large orange
1 cup sour cream

1¾ cups flour
1 teaspoon baking powder
1 teaspoon baking soda
3 egg whites

Cream butter, yolks, sugar and orange rind until well blended. Add sour cream. Sift together flour, baking powder and soda and add to the above mixture. Beat egg whites until stiff; slowly fold them into the above batter. Pour into greased tube pan or bundt mold. Bake in 325-degree oven for 40 minutes. Cool on rack for 5 minutes; turn out onto cake plate and pour orange syrup over cake while it is still warm. Fresh strawberries and whipped cream make a nice garnish.

Orange Syrup

Juice of 2 large oranges
¾ cup sugar

Juice of 1 lemon
Dash of salt

Combine all 4 ingredients and boil for 4 minutes.

Linda Armstrong Andrews
(Mrs. Richard C.)

ORANGE CAKE

Serves: 6

1 cup sugar
½ cup butter
2 egg yolks
½ teaspoon vanilla
¼ cup orange juice
Grated rind of ½ orange
   (optional)

1½ cups cake flour
1½ teaspoons baking powder
¼ cup milk
2 egg whites, beaten stiff
Whipped cream, sweetened

Cream sugar and butter. Add egg yolks, beaten in one at a time. Add vanilla, orange juice and rind. Sift flour and baking powder together three times; add to mixture alternately with milk, beating well after each addition. Fold in egg whites. Grease a 12 x 3½-inch baking pan or an 8-inch square pan and place waxed paper on the bottom. Pour in batter and bake at 350 degrees for 45 minutes. Frost top with whipped cream before serving. Or use favorite butter-cream frosting, substituting orange juice for milk.

Mildred A. Muir

PUMPKIN CAKE ROLL

Serves: 8

3 eggs
1 cup sugar
⅔ cup canned pumpkin
1 teaspoon lemon juice
¾ cup flour
1 teaspoon baking powder

2 teaspoons cinnamon
1 teaspoon ginger
½ teaspoon nutmeg
½ teaspoon salt
1 cup finely chopped nuts

Filling

1 cup powdered sugar
2 (3-ounce) packages cream
  cheese

4 tablespoons butter
½ teaspoon vanilla

Beat eggs on high speed of mixer for 5 minutes. Gradually beat in sugar. Stir in pumpkin and lemon juice. In a separate bowl, stir together flour, baking powder, cinnamon, ginger, nutmeg and salt. Fold into pumpkin mixture. Spread on greased and floured 15 x 10 x 1-inch jelly roll pan. Top with nuts. Bake at 375 degrees for 15 minutes. Turn onto towel sprinkled with powdered sugar. Starting at narrow end, roll towel and cake together. Cool and unroll. For filling, combine sugar, cream cheese, butter and vanilla. Beat until smooth. Spread over cake. Roll and chill.

Susan Welky Corey
(Mrs. John B.)

MARION BEESON'S PARTY CAKE

Yield: 13 x 9 x 2-inch Cake

2 eggs, lightly beaten
1 cup sour cream
2 cups sugar
1 teaspoon vanilla
4 (1-ounce) squares unsweetened
  chocolate

8 tablespoons butter
2 cups flour
1 cup boiling water
1 heaping teaspoon soda

Preheat oven to 350 degrees. Mix together, eggs, sour cream, sugar and vanilla. Melt chocolate and butter. Add to above mixture. Add flour and mix well. Then combine baking soda and boiling water. Add quickly to cake batter. Pour in a 9 x 13 x 2-inch pan and bake for 30 to 35 minutes. Frost with favorite buttercream icing.

Carol Potter Day
(Mrs. Richard B.)

FRESH APPLE POUND CAKE

Serves: 8

1¼ cups cooking oil
2 cups sugar
3 eggs
2 teaspoons vanilla
3 cups flour
1 teaspoon baking soda

1 teaspoon salt
¾ teaspoon cinnamon
1 cup chopped pecans
3 medium apples, peeled
and diced

Combine, oil, sugar and eggs. Beat at medium speed for 3 minutes. Add vanilla. Combine dry ingredients; add to above mixture. Fold in pecans and apples. Bake in greased, floured tube pan at 325 degrees for 1 hour and 20 minutes or until done.

Jean Potter Benton
(Mrs. Don C., III)

BARBARA'S APPLE CAKE

Serves: 6

Apple Mixture

4 tablespoons cinnamon
5 large cooking apples, peeled
and cut into chunks
1 cup raisins

1 cup coarsely chopped nuts
6 tablespoons brown sugar
2 tablespoons sugar

Batter

3 cups flour
2 cups sugar
1 teaspoon salt
3 teaspoons baking powder

4 eggs
¼ cup orange juice
1 cup oil
3 teaspoons vanilla

Mix together apple mixture and set aside. Mix together batter ingredients. Grease and flour a 10-inch tube pan. Pour ½ of batter into pan; cover with ½ of apple mixture. Add other ½ of batter and top with remainder of apple mixture. Bake in preheated 350-degree oven for 1 hour.

Shelley Stuart Carvel
(Mrs. H. Steven)

PRUNE CAKE

Serves: 12

1½ cups sugar
1 cup vegetable oil
3 eggs
1 cup buttermilk
1 teaspoon baking soda
1 cup cooked, chopped prunes
1 cup chopped pecans

2 cups flour
1 teaspoon vanilla
1 teaspoon allspice
1 teaspoon cinnamon
1 teaspoon nutmeg
1 teaspoon salt

Combine sugar and oil. Add eggs and mix well. Add the combination of soda and buttermilk. Add the remaining ingredients and mix well. Pour into a greased 13 x 9 x 2-inch baking pan. Bake 350 degrees for 35 to 40 minutes. Toward the end of baking time, prepare the following sauce.

Sauce

½ cup butter
1 cup sugar
½ teaspoon soda

½ cup buttermilk
1 teaspoon vanilla
1 tablespoon light corn syrup

Combine the ingredients in a saucepan and bring to a boil. Cook over medium heat for 12 to 15 minutes, stirring occasionally. Pour over cake while hot.

Rebecca Bilbrey Sweeney
(Mrs. Eugene G., Jr.)

CANDIED FRUIT CAKE

Yield: 3 cakes

1½ pounds pitted dates
1 pound candied whole cherries
1 pound candied pineapple
 (cut up)
2 cups flour

2 teaspoons baking powder
¼ teaspoon salt
4 eggs
1 cup sugar
2 pounds pecans

Place dates, cherries and pineapple in very large bowl. Sift flour, baking powder and salt over fruit, coating each piece. In separate bowl beat eggs until frothy. Add sugar and continue beating. Add to fruit, then add pecans. Mix well and pack into three 9 x 5 x 3-inch loaf pans that have been greased and lined with greased brown paper. Bake at 300 degrees for 1¼ hours. Cool.

Nancy Montgomery Beebe
(Mrs. Michael)

OLD FRENCH FRUIT POUND CAKE

Yield: One 10-inch tube pan or
Two 10 x 4 x 2-inch loaf pans

1 cup butter or margarine
1½ cups sugar
1 cup ground almonds
5 large eggs
2 cups flour
¼ teaspoon ground allspice
1½ teaspoons cinnamon
1 (16-ounce) container mixed
  candied fruit

1 (4-ounce) container candied
  orange peel
1 (16-ounce) box currants
¼ cup brandy
Waxed paper and shortening to
  prepare pan(s)
Brandy

Thoroughly grease bottom and sides of pan(s). Line with waxed paper cut to fit. Lightly grease waxed paper. Cream butter and sugar. Add ground almonds. Add eggs 1 at a time, beating well after each addition. Sift flour with spices. Stir fruit mixture into flour, tossing lightly to coat fruit. Combine with butter and sugar mixture. Stir in brandy. Pour into prepared pan(s). Bake at 300 degrees for 1½ to 1¾ hours or until cake tester comes out clean. Cool before removing from pan. Brush with brandy and wrap cake in foil or plastic wrap. Serve in thin slices.

Carol Potter Day
(Mrs. Richard B.)

BAVARIAN APPLE TORTE

Serves: 6

½ cup butter
⅓ cup sugar
¼ teaspoon vanilla
1 cup flour
1 (8-ounce) package cream
  cheese, softened
¼ cup sugar

1 egg
½ teaspoon vanilla
⅓ cup sugar
½ teaspoon cinnamon
4 cups peeled apple slices
¼ cup almonds

Cream butter, ⅓ cup sugar and ¼ teaspoon vanilla. Blend in flour to form crumbs. Spread dough onto bottom and sides of 9-inch spring-form pan. Combine cream cheese and ¼ cup sugar and mix well. Blend in egg and ½ teaspoon vanilla. Pour into pastry-lined pan. Combine last ⅓ cup sugar and cinnamon and toss in apples. Spoon over cream cheese layer. Sprinkle with almonds. Bake at 450 degrees for 10 minutes. Reduce heat to 400 degrees and bake for 25 minutes. Cool before removing from pan. Serve with vanilla ice cream.

Kathleen Foshay Hanson
(Mrs. Robert F.)

QUEEN ELIZABETH CAKE

Serves: 8

1 cup boiling water
1 cup chopped dates
1 teaspoon baking soda
1 cup sugar
¼ cup butter
1 egg, beaten

1 teaspoon vanilla
1½ cups flour
1 teaspoon baking powder
⅓ teaspoon salt
⅓ cup chopped nuts

Icing

5 tablespoons brown sugar
5 tablespoons cream
2 tablespoons butter

¼ cup shredded coconut
¼ cup chopped nuts

Pour boiling water over chopped dates and baking soda. Let stand. Meanwhile, mix together remaining cake ingredients. Fold this mixture into the date mixture and pour into a 12 x 9 x 2-inch baking pan. Bake at 375 degrees for 35 minutes. For icing, boil sugar, cream and butter for 3 minutes. Then spread on cool cake. Sprinkle with coconut and nuts.

This is the only cake that the Queen makes herself. Her one request is that the recipe not be passed on, but sold for only charitable purposes.

Elizabeth Oldham Sawyer
(Mrs. Stewart)

VI'S MOIST COCONUT CAKE

Serves: 6 to 8

1 yellow cake mix

Bake in three 9-inch layers.

Sour Cream Filling

2 cups powdered sugar
2 cups sour cream
1 (9-ounce) container non-dairy
    whipped topping

1 teaspoon vanilla
3 cups coconut

Fold together all filling ingredients. Spread between cake layers generously. Put in covered cake container and refrigerate at least 3 days before serving.

Katie Danoski Freilinger
(Mrs. James E.)

GUY'S CHEESECAKE WITH STRAWBERRY GLAZE

Serves: 12

Butter
Graham cracker crumbs
4 (8-ounce) packages cream
   cheese

1 cup heavy cream
1 teaspoon vanilla
1½ cups sugar
4 eggs

Strawberry Glaze

4 cups strawberries
⅓ cup sugar
¼ cup water

1 tablespoon cornstarch
1 teaspoon butter

Butter a 9-inch spring-form pan and press graham cracker crumbs on bottom and sides. Beat remaining ingredients and turn mixture into prepared pan. Place cake pan in a pan containing ½-inch boiling water. Bake at 300 degrees for 2 hours. Turn oven off and bake 1 hour longer. Remove from oven and let rest for 2 hours. Invert onto plate and refrigerate overnight. Glaze cooled cake. To make glaze, wash and hull berries. Crush enough to make 1 cup. Boil crushed berries, sugar, water and cornstarch for 2 minutes, stirring constantly. Add butter. Strain and cool. Arrange whole berries on top of cheesecake and pour glaze over. Chill.

Suzanne A. LaDouceur Hatfield
(Mrs. Paul L.)

"NEW YORK" CHEESECAKE

Serves: 8 to 10

2 (8-ounce) packages cream
   cheese
1 (16-ounce) container ricotta
   cheese
1½ cups sugar
4 eggs

3 tablespoons flour
3 tablespoons cornstarch
2 teaspoons vanilla
¼ cup margarine, melted
1 pint sour cream

Mix cream cheese and ricotta together. Add sugar gradually. Beat in eggs one at a time, add flour, cornstarch, vanilla and margarine. Mix well. Fold in sour cream. Pour into a greased 10-inch springform pan. Bake in a preheated 325-degree oven for 1 hour, then turn off oven and leave cake for 2 hours. Serve plain or with a fruit glaze.

Patricia Tofuri Bicknell
(Mrs. Brian P.)

CHOCOLATE RIPPLE CHEESECAKE

Serves: 8 to 10

¾ cup flour
2 tablespoons sugar
¼ teaspoon salt
¼ cup margarine
1 (1-ounce) envelope
  unsweetened chocolate
3 (8-ounce) packages cream
  cheese

1 cup sugar
¼ cup flour
2 teaspoons vanilla
6 eggs
1 cup sour cream
2 (1-ounce) envelopes
  unsweetened chocolate

Combine ¾ cup flour, 2 tablespoons sugar, and salt; cut in margarine until particles are fine. Stir in 1 envelope chocolate, press over bottom of 9-inch spring-form pan. Bake 10 minutes at 400 degrees. In large mixing bowl at low speed blend cream cheese with sugar. Add ¼ cup flour and vanilla. Add eggs one at a time. Beat in sour cream. In a small bowl, combine 1½ cups of cheese mixture with 2 envelopes of chocolate. Pour half of plain cheese mix over baked crust in pan. Drizzle half of chocolate mix on top. Cover with remaining plain mix; then rest of chocolate. Cut through batter with spatula to marbleize chocolate with plain mixture. Bake in 500-degree oven for 12 minutes; turn heat down to 200 degrees and bake 1 hour longer. Cool away from drafts 2 to 3 hours. Refrigerate for at least 8 hours before serving.

Deborah F. Hammond

PERFECT POUND CAKE

Yield: 12 servings

1 cup butter, softened
3 cups sugar
1 teaspoon vanilla
½ teaspoon salt
6 eggs, separated

¼ teaspoon baking soda
3 cups flour
8 ounces sour cream
Powdered sugar

Cream butter and sugar. Add vanilla and salt. Blend in egg yolks one at a time. Sift dry ingredients together and add alternately with sour cream. Beat egg whites until stiff and fold into above mixture. Bake in a greased tube pan at 325 degrees for 1 hour and 15 minutes. Cool in pan for 30 minutes before turning out on rack. Sprinkle with powdered sugar before serving.

Susan Messia Harrod
(Mrs. Peter E.)

CHOCOLATE CHEESECAKE

Serves: 10 to 12

2 (8½-ounce) packages chocolate
  wafer cookies
½ teaspoon cinnamon
½ cup butter, melted
1 cup sugar
4 eggs
3 (8-ounce) packages cream
  cheese, softened

16 ounces semi-sweet chocolate
1 teaspoon vanilla
2 tablespoons cocoa
3 cups sour cream
¼ cup butter, melted
Whipped cream
Candied lilacs

Preheat oven to 350 degrees. Crush chocolate wafers and mix with cinnamon and melted butter. Press crumbs firmly into a 9-inch spring-form pan. Chill. Beat sugar and eggs until fluffy. Add cream cheese and beat until well mixed. Melt chocolate and add to egg mixture. Add vanilla, cocoa and sour cream beating constantly. Add melted butter and mix well. Pour mixture into chilled crust and bake for 45 minutes. Chill overnight in refrigerator. Before serving, pipe with whipped cream and garnish with candied lilacs, if desired.

Sally Grindell Vamvakias
(Mrs. James G.)

VANILLA ALMOND CRUNCH

Serves: 10

4 ounces slivered almonds
¼ cup butter
1 cup crushed rice cereal squares
½ cup light brown sugar

½ cup flaked coconut
⅛ teaspoon salt
1½ quarts vanilla or coffee ice
  cream, softened

Toast the nuts in the butter in a small saucepan over medium-low heat. Set half the toasted nuts aside for garnish. Combine the rest of the toasted almonds, the crushed rice cereal, the sugar, coconut, and salt. Pat the mixture into a 7 x 11 x 2-inch pan and bake for 5 minutes at 375 degrees. Cool completely. Spread the softened ice cream over the cooled crust. Garnish with the reserved toasted almonds. Freeze. Serve with butterscotch or chocolate sauce. Can also be made in a 9 x 13 x 2-inch pan using 2 quarts of ice cream—there will be enough crust. This will serve 15.

Patricia Pugh Britt
(Mrs. Michael E.)

BAKLAVA

Syrup

2½ pounds sugar
3 quarts water

½ cinnamon stick

Pastry

2 pounds melted butter
2 pounds phyllo
4 pounds walnuts, finely ground
1 (6-ounce) box zwieback, finely
   ground

Whole cloves for garnish
2 pounds honey
2 ounces lemon juice

First Day
Prepare sugar syrup by boiling sugar, cinnamon stick in water for 3 hours or until thick enough to form a flat ball. Set aside to cool for 24 hours.

Second Day
Melt butter and coat bottom of 16 x 18-inch pan with brush. Place 7 to 8 leaves of phyllo in pan, brushing tops of leaves with butter. Cover with mixture of ground walnuts and zwieback. Then cover with 1 phyllo leaf, butter, walnuts etc. Repeat until 15 leaves are layered. Top with 7 to 8 phyllo leaves spread with butter. Cut phyllo through to bottom of pan, going straight across narrow part of pan. Cut on diagonal. Place one whole clove in the center of each diamond. Bake at 350 degrees for 2 hours, checking frequently to make sure the bottom is browned by lifting up edges with a knife. Top should appear to be toasty golden brown. Remove from oven and pour honey on top. Let stand for 10 minutes. Add lemon juice to syrup. Pour over top and allow to soak for 24 hours. Prepare this recipe at least 2 days ahead of time.

Mrs. Katrina Mavadonas

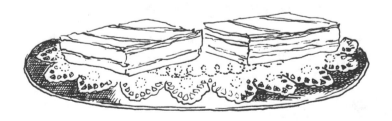

GALACTOBURIKO
(CUSTARD FILLED DIAMONDS)

Serves: 12 to 18

½ cup ready-to-cook cream of
    wheat (not instant)
½ cup sugar
⅓ cup flour
4 eggs, beaten
2 teaspoons vanilla
4 cups milk
⅔ cup sugar

½ cup butter or margarine,
    melted
½ to ¾ cup butter or margarine,
    melted
10 (12 x 9-inch) sheets phyllo
    (cut phyllo to fit pan)
½ recipe Honey-Lemon Syrup,
    cooled

In a bowl, stir together cream of wheat (not cooked), ½ cup sugar, and the flour. Add eggs and vanilla; mix well. In saucepan combine milk and ⅔ cup sugar; bring to boiling, stirring constantly. Very slowly add about 1 cup of hot milk mixture to egg mixture, stirring constantly. Return all to milk mixture in saucepan. Cook and stir until bubbly. Remove from heat; blend in first ½ cup butter or margarine. Cool. Brush bottom of 13 x 9 x 2-inch baking dish with some of melted butter (or margarine). Overlay 2 sheets of phyllo in bottom of dish so that about half the length of sheets extends over RIGHT side of the dish. Brush each sheet with melted butter before adding the next. Repeat with 2 more sheets of phyllo, extending them over the LEFT side of the dish. Place a fifth sheet of phyllo over the bottom of the dish, covering all other sheets. Spoon in cooled custard, spreading evenly. Cover custard by folding over the extended sheets of phyllo, brushing the top of each one with butter after folding. Top with the remaining 5 sheets of phyllo, brushing with butter between each layer. With a sharp knife, score top in diamond pieces. Bake at 375 degrees for 45 to 50 minutes or until golden. Place dish on rack. Pour COOLED lemon-honey syrup over diamonds. Do not cover. Let stand until syrup is nearly absorbed. Serve warm or chilled.

Honey-Lemon Syrup

3 cups sugar
½ cup honey
1 teaspoon shredded lemon peel

3 tablespoons lemon juice
2 inches stick cinnamon
2 cups water

In saucepan, combine all ingredients and water. Bring to boiling, reduce heat. Simmer, uncovered 10 minutes. Remove cinnamon. Makes 4 cups.

Sally Grindell Vamvakias
(Mrs. James G.)

STRAWBERRY BLITZ TORTE

Serves: 6 to 8

¼ cup shortening
½ cup sugar
½ teaspoon vanilla
2 egg yolks
1 cup cake flour
1½ teaspoons baking powder
¼ teaspoon salt

½ cup milk
2 egg whites
½ cup sugar
¼ cup slivered almonds
2 cups whipped cream
1 quart fresh strawberries,
   sweetened and halved

Cream shortening. Gradually add sugar and vanilla; cream until fluffy. Beat in egg yolks. Sift together flour, baking powder and salt. Add to creamed mixture alternately with milk, beating after each addition. Pour into 2 waxed paper-lined 8 x 1½-inch round pans. Beat egg whites until frothy. Gradually add sugar; beat until stiff peaks are formed. Spread evenly over cake batter. Sprinkle with almonds. Bake at 350 degrees for 30 to 35 minutes. Cool in pans for 10 minutes. Cool on rack. With meringue side up, spread 1 layer with whipped cream, then drained strawberries. Add second layer and top with remaining whipped cream and strawberries. Serve immediately.

Jeri Dyer Edgar
(Mrs. Joseph H., Jr.)

MOUNT KATAHDIN

Serves: 12

½ gallon harlequin ice cream
1 pint vanilla ice cream
1 cup hot fudge sauce
1 (16-ounce) box frozen
   strawberries, thawed

1 cup cream, whipped
Nuts (optional)
Cherry

Remove harlequin ice cream from container. Place on serving plate and use as the base. Scoop vanilla ice cream into balls and pile into mound on top of base. Return to freezer until ready to use. Before serving, ladle hot fudge sauce over ice cream. Then pour on thawed strawberries. Add whipped cream and nuts. Cherry on top. Light a sparkler, stick on top of mountain and serve immediately.

India Horton Weatherill
(Mrs. Robert H.)

GREAT VANILLA ICE CREAM

Yield: 1 quart

1 cup plus 2 tablespoons
   light cream
6 large egg yolks
5½ tablespoons sugar
1 cup whipping cream

5½ tablespoons sugar
1 whole vanilla bean, split
   down center
¼ cup butter
½ teaspoon vanilla extract

In a small heavy-bottomed saucepan, slowly bring light cream to a boil. Place in refrigerator overnight or chill in freezer briefly (do not freeze). Cream egg yolks and 5½ tablespoons sugar; set aside. In 2-quart saucepan combine whipping cream, remaining sugar and vanilla bean and bring slowly to a boil, stirring frequently. Remove bean. Using point of knife, scrape vanilla grains, from inside hull, into cream mixture. Add ⅓ of this mixture to yolk mixture, whisking constantly. Add this to remaining vanilla/cream in saucepan and bring to just under boiling point. Remove from heat and whisk in butter. Immediately place pan in cold water or over ice. Stir until cool. Beat in chilled light cream and vanilla. Place in ice cream maker and churn.

Judith Bishop Condron
(Mrs. Arthur)

FRENCH CHOCOLATE NUT SOUFFLÉ

Serves: 8

1 tablespoon unflavored gelatin
1 cup milk
1 (6-ounce) package semi-sweet
   chocolate chips
1 cup sugar, divided

¼ teaspoon salt
4 eggs, separated
1 cup whipped cream
6 to 7 ounces chopped nuts
Whole nuts to garnish

Sprinkle gelatin over milk in saucepan to soften. Stir in chocolate, ½ cup sugar, salt and egg yolks until blended. Heat over low heat stirring constantly until gelatin is dissolved and chocolate is melted. Cool. Beat egg whites to peaks. Gradually add ½ cup sugar, beating to stiff peaks. Fold egg whites, whipped cream, chocolate mixture and nuts together. Pour into 1½-quart soufflé dish. Garnish with whole nuts. Chill.

Martha Andrew Timothy
(Mrs. Robert P.)

LIME SOUFFLE

Serves: 6

1 teaspoon vegetable oil
1 cup lime juice, strained
1 envelope unflavored gelatin
1 cup evaporated milk
6 egg yolks

1¼ cups sugar
4 tablespoons finely grated
   lime rind, divided
4 egg whites
½ cup coconut

Out of waxed paper make a 2-inch collar for a 1-quart soufflé dish. Coat inside of dish and collar with oil. Pour lime juice into oven-proof glass bowl, sprinkle in gelatin and let soften 2 to 3 minutes. Place bowl into a skillet of simmering water. Stir over low heat until gelatin is dissolved. Remove skillet from heat, do not remove bowl from skillet. In another pan, simmer evaporated milk. Remove from heat. Beat egg yolks. Slowly add sugar to yolks and continue beating until mixture is thickened. Beating constantly, slowly pour milk into yolks and return mixture to saucepan. Stir over low heat until it coats a spoon. Remove from heat and stir in gelatin and 3 tablespoons of lime rind. Transfer to deep bowl and cool. Beat egg whites until peaks form. Slowly fold whites into custard mixture. Pour into prepared dish. Refrigerate for 3 hours. Preheat oven to 325 degrees. Spread coconut on baking pan and toast 15 to 20 minutes. Garnish soufflé with coconut and remaining rind. Remove collar and serve.

Barbara Dwyer Newcomb
(Mrs. John)

ORANGE SOUFFLÉ

Serves: 6 to 8

1 tablespoon gelatin
¼ cup cold water
3 eggs, separated
1 cup sugar
1 teaspoon lemon juice

⅓ cup orange juice
Grated orange rind
1 tablespoon orange liqueur
2 cups heavy cream

Sprinkle gelatin over water. It will become opaque and firm. Melt gelatin over low heat. In a bowl, beat yolks until lemon colored. Add sugar and beat until light. Beat in juices, grated rind and liqueur. Add hot gelatin in a thin stream, beating mixture constantly. Allow mixture to cool. Beat egg whites and whip cream. Fold both into orange mixture. Pour into 1 quart soufflé dish with collar and chill 5 to 6 hours.

Roselle Flynn Johnson
(Mrs. Steven M.)

PLUM PUDDING

Serves: 16

½ cup currants
½ cup raisins
⅓ cup brandy
½ cup sugar
3 cups flour
1 teaspoon soda
1½ teaspoons salt
½ teaspoon ground cloves
½ teaspoon ginger
½ teaspoon nutmeg

1 teaspoon cinnamon
1 apple, grated
¼ cup citron
¼ cup orange peel
½ cup chopped nuts
1 cup suet
1½ cups milk
½ cup molasses
½ cup brandy

Soak currants and raisins in ⅓ cup of brandy overnight. Sift dry ingredients into large bowl. Add apple, soaked fruit, citron, peels and nuts. Stir in suet, milk and molasses. Pour into 2 buttered 1½-quart molds. Place on rack in bottom of deep pot. Add enough water to cover ½ the mold. Steam for 3 hours. Cool and wrap in cheese cloth soaked in brandy. Keep wrapped for at least 2 weeks.

Sharon Smith Bushey
(Mrs. Donald J.)

BRITT'S HOLIDAY PUDDING

Serves: 4 to 6

½ cup butter
1 cup sugar
2 eggs, beaten
1 cup milk
4 tablespoons flour

¼ teaspoon salt, scant
2 teaspoons baking powder
½ pound chopped dates, dust
   with small amount of flour
1 cup chopped nuts

Cream together the butter and sugar. Combine the eggs and milk and add to creamed sugar and butter. Combine flour, salt, and baking powder and add to the above. Stir the dates and nuts into mixture and pour into a well-greased 9 x 5 x 3-inch loaf pan and bake for 90 minutes at 325 degrees. This can be doubled.

Martha E. Britt
(Mrs. Edward)

BLUEBERRY SHAKER PUDDING

Serves: 6

2 tablespoons butter
½ cup sugar
1 cup flour
1 teaspoon baking powder
½ teaspoon salt

½ cup milk
¾ cup sugar
1 cup water
2 cups blueberries
1 tablespoon butter

Cream together 2 tablespoons butter and ½ cup sugar. Add flour, baking powder, salt and milk. Beat together and pour into a greased 2½ quart casserole. Boil together for 3 minutes ¾ cup sugar, water, blueberries and butter. Pour over batter and bake at 375 degrees for 1 hour. Serve cold with vanilla ice cream.

Judith Topham Flaker
(Mrs. James R.)

BLUEBERRY MOUSSE

1 (3-ounce) package grape
  or blackberry gelatin
1 (3-ounce) package lemon
  gelatin
2 cups boiling water

2 cups heavy cream, whipped
2 teaspoons vanilla
3 cups fresh blueberries
Whipped cream to garnish
Blueberries to garnish

Dissolve gelatin in boiling water. Cool and chill until slightly thickened. Fold in whipped cream, vanilla and blueberries. Pour into a 2-quart mold. Chill until firm. Unmold and garnish with additional whipped cream and blueberries.

Jean Smith
(Mrs. Robert)

SOUR CREAM BRULÉE

Serves: 6

3 cups sour cream
1 teaspoon vanilla
¼ teaspoon nutmeg

1¼ cups brown sugar, sieved
1 pint strawberries, fresh or
  frozen

Mix sour cream, vanilla and nutmeg together and put in an 8-inch square pan. Sprinkle brown sugar over mixture and broil 5 inches from heat until bubbly. Watch carefully. Chill up to 3 hours (no more). Cover with strawberries and serve immediately.

Joan Shepherd
(Mrs. Robert)

PECAN PUDDING

Serves: 8 to 12

3 eggs
1 cup dark corn syrup
½ cup sugar
2 tablespoons melted butter
½ cup flour

⅛ teaspoon cream of tartar
1 teaspoon vanilla
1 cup chopped pecans, divided
Whipped cream

Beat eggs until thick. Mix in syrup, sugar and butter. Sift together flour and tartar and add to above mixture. Fold in vanilla and ½ cup pecans. Pour into greased 8 x 8-inch baking pan. Sprinkle ½ cup pecans over the top. Bake at 375 degrees for 35 to 40 minutes. Serve cold with whipped cream.

Barbara Wemyss Lechman
(Mrs. Charles A.)

BROWNIE PUDDING

Serves: 8

1 cup flour
2 teaspoons baking powder
1 teaspoon salt
⅔ cup sugar
2 tablespoons cocoa
½ cup milk

2 teaspoons melted shortening
1 teaspoon vanilla
½ cup chopped nuts
1 cup white or brown sugar
4 tablespoons cocoa
1½ cups boiling water

Preheat oven to 350 degrees. Sift together flour, baking powder, salt, sugar and cocoa. Add milk, shortening, vanilla and nuts and mix until smooth. Pour into greased 1½-quart baking dish. Mix together sugar and cocoa and sprinkle over top of batter. Pour boiling water over all. Bake uncovered for 30 to 40 minutes. Finished pudding will have cake top with sauce in bottom of pan.

Leslie MacDougall Webber
(Mrs. Walter E.)

MARSHMALLOW MINT FIDELIO

Serves: 4 to 6

16 marshmallows, quartered
⅔ cup crème de menthe

1 pint whipping cream, whipped

Melt the marshmallows and the crème de menthe in top of a double boiler. Allow this mixture to cool slightly. Fold the cooled marshmallow mixture into the whipped cream. Pour into individual serving dishes and freeze. Serve with Four Star Hot Fudge Sauce.

Patricia Pugh Britt
(Mrs. Michael E.)

INDIAN PUDDING

Serves: 6

3 cups milk
4 tablespoons corn meal
   (preferably undegerminated
   corn meal)
1 cup molasses
3 tablespoons butter
¾ teaspoon salt

¾ teaspon ginger
¼ teaspoon clove
¼ teaspoon mace
1 teaspoon vanilla
½ teaspoon cinnamon
1 egg, well-beaten

Mix small amount of cold milk into corn meal to make a thin paste. Scald balance of milk, stir in corn meal mixture. Place in double-boiler over boiling water and cook for 15 minutes. Stir in remaining ingredients and pour batter into well-greased 10-inch soufflé dish. Bake at 325 degrees for 1½ to 2 hours. Serve hot with hard sauce, cream (whipped or liquid) or ice cream.

India Horton Weatherill
(Mrs. Robert H.)

POT DE CRÈME

Serves: 6 to 8

3 cups heavy cream
½ cup sugar
1 tablespoon instant coffee
   granules

5 egg yolks
1 teaspoon vanilla
Chocolate shavings

Cook cream, sugar and coffee until hot. Do not boil. Slowly add to egg yolks, which have been mixed well in another bowl. Add vanilla. Pour into individual pots and place them in a pan with 1 inch of water. Cook at 325 degrees for 25 to 30 minutes. Cool and refrigerate. To serve, add chocolate shavings, if desired.

Nancy Montgomery Beebe
(Mrs. Michael)

WHITE WINE SHERBET

Serves: 6 to 8

2 pints lemon sherbet, softened
1½ cups white wine

Seedless green grapes
Unhulled strawberries

Stir the softened sherbet into the wine. Pour into a decorative 6-cup mold which has been lined with plastic wrap. Freeze overnight. Unmold onto chilled tray and garnish with the grapes and strawberries. Serve immediately.

Patricia Pugh Britt
(Mrs. Michael E.)

DEB'S BLUEBERRY BUCKLE

Yield: One 8-inch cake

¾ cup sugar
1 egg
2 cups flour
½ teaspoon salt
¼ cup soft shortening

½ cup milk
2 teaspoons baking powder
2 cups small Maine blueberries,
   fresh or frozen

Topping

½ cup sugar
½ teaspoon cinnamon
¼ teaspoon freshly grated
   nutmeg

⅓ cup flour
¼ cup soft butter or margarine

Mix together all the ingredients for the cake except the blueberries. Gently fold in the blueberries last. Batter will be stiff. Pour batter into a greased 8-inch square pan. Sprinkle top with the crumb topping. Bake in a 375-degree oven for 45 to 60 minutes.

Bonnie Bonjean Dowling
(Mrs. Patrick)

CHOCOLATE MOUSSE

Yield: 4 to 6 servings

1 (6-ounce) package semi-sweet
   chocolate chips
2 tablespoons coffee liqueur
1 tablespoon orange juice
2 whole eggs
2 egg yolks
1½ teaspoons vanilla extract

¼ cup sugar
1 cup heavy cream
Additional whipped cream
   for garnish
Candied lilacs or violets
   for garnish

Melt chocolate, liqueur, and orange juice over very low heat and set aside In a blender, combine whole eggs, egg yolks, vanilla and sugar and blend for 2 minutes. Add cream and blend for another minute. Add chocolate mixture and blend until smooth. Top with whipped cream and a candied lilac.

Carol Potter Day
(Mrs. Richard B.)

KELA KA RAYTA

Serves: 4 to 6

2 tablespoons butter
2 tablespoons honey
½ cup shredded unsweetened
  coconut

1 cup plain yogurt
½ teaspoon ground coriander
3 medium bananas, sliced
⅛ cup wheat germ

Melt butter in skillet. Mix butter and honey. Add coconut and simmer 5 minutes. Remove from heat and add 2 tablespoons yogurt; mix. Add remaining yogurt, coriander and bananas. Mix. Cover and refrigerate 2 hours before serving. Sprinkle with wheat germ. Wonderful with curry! A simple Indian dessert. Serve with Murgh Masallam. (See index)

Suzanne Bernard Ewing
(Mrs. Robert M.)

ORANGES SUPREME

Serves: 6

6 large oranges
1 cup pitted and chopped dates
1 cup drained and diced canned
  peaches
1 cup drained canned crushed
  pineapple

¼ cup drained and diced
  maraschino cherries
¼ cup Brandy, or to suit taste
4 pints vanilla ice cream, must
  be very hard

Cut oranges into petals about ⅔ of the way down and remove the pulp, leaving an orange shell. Use pulp for salad, children's snacks, etc. In a bowl combine the fruits, dates, and brandy. Pack some ice cream into the bottom of each empty orange shell. Pour ⅓ cup of the fruit mixture on top of the ice cream. Pack shells with more ice cream, then press the "petals" into the ice cream. Top with a little fruit mixture and place in freezer trays. When completely frozen, pack in plastic bags. Remove from freezer 15 minutes before serving. Can be made 3 weeks ahead of time.

Patricia Pugh Britt
(Mrs. Michael E.)

PIE IN A PAN

Serves: 15

½ cup butter
2 tablespoons sugar
1 cup flour
1 (8-ounce) package cream
  cheese
1 cup powdered sugar
1 cup frozen dairy topping

2 (4-ounce) packages instant
  chocolate pudding
2 cups milk
1-2 cups dairy topping or
  whipped cream

Blend together butter, sugar and flour and pat into a 9 x 13-inch glass baking dish and prick with a fork. Bake in 350-degree oven for 15 minutes. Cream together cheese and powdered sugar; fold in 1 cup dairy topping and spread on cooled crust. Mix pudding and milk and beat for 2 minutes and spread on cheese mixture. Frost with layer of whipped cream or dairy topping and chill until firm. Lemon pudding may be substituted.

Sally Grindell Vamvakias
(Mrs. James)

BANANA SPLIT DESSERT

Serves: 9

1 cup margarine, divided and
  softened
2 cups graham cracker crumbs
1 (8-ounce) package cream
  cheese, softened
1½ pounds powdered sugar
3 bananas, sliced

1 (6½-ounce) can crushed
  pineapple, drained
1 (9.6-ounce) container frozen
  dairy topping, thawed
½ cup chopped walnuts
9 maraschino cherries

Melt ½ cup margarine and mix with 2 cups graham cracker crumbs. Press mixture in 9-inch square pan. Chill. With electric mixer, blend remaining ½ cup margarine with cream cheese and powdered sugar until smooth. Pour mixture over graham cracker crust. Layer with sliced bananas, crushed pineapple, dairy topping and chopped nuts. Garnish with cherries.

Shirley Thompson Leighton
(Mrs. Thomas M.)

ALMOND TORTONI FRENNING

Serves: 4

1 egg white
⅛ teaspoon salt
1 tablespoon instant coffee
2 tablespoons sugar
1 cup heavy cream

⅛ teaspoon almond extract
1 teaspoon vanilla
¼ cup sugar
¼ cup toasted chopped almonds

Combine egg white with salt and coffee. Beat until foamy. Gradually add the 2 tablespoons sugar; beat until stiff. Set aside. Whip cream until stiff, adding extracts and the ¼ cup sugar. Fold in the egg white mixture and the almonds, reserving 1 tablespoon almonds for garnish. Pour into parfait glasses, sprinkle with almonds and freeze. Serve with delicate cookies.

Susan Hall Haynes
(Mrs. J. David)

BAKED BLUEBERRY TOPPING FOR CHEESECAKE

1½ teaspoons flour
⅛ cup sugar
1 tablespoon lemon juice

1 pint fresh blueberries, washed
and drained well

Combine flour, sugar, and lemon juice. Add the blueberries, stirring carefully. Place in a covered casserole and cook in a 350-degree oven for 45 minutes or until thick. Spoon over cheesecake.

Charleen Campbell Malone
(Mrs. Joseph)

FOUR STAR HOT FUDGE SAUCE

Yield: 3 cups

2 cups sugar
4 heaping tablespoons cocoa
4 tablespoons butter

Pinch of salt
1 (13-ounce) can evaporated milk
2 teaspoons vanilla

Combine sugar, cocoa, butter, and salt (in given order) in a heavy saucepan and stir with a wooden spoon over low heat for 2 minutes. Do not let sugar melt. Add the evaporated milk, increase heat, and bring to a boil, stirring constantly. Boil rapidly for 1 minute (begin timing after mixture comes to a full rolling boil) again stirring constantly. Remove from heat and stir in vanilla. Keeps 3 weeks in refrigerator. Can be gently reheated.

Patricia Pugh Britt
(Mrs. Michael E.)

BUTTERSCOTCH SAUCE

Yield: 2 cups

1¼ cups light brown sugar
4 tablespoons butter

⅔ cup corn syrup
¾ cup half and half

Combine brown sugar, butter and corn syrup in a pan and cook over medium heat, stirring constantly. Cook until mixture reaches 232 degrees on a candy thermometer. Remove from heat and add the half and half. Stir well. Keeps well in refrigerator up to 10 days.

Patricia Pugh Britt
(Mrs. Michael E.)

FUDGE SAUCE

Yield: 3 to 4 cups

5 squares unsweetened chocolate
½ cup butter
3 cups powdered sugar

1 (13-ounce) can evaporated milk
1¼ teaspoon vanilla

Melt chocolate and butter over low heat. Remove from heat and alternately mix in sugar and milk. Boil over moderate heat for 8 minutes, stirring constantly. Remove from heat and stir in vanilla. Better reheated.

Nancy Montgomery Beebe
(Mrs. Michael)

MOM'S EGGNOG SAUCE

Yield: 1½ cups

½ cup sugar
2 eggs, separated
Pinch salt

1 cup heavy cream
½ teaspoon vanilla
2 teaspoons rum

Gradually add ¼ cup sugar to beaten egg yolks. Whisk well. In separate bowl, beat egg whites until they stand in peaks. Gradually beat in ¼ cup sugar and pinch of salt. Fold into egg mixture. Whip cream until stiff. Flavor with vanilla and rum. Fold into egg mixture. This is good for plum pudding or any steamed pudding.

Sharon Smith Bushey
(Mrs. Donald J.)

GIFTS

SALTY TOPAZ

30 ounces golden raisins
30 ounces dark raisins
8 ounces dried apricot halves,
    quartered

24 ounces salted cashews

Combine all the above ingredients in a plastic container with a tight fitting lid. Shake to combine well and distribute the salt from the cashews.

Patricia Pugh Britt
(Mrs. Michael E.)

SPICED NUTS

Yield: 2½ cups

1½ cups dry roasted peanuts
½ cup almonds
½ cup walnut halves
1 tablespoon pumpkin pie spices

½ teaspoon salt
1 egg white, slightly beaten
1 teaspoon water
¾ cup sugar

Combine all ingredients, mixing well. Spread on greased cookie sheet. Bake at 300 degrees for 20 to 25 minutes. Remove from cookie sheet while still warm.

Sharon Smith Bushey
(Mrs. Donald J.)

SUGARED NUTS

Yield: 2 pounds

2 cups light brown sugar
1 cup sugar
1 cup sour cream
2 teaspoons vanilla

2 cups walnut halves
1 cup pecan halves
1 cup unblanched almonds

Combine sugars and sour cream in a large saucepan. Cook over medium heat until sugar is dissolved. Continue cooking without stirring to 238 degrees F. on candy thermometer (soft ball). Remove from heat. Add vanilla and nuts. Stir gently to coat. Turn onto large piece of waxed paper and separate nuts with a fork. Let dry.

Kathleen Foshay Hanson
(Mrs. Robert)

BREAD AND BUTTER PICKLES

Yield: 8 pints

6 quarts sliced cucumbers
6 white or yellow onions, sliced
2 green peppers, sliced into
   thin strips
3 cloves garlic, minced
⅓ cup pickling salt

2 trays ice cubes
5 cups sugar
3 cups vinegar
1½ teaspoons celery seed
1½ teaspoons mustard seed
1½ teaspoons turmeric

Put vegetables and salt in large enameled or stainless steel pan. Cover with 2 trays ice cubes. Mix well and put in refrigerator for 3 hours. Drain well. Mix remaining ingredients with vegetables and bring to a boil. Seal at once in hot sterilized jars according to manufacturer's directions.

Jane (Ba) Davidson Kopp
(Mrs. Donald)

SHERRIED PEPPERS

Hot red or green peppers   Medium dry sherry

Cut the hot peppers lengthwise and carefully pack into attractive jars. Cover with sherry and close tightly. Let stand 4 to 5 days. Sprinkle on salads or add to soups, stews and gravies.

The Committee

CRISPY CUCUMBER PICKLES

Yield: 5 pints

16 (4-inch) pickling cucumbers
2½ cups granulated sugar
2 cups cider vinegar
1 cup water
1 tablespoon pickling salt

1½ tablespoons mustard seed
1 tablespoon mixed pickling
   spice (with red pepper
   removed) tied securely in
   small cheesecloth bag)

Wash cucumbers and slice very thinly (3mm slicing disk of food processor works very well). Bring remaining ingredients to a boil in large stainless steel or enameled pan. Add the sliced cucumbers and bring to a boil again. Boil for only 2 minutes. Remove cheesecloth bag and ladle into hot, sterilized jars. Seal according to manufacturer's directions.

Carol Potter Day
(Mrs. Richard B.)

DUTCH SALAD

Yield: 8 to 10 pints

4 cups chopped cabbage
4 cups chopped onion
4 cups cubed cucumber
4 cups cauliflowerets
1 sweet red pepper, chopped
1 sweet green pepper, chopped
1 cup pickling salt

4 cups vinegar
4 cups water
5 cups sugar
1 cup flour
6 tablespoons dry mustard
1 tablespoon turmeric

Mix vegetables together in large enameled or stainless steel pot. Sprinkle salt over vegetables. Let sit overnight. Cook in boiling water for about 5 minutes. Vegetables should be crisp. Drain and rinse with cold water until vegetables are cool. Make a paste of remaining ingredients and cook until thick, about 10 minutes. Divide vegetables among sterilized hot jars and pour paste over vegetables. Seal.

Shirley Brearley

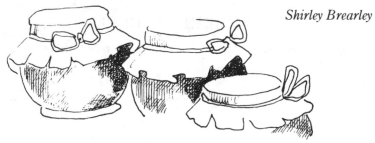

ZUCCHINI RELISH

Yield: 8 pints

12 cups sliced zucchini
4 cups sliced onions
5 tablespoons pickling salt
1 sweet red pepper, chopped
   fine
1 sweet green pepper, chopped
   fine
2½ cups cider vinegar

4 cups sugar
1 tablespoon dry mustard
¾ teaspoon nutmeg
¾ tablespoon cornstarch
¾ teaspoon turmeric
1½ teaspoons celery salt
½ teaspoon black pepper

Grind zucchini and onions together. Sprinkle with salt. Let stand overnight in stainless steel or enameled pan. Rinse with cold water and drain. Combine remaining ingredients in the same pan and bring to a full boil over high heat. Reduce heat and cook slowly for 1 hour. Pour into hot sterilized jars and seal.

Phyllis Treworgy
(Mrs. Audway)

SUMMER SQUASH PICKLE

Yield: 4 pints

⅔ cup pickling salt
3 quarts water
8 cups thinly sliced summer
    squash
2½ cups sugar

2 cups cider vinegar
2 teaspoons mustard seed
3 medium onions, thinly sliced
2 green peppers, cut in strips

In large bowl, combine salt and water. Add squash and weight down with a plate so the squash are completely covered by water mixture. Refrigerate for 3 hours. Mix sugar, vinegar, mustard seed in large enamel or stainless steel pot and bring to a boil, stirring until sugar is dissolved. Drain squash well. Add squash, pepper and onion to pot. Bring mixture just to a boil. Cool and store in refrigerator. These pickles keep several weeks in refrigerator.

Jane (Ba) Davidson Kopp
(Mrs. Donald)

TOMATO MARMALADE

Yield: about 8 cups

5 pounds ripe tomatoes
½ cup cider vinegar
3 pounds sugar

2 teaspoons whole cloves
2 unpeeled oranges, finely
    chopped

Chop tomatoes and cover with vinegar. Let stand overnight. Drain well. Add the sugar, cloves, and oranges. Cook slowly until thickened about 30 minutes. Pour into hot sterilized jars and seal.

Janie Sanborn

GREEN PEPPER JELLY

Yield: 8 to 10 half pints

1½ cups chopped green pepper
1½ cups cider vinegar
6½ cups sugar

25 shakes hot pepper sauce
3 to 5 drops green food color
1 (6-ounce) bottle liquid pectin

Combine first 4 ingredients in stainless steel or enameled pan. Bring to a full boil over high heat. Remove and set aside for 20 minutes. Return to heat and bring to a full rolling boil for 2 minutes. Remove from heat and add liquid pectin and food color. Stir and skim and pour into hot sterilized jars. Seal according to manufacturer's directions. Spread jelly over cream cheese and serve with crackers for a last minute hors d'oeuvre.

Carol Potter Day
(Mrs. Richard B.)

ROSE HIP JAM

Yield: 2 cups

3 cups fully ripe rose hips
1 orange
1 lemon

1 cup water
1½ cups sugar

Remove stiff hairs from calyx end of rose hips. Split open and scrape out the seeds. Wash hips and measure 1½ cups. Cut peel from orange and lemon into thin slivers. Add to water and boil for 5 minutes. Add sugar and stir until dissolved. Add juice from the orange and lemon and add the rose hips. Cover and simmer for 15 minutes. Uncover and cook until hips are clear and transparent and the syrup is thick. Pour into hot sterilized jars and seal.

Judy McDonald Dooley
(Mrs. Edmund)

PARSLEYED VERMOUTH JELLY

Yield: Five (8-ounce jars)

2 cups dry vermouth
3 cups sugar

1 (6-ounce) bottle liquid pectin
½ cup chopped parsley

Combine vermouth and sugar in top of double-boiler over boiling water and stir constantly for about 5 minutes, skimming foam off top. Remove from heat and stir in pectin and parsley. Mix well. Allow to stand 5 minutes. Ladle into hot sterilized jars and seal. Excellent with cold meat.

Carol Potter Day
(Mrs. Richard B.)

GREEN TOMATO RELISH

Yield: 8 pints

1 peck green tomatoes
4 large red sweet peppers
1 hot green pepper
6 medium onions
½ cup pickling salt

6 cups cider vinegar
7 cups sugar
1 teaspoon ground clove
1 teaspoon celery seed
2 teaspoons ground cinnamon

Grind tomatoes, peppers, and onions. Drain off juice. Cover with salt and let stand 1 hour. Rinse and drain well. Combine remaining ingredients and vegetables and cook until mixture looks dark and thick (about 30 minutes). Pour hot relish into sterilized hot jars and seal according to manufacturer's directions.

Jane (Ba) Davidson Kopp
(Mrs. Donald)

GINGERED RHUBARB JAM

Yield: 3½ cups

3 tablespoons finely cut
   candied ginger
4 cups diced fresh rhubarb

2 tablespoons lemon juice
3 cups sugar
Red food coloring, if desired

Combine all ingredients, except food coloring, in a large enamel pan and let stand for at least 30 minutes or until the sugar is moistened by the juices. Cook over moderately high heat stirring often until thick and clear—about 20 minutes. (Time seems to vary considerably depending on humidity, etc.) Skim off any foam, add coloring, if desired. Ladle into hot sterilized jars or glasses and seal at once according to manufacturer's directions. Delicious on roast pork and lamb.

Eileen A. Pugh
(Mrs. Richard F.)

RUM BALLS

Yield: 40 to 50 balls

1 cup crushed vanilla wafers
1⅔ cups chopped walnuts
   or pecans
1 cup powdered sugar
2 tablespoons cocoa

2 tablespoon light corn syrup
¼ cup rum
1 cup chocolate sprinkles
   or coconut

Combine crushed wafers and chopped nuts with sugar and cocoa. Stir in corn syrup and rum and mix. Wet hands and form mixture into balls, size of large olives. Roll in chocolate sprinkles or coconut and freeze on flat tray. When firm, pack in large container. Keep frozen until ready to serve.

Shelley Stuart Carvel
(Mrs. H. Steven)

PEANUT BUTTER CUPS

Yield: 32

½ pound margarine, melted
2 cups peanut butter
2 cups crushed graham crackers
1 pound powdered sugar

1 (6-ounce) package semi-sweet
   chocolate chips
¼ pound margarine

Mix first 4 ingredients thoroughly. Pack in 9 x 13-inch slightly greased pan. Melt chocolate bits and margarine. Frost and chill. Cut into small pieces using knife dipped in hot water.

Jane (Ba) Davidson Kopp
(Mrs. Donald)

PENUCHI FUDGE

Yield: 64 pieces

2 cups brown sugar
½ cup milk
2 tablespoons butter

⅛ teaspoon salt
1 cup chopped walnuts
1 teaspoon vanilla

Combine sugar and milk in a medium saucepan and cook until 234 degrees on candy thermometer. Add butter, salt and nuts. Beat until cool and add vanilla. Pour into 8 x 8-inch pan and mark when it begins to harden.

Deborah Spring Reed
(Mrs. Verner Z., III)

FAILPROOF CHOCOLATE FUDGE

Yield: 2 dozen pieces

4½ cups sugar
1 (13-ounce) can evaporated milk
2 cups chopped walnuts
1 cup butter

3 cups semi-sweet chocolate
  chips
3 tablespoons vanilla

Bring sugar and milk to a boil in large pot. Boil hard for 6 minutes. Remove from heat, add remaining ingredients. Pour into greased 12 x 8 x 2-inch pan.

Nancy Montgomery Beebe
(Mrs. Michael)

NANA'S CHOCOLATE FUDGE

Yield: 36 pieces

Butter
2 cups sugar
⅔ cup milk
1 cup marshmallow cream
1 cup peanut butter

1 (6-ounce) package semi-sweet
  chocolate chips
1 teaspoon vanilla
1 cup chopped walnuts

Butter sides of 2-quart pan. Combine sugar and milk and heat over medium heat until sugar dissolves, stirring constantly. Cook to soft ball stage on candy thermometer, stirring occasionally. Remove from heat and add remaining ingredients. Put in 9 x 9-inch pan and refrigerate. This fudge tastes best cold.

V. Albenia Zamarchi King
(Mrs. Russell C.)

THELMA'S GINGER FUDGE

Yield: 36 pieces

2 cups sugar
1 cup medium cream
1 teaspoon light corn syrup

1 teaspoon vanilla
2 (2-ounce) jars preserved
   or crystallized ginger

Cook sugar, cream and syrup to 230 degrees or soft ball stage on the candy thermometer (232 degrees on damp day). Remove from heat. Add vanilla and 1 jar of ginger; beat with wooden spoon until cool. Pour onto marble slab and work or knead until it creams, adding and working in remaining ginger pieces. Pour into 8-inch square pan and cut into small pieces. For Christmas giving, add small pieces of green and red cherries.

Deborah Spring Reed
(Mrs. Verner Z., III)

NEEDHAMS

Yield: 48 pieces

Centers

½ cup margarine
¾ cup unseasoned mashed
   potatoes
½ teaspoon salt
2 (16-ounce) boxes powdered
   sugar

1 (12-ounce) package flaked
   coconut
2 teaspoons vanilla

In a large pan melt the margarine. Add remaining ingredients and mix well. Spread mixture in a 9 x 13-inch buttered pan. Refrigerate until hard (2 to 3 hours). Cut into squares and refrigerate, covered, overnight.

Dipping Chocolate

1 (12-ounce) bag semi-sweet
   chocolate chips
4 (1-ounce) squares unsweetened
   chocolate

⅓ cup paraffin

Melt paraffin in top of double-boiler. Add chocolates and stir until melted. Dip centers in chocolate using toothpicks. Put on waxed paper to set.

Lee Morse Edwards
(Mrs. Dwight)

EASTER EGGS

Yield: 3 dozen

Coconut filling or
Peanut butter filling
1 (12-ounce) package semi-sweet
   chocolate chips

1 (2-inch) square paraffin

Prepare coconut or peanut butter filling. (If using both, double the chocolate dip). Chill at least 30 minutes. Shape into egg shapes and chill for another 30 minutes. Melt chocolate and wax in double boiler over hot but not boiling water. Dip eggs into chocolate. Cool on waxed paper.

Coconut Filling

¼ cup melted butter
1 (14-ounce) can sweetened
   condensed milk
1 (16-ounce) box powdered sugar

1 (14 or 16-ounce) package
   coconut
1 teaspoon vanilla or ½ teaspoon
   almond extract

Combine all ingredients and proceed with Easter Egg recipe.

Peanut Butter Filling

1½ cups peanut butter
½ cup margarine, melted

12 ounces powdered sugar

Add peanut butter to margarine. Add powdered sugar and mix well. Proceed with Easter Egg recipe.

CHRISTMAS TREE FUDGE

Yield: 2¼ pounds

2¼ cups sugar
¾ cup evaporated milk
⅓ cup light corn syrup
2 tablespoons butter
1 (12-ounce) package semi-sweet
   chocolate chips

1 teaspoon vanilla
1 cup chopped nuts, raisins
   or coconut
Gum drops
Miniature marshmallows

Combine sugar, milk, corn syrup and butter in pan. Bring to a boil, stirring constantly. Remove from heat. Add chocolate chips and vanilla and stir until smooth. Add nuts. Turn into greased Christmas tree pan. Decorate with thin strips of gum drops and miniature marshmallows.

Antoinette Figuers Pierce
(Mrs. Thomas M.)

CHRISTMAS CHOCOLATES

Yield: 5 pounds

Maple Cream Filling

3 (16-ounce) packages powdered
   sugar
1 (14-ounce) can sweetened
   condensed milk

1 cup butter
2 tablespoons maple flavoring
½ cup ground nuts, optional

Mix all ingredients together well. Chill overnight. Roll into small bite-size balls and dip with toothpick into melted chocolate mixture. Put onto cookie sheet to harden. Variation: Omit maple flavor, add orange extract.

Chocolate Dip

4 (1-ounce) squares unsweetened
   chocolate
4 (6-ounce) packages semi-sweet
   chocolate chips

¾ square paraffin

Melt chocolates and wax in double-boiler. Keep hot while dipping balls.

Linda Armstrong Andrews
(Mrs. Richard C.)

CHOCOLATE POTATO CHIPS

Yield: 1½ pounds

1 (14-ounce) bag potato chips
4 ounces bitter chocolate
1 (12-ounce) package semi-sweet
   chocolate chips

Square of paraffin wax
(2½ x 3¾-inches)

Melt all ingredients together in top of double-boiler. Stir well until smooth (may need to whisk a little). Keep mixture hot while dipping chips. Use tongs or fingers for dipping chips—shake excess off and rest on waxed paper. Redip for any spots not covered after chips have cooled. Store in tightly covered tin in a cool place.

The Committee

PUGHIE'S SEASONED SALT

3 pounds Kosher salt
3 pounds butcher grind pepper
½ pound monosodium glutamate

½ pound garlic powder
2 tablespoons paprika

Combine all the above ingredients thoroughly. Seal in tightly covered container. Repackage in attractive containers to give as gifts. Use this seasoning very liberally on chicken, pork or beef before broiling or baking.

Richard F. Pugh

CHAMPAGNE MUSTARD

Yield: 1¾ cups

⅔ cup dry mustard
1 cup sugar
3 eggs

⅔ cup champagne or white
   wine vinegar

In the top of a double-boiler, combine dry mustard and sugar. Beat in eggs and vinegar. Place over boiling water and stir for 6 to 8 minutes until slightly foamy and thickened. Do not freeze.

Carol Potter Day
(Mrs. Richard B.)

HONEY MUSTARD

Yield: 2 cups

2 cups dry white wine
1 cup finely chopped onion
2 cloves garlic, minced
1 (4-ounce) can dry mustard

2 tablespoons honey
1 tablespoon vegetable oil
2 teaspoons salt
3 to 4 drops hot pepper sauce

Combine wine, onion and garlic in a small pan. Heat to boiling and simmer 5 minutes. Set aside and cool. Strain mixture into dry mustard and return to pan stirring constantly until very smooth. Blend honey, oil, salt and hot pepper sauce and add to mustard. Heat slowly, stirring constantly, until mixture thickens. Cool and pour into non-metal containers. Cover and refrigerate at least 24 hours before serving.

Carol Potter Day
(Mrs. Richard B.)

VENDOR PRETZELS

Yield: 18 pretzels

1 envelope yeast
1½ cups warm water
2 tablespoons oil
1 tablespoon sugar

4 cups flour
1 teaspoon salt
2 eggs, beaten
Coarse salt

Dissolve yeast in warm water. Add oil, sugar, flour and salt. Knead on floured board until smooth. Divide into 18 pieces and roll into ropes. Form into desired shapes. Arrange on cookie sheets lined with foil. Brush pretzels with beaten eggs and sprinkle with coarse salt. Bake at 425 degrees 12 to 15 minutes.

Clay A. Bouton

STRAWBERRY BUTTER

Yield: 1½ cups

8 ounces cream cheese
4 ounces butter or margarine
½ to ¾ cup powdered sugar

1 teaspoon vanilla
8 large strawberries, mashed

Cream the cream cheese, butter, and the powdered sugar until light and fluffy. Add the vanilla and the strawberries and beat well to blend thoroughly. Serve with croissants or on wheat thins.

The Committee

BARNEY'S BEST BISCUITS

Yield: 26

3½ cups whole wheat flour
2½ cups rolled oats
3 tablespoons wheat germ
¼ cup instant nonfat dry milk
4 tablespoons rendered chicken
 fat or bacon grease

1 egg
1 cup pureed carrots or spinach
2 cups chicken or beef stock
1 teaspoon salt

Combine all the above ingredients thoroughly. The dough will be quite sticky. Turn dough out onto a heavily floured board and pat out to ¼-inch thickness. Cut with dog biscuit cutter and place on a greased cookie sheet. Prick with fork and bake in a 325-degree oven for 60 minutes. Cool on wire racks. Makes 26 dog biscuits 4½-inches long.

A baker's dozen for 2 of your favorite canines!

Carol Potter Day
(Mrs. Richard B.)

EASY PLAY CLAY

Yield: About 2 cups

1 cup flour
1 cup salt
1 tablespoon cream of tartar
1 tablespoon oil

1 cup water
Red or green food coloring
¼ teaspoon peppermint extract

Combine all ingredients in a saucepan over medium heat. Stir constantly for 3 to 5 minutes. Mixture will form a ball. When cool, knead until smooth. Keeps well in an airtight container.

The Committee

BARBEQUE SAUCE

Yield: 2 cups

2 tablespoons margarine
3 tablespoons chopped onion
½ cup chopped celery
4 tablespoons light brown
   sugar
2 tablespoons vinegar

1 tablespoon Worcestershire
   sauce
¼ cup lemon juice
1 cup catsup
1 teaspoon dry mustard
Hot pepper sauce, to taste

Melt butter and sauté onion and celery until tender. Add remaining ingredients, reduce heat and simmer 30 to 45 minutes, stirring frequently. A double recipe makes almost 1-quart of sauce which can be bottled, refrigerated, and given as gifts.

Annette Evans
(Mrs. Ronald)

MASTE BALLS

(Maste being the apple and spice pulp left after jelly-making)

¾ cup dried spices (use equal
   portions of the following
   spices to make up the ¾ cup)
Allspice, ground
Cinnamon, ground
Cloves, ground
Ginger, ground

Mace, ground
Nutmeg, ground
½ teaspoon powdered orris root
   (available at drugstore)
½ cup applesauce, canned
Whole cloves or small pieces
   of stick cinnamon

Combine the spices with the orris root, mix thoroughly until no white shows. Stir spices into applesauce until the bowl is dry. Divide mixture into 10 quarter-size or 20 dime-sized balls. Do not double recipe! Proceed as follows: cut thin ribbon or yarn into 18-inch lengths, fold in half and tie ends; insert small crochet hook down through the center of the maste ball, catch fold of ribbon and draw ribbon up through the ball; anchor ribbon with a whole clove or a piece of cinnamon; decorate with bows or strawflowers, if desired; and hang overnight to dry. If the balls crack or become too dry when making, rub with a bit of applesauce. These smell wonderul and took the place of pomander balls in Colonial days when oranges and lemons were not available. As the spicy smell fades, roughen the surface of the maste ball with an emery board to expose a new surface and freshen the scent.

The Committee

CHERRY LIQUEUR SALONIKA

Yield: Approximately 1½ gallons

5 pounds sweet cherries,
   unpitted
7½ cups sugar
3 sticks cinnamon

13 whole cloves
35 ounces inexpensive brandy
1 gallon glass jar with lid

Combine all the above ingredients except brandy in a glass jar with a tight fitting lid. Jar will be ¾ full. Place plastic wrap between the lid and the jar. Set the jar in the sun for 5 or 6 days, stirring each day. On the 6th or 7th day, add 1 cup of brandy and stir well. Stir daily. Every 4th day add 1 additional cup of brandy until all the brandy is used. Allow to remain in the sun for as long as possible (a month is the minimum time), stirring daily. The longer this remains in the sun, the better. When ready to bottle, strain and reserve the brandied cherries to use in desserts, over ice cream, etc.. The liqueur has magnificent color and superb taste.

Patricia Pugh Britt
(Mrs. Michael E.)

ORANGE LIQUEUR

Yield: 3 cups

Peel of 2 large oranges
1 cup water
1 cup light corn syrup
3 tablespoons dark corn syrup
⅓ cup sugar

3 teaspoons vanilla extract or
1 vanilla bean, split
¼ cup pure orange extract
2 cups vodka

Cut peel from oranges and put in a medium saucepan with water, corn syrups, sugar and vanilla. Bring to a boil and boil for 8 to 10 minutes, stirring occasionally. Remove from heat and stir in orange extract. When cool add vodka and pour into a jar with a tight fitting lid. Let stand 2 to 3 weeks before using.

Carol Potter Day
(Mrs. Richard B.)

VODKA COFFEE LIQUEUR

Yield: 6 cups

2½ cups sugar
12 teaspoons instant coffee
4 cups water

3 teaspoons vanilla
1 fifth vodka

Combine sugar, coffee and water. Bring to a boil. Reduce heat and simmer slowly uncovered for one hour. Let cool. Add three teaspoons vanilla extract (not imitation flavoring) and one fifth vodka. Pour into bottles. Keep tightly closed. Can be used immediately.

Lee Morse Edwards
(Mrs. Dwight H.)

FRUIT BRANDY

Serves: A lot!

⅓ cup water
1 cup sugar
1 quart vodka

**Fresh fruit, such as peaches,
oranges or pears**

Simmer sugar and water to soft ball stage. Pour this mixture into a large jar. Add vodka and mix. Pierce fruit with fork (three or four times) and place either two peaches, oranges or pears in jar. Seal tightly. Let stand 2 to 3 months. Remove and discard fruit before using. Makes an unusual Christmas hostess gift when put into smaller jars at the end of two to three months.

Jane Verwohlt Berry
(Mrs. John F.)

CRANBERRY CORDIAL

Yield: 2½ cups

1 (12-ounce) package fresh
  cranberries

2 cups sugar
1 cup vodka

Rinse cranberries and chop in blender in batches. Put in a large mixing bowl and stir in sugar. Spoon into a large jar, cover tightly, and store in a cool place for 6 to 8 weeks. Line a strainer with damp cheesecloth and place over a mixing bowl. Pour the mixture into the strainer, cover with plastic wrap and let it drip for at least 8 hours. Do not press or the liquid will be cloudy. Stir in vodka and pour in bottle. Serve plain or mixed with club soda.

Lee Morse Edwards
(Mrs. Dwight)

GINGERBREAD HOUSE

Yield: 1 house and yard

Cardboard for patterns
1 (16 x 16-inch) board (plywood,
  heavy cardboard or sturdy
  cookie sheet) to hold house
  and yard
Aluminum foil
3 (13-ounce) boxes gingerbread
  mix
Flour
Approximately 4 pounds
  powdered sugar

4 teaspoons cream of tartar
8 egg whites, at least
Colorful candies for trim: cut
  rock for tiling roof, starlight
  mints, tiny candy canes,
  gumdrops, red cinnamon dots.
  (Do not use chocolate candies)
Tiny ornaments for yard and
  house: wreaths, tiny trees,
  little skiers, birds, snowman
  (Use your imagination!)

Make cardboard patterns for house, as shown in illustration. Cover board with foil, secure with tape. Make gingerbread mix according to directions on package for rolled gingerbread cookies. (i.e. Add enough water to moisten mix.) Add more flour to make a good stiff dough. Grease cookie sheets well. Roll out big piece of dough to ¼-inch thick (no thinner). Put cardboard pattern over dough and cut around it with very sharp knife. Remember to cut out and bake doors and windows too. (The inside of window makes 2 shutters.) Carefully transfer pieces to cookie sheets and bake in 350 to 375 degree oven for 15 to 20 minutes, or until quite firm. Gently remove pieces from cookie sheet and cool on rack. Cut and bake remaining pieces for house. When ready to assemble house, make up 1 batch of "cement". (You will use all of 4 batches, but it hardens quickly, so make up only 1 batch at a time.)

"Cement" (One Batch)

2 egg whites   2½ cups powdered sugar
1 teaspoon cream of tartar

Using an electric mixer, beat egg whites to soft peaks. Add cream of tartar and powdered sugar. Continue beating for 7 minutes. Cover if not using immediately. Spread cement on the board in a rectangular patch that extends an inch beyond the size of your pieces. Spread cement along the bottom and along the adjoining upright edges of one front wall and one side wall. Set into cement patch firmly. (Be sure walls are set at right angles and *firm*.) Now add third and fourth walls, being sure to cement upright edges and bases. You can put in corner candy trims now. Also, with exterior walls standing, decorate interior of house if you want anything in there (children love to find something inside!) Be sure to put cement on anything you are fixing in place. You don't need to be neat when applying cement because it all looks like snow anyway. Let dry 20 minutes or until hardened. Now add roof and chimney. Spread cement on all top edges of walls. Now put on roof pieces, cementing along top edges where they meet. Run a line of bright candy across the roof peak. When roof pieces are set FIRMLY, set in chimney pieces. Decorate chimney and "tile" roof with cut rock candies. When house is completely decorated, do yard, finishing with candy cane fence around outer edges. Lay a path to front door with round candies and add all the little decorations you want. When house and yard are complete, sift powdered sugar over the entire creation for a "fresh snowfall!"

Bonnie Bonjean Dowling
(Mrs. Patrick)

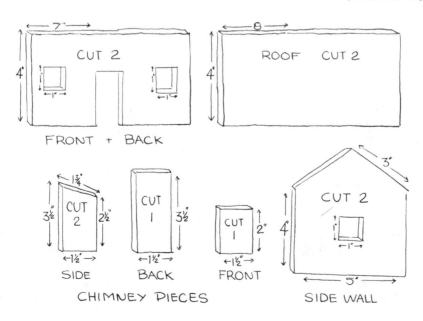

INDEX

A

Almond Tortoni Frenning 267
Anadama Bread 192
Angel Biscuits 195
Antipasto 42
Antojitos (Stuffed Tortillas) 42

Appetizers

Antipasto 42
Antojitos (Stuffed Tortillas) . . . 42
Artichoke Squares 40
Asparagus Canapés 40
Bacon Date Roll-ups 43
Baked Brie 49
Best Marinated Mushrooms
Ever 55
California Crispies 41
Cheese Bombay 50
Cheese Stuffed Mushrooms . . 54
Chestnut Bacon Rolls 58
Chili Con Queso 62
Chili Rellenos 43
Chinese Barbecued Spareribs . 52
Chinese Chicken Wings 52
Chinese Delights 53
Chocochip Paté . . . . . ., ... 58
Chopped Chicken Livers
Hollister 57
Cocktail Cauliflower 60
Cousin Molly's Pepper Jam . . . 47
Curried Cheese on Rye 49
Curry Dip for Raw Vegetables 59
Dolmathes (Stuffed Grapevine
Leaves) 46
Eggrolls 54
Fish Dip 61
Greek Zucchini 51
Green Pelican Cheese 50
Hot Artichoke Dip 62
Hot Crabmeat Dip 60
Hummus 62
Jalapeño Pepper Spread 47
Jane's Cheese Puffs 49
Liver Paté 57
Lobster Dip 61
Marinated Broccoli 51

Mini-Quiche Appetizers 41
Peach Melbas 45
Peanut Kisses 43
Pickled Pineapple 53
Poor Man's Salmon Mousse . . 47
Potted Shrimp 60
Russian Chicken Livers 56
Salmon Party Log 44
Salty Topaz 270
Smoked Oyster Dip 61
Spicy Cheese Twists 48
Stuffed Mushrooms 55
Surprise Dip 58
Sweet and Sour Meatballs 44
Three Cheese Squares 48
Treasure Bits 45
Vegetable Platter 59
Youngstown Club Cheese 50
Apple Knobby Cake 240

Apricot

Apricot Bars 221
Apricot Brandy Poundcake . . . 243
Apricot Bread 198
Apricot-Glazed Chicken
Breasts 148
Apricot Sauce for Lamb 187
Art's Elegant Potato Soup 74

Artichoke

Artichoke and Spinach
Casserole 108
Artichoke Pimento Salad 85
Artichoke Squares 40
Hot Artichoke Dip 62

Asparagus

Asparagus Au Naturel 109
Asparagus Canapés 40
Asparagus-Cauliflower Au
Gratin 109
Asparagus Parmesan 108
Cream of Asparagus Soup 65
Athenian Lamb 185
Austrian Ham Strudels 98
Avocado Soup 65

B

Bacon Date Roll-ups 43
Baked Acorn Squash 127
Baked Beans 110
Baked Blueberry Topping for
   Cheesecake 267
Baked Brie 49
Baked Crab 140
Baked Haddock 141
Baked Haddock with Crabmeat .146
Baked Haddock with
   Curry Sauce 146
Baked Pineapple 106
Baked Pumpkin 123
Baked Stuffed Potatoes 122
Baked Swordfish and
   Mushrooms 144
Baked Vegetable Casserole 131
Bakie's Pecan Pie 235
Baklava 255
Banana Split Dessert 266
Barbara's Apple Cake 248
Barbecue Sauce 283
Barney's Best Biscuits 282
Bartender's Rum Collins 34
Bavarian Apple Torte 250
Beacon Hill Cookies 210

Beans

Baked Beans 110
Bean Salad 90
Dilled Green Beans 110
Green Beans Clarion 111
Italian Style String Beans 111
Party Casserole 128
Scandanavian Baked Beans ...110

Beef

Beef Birds 173
Beef in Sour Cream 171
Beef Rouladen 167
Chinese Beef and Radishes ...173
Chinese Curried Beef 169
Cold Filet of Beef with Sour
   Cream Filling 167
Contrefilet 168
Foolproof Roast Beef 166

Hobo Steak 169
Louisiana Beef Stew 178
New England Boiled Dinner ..170
Marinade for Beef 187
Perked Pot Roast 172
Pot Roast Autrichienne 171
Pot Roast Indienne 172
Ruth Howard's Boeuf
   Bourguignon 166
Teriyaki Steak 168

Beef, Ground

Cheese Meat Loaf 176
Chili 178
Grandmother Muskie's Polish
   Meatloaf 174
Italian Meat Pie 176
"Joe's" Yummy Special 177
Lasagna Alla Carola 174
Layered Meat Loaf 175
Matchless Meat Loaf 175
Nasty Nacho Casserole 177

Beets

Beets in Orange Sauce 112
Pickled Beets 112
Belgian Carrots 115
Bengal Chicken Curry 150
Best Marinated Mushrooms
   Ever 55

Beverages

Bartender's Rum Collins 34
Bloody Mary Mix 34
Brandied Champagne Punch .. 35
Champagne Punch 36
Cherry Liqueur Salonika 284
Cranberry Cordial 285
Cranberry Damsel 33
Egg Nog 37
Father Kerr's Christmas Punch 34
Fish House Punch 36
Fruit Brandy 285
Goombay Smash 33
Lemon Coconut Cooler 32
Magic Morning Surprise 32
Morning Cup 33
Mulled Wine 35

Orange Liqueur 284
Party Punch 37
Peach Fuzzies 32
Plaza Suite 32
Russian Tea 38
Sparkling Rum Fruit Punch . . . 36
Strawberry Wine Slush 37
Twenty-Four Hour Cocktail . . 35
Vodka Coffee Liqueur 285
Yarmouth Spiced Tea 38
Blender Bérnaise Sauce 188
Blender Hollandaise Sauce 132
Bloody Mary Mix 34
Blue Ribbon Brownies 221
Blueberry
Baked Blueberry Topping for
Cheesecake 267
Blueberries Aragonaise 106
Blueberry-Corn Cakes 96
Blueberry Drop Cookies 210
Blueberry Mousse 261
Blueberry Shaker Pudding . . . 261
Blueberry Sour Cream Cake . 242
Deb's Blueberry Buckle 264
Old Fashioned Blueberry
Cake 236
Portland Country Club's
Blueberry Cake 205
Special Blueberry Muffins 206
Bohemian Vegetable Soup
(Cream) 75
Brandied Champagne Punch 35
Bread and Butter Pickles 271
Breads
Biscuits
Angel Biscuits 195
Barney's Best Biscuits 282
Sausage Biscuits 104
Breads
Anadama Bread 192
Apricot Bread 198
Bulgur Yeast Bread 192
Carrot Bread 200
Corn Bread 197
Fruited Eggnog Bread 202
Gram's Date and Nut Bread 201

Maine Potato Bread 194
No-Fail Whole Wheat Bread 191
Oatmeal-Sesame Bread 195
Orange French Toast 101
Popovers 205
Poppy Seed Tea Bread 202
Pumpkin Bread 199
Refrigerator-Rise Oatmeal
Bread 190
Russian Black Bread 193
Shredded Wheat Bread 190
Spider Corn Cake 198
Strawberry Nut Bread 201
Zucchini Bread 200
Coffeecakes
Christmas Cranberry Cake . 204
Danish Coffee Cake 204
Lemon Tea Cake 203
Portland Country Club's
Blueberry Cake 205
Rhubarb Coffee Cake 203
Muffins
Date Bran Muffins 206
French Donut Muffins 207
Special Blueberry Muffins . . 206
Pancakes
Blueberry-Corn Cakes 96
Pancakes Allemagne 101
Rolls
Cinnamon Crescents 207
Ellen's Herbert Hotel Rolls . 196
Kingfield Whole Wheat
Rolls 197
Willa Allen Dowling's
Cinnamon Twists 208
Breakfast Soufflé 97
Britt's Holiday Pudding 260
Broccoli
Broccoli and Bleu Cheese 112
Broccoli Deluxe 113
Broccoli Surprise 113
Crazy Quiche 103
Tania's Broccoli Salad 84
Brownie Pudding 262

Brunch
Austrian Ham Strudels 98
Baked Pineapple 106
Blueberries Aragonaise 106
Blueberry-Corn Cakes .. 96
Breakfast Soufflé 97
Chicken Livers and Mushrooms
  in Madeira Sauce 95
Chicken Mushroom Crepes with
  Mock Mornay Sauce 94
Christmas Breakfast 99
Christmas Sausage 105
Crab Open-Faced Sandwiches 100
Crazy Quiche 103
Eggs-A-Plenty 98
Eggs Augenstein 96
Favorite Quiche 102
Fruit Compote 105
Grilled Apple Sandwiches 100
Kelsey's Christening Brunch .. 99
Nana Carey's Nutmeg Sauce ..106
Oeufs Avec Crabe 97
Orange French Toast 101
Pancakes Allemagne 101
Party Salad Loaf 101
Sausage Biscuits 105
Spinach Pie 102
Spinach Quiche 103
Tomato Pie 104
Brunswick Stew 160
Brussels Sprouts
Herbed Brussels Sprouts 114
Bulgur Yeast Bread 192
Butterscotch Sauce 268

C

Cabbage
Stuffed Cabbage À La
  Moosewood 114
Zesty Slaw 87
Caesar Salad 86
Cakes
Apple Knobby Cake 240
Apricot Brandy Poundcake ...243
Barbara's Apple Cake 248
Blueberry Sour Cream Cake .242
Candied Fruit Cake 249

Carrot Cake 243
Cassata Torte 237
Chocolate Apple Walnut Cake .244
Chocolate Zucchini Cake 245
Fresh Apple Pound Cake 248
Hundred Dollar Chocolate
  Cake 245
McLellan Cake 237
Marie's Oatmeal Cake 240
Marion Beeson's Party Cake .247
Old Fashioned Blueberry
  Cake 236
Old French Fruit Pound Cake .250
Orange Cake 246
Orange Ring Cake 246
Perfect Pound Cake 253
Portland Country Club
  Blueberry Cake 205
Prune Cake 249
Pumpkin Cake Roll 247
Queen Elizabeth Cake 251
Reine De Saba 241
Serendipity Cake 242
Sour Cream Chocolate Chip
  Cake 236
Vi's Moist Coconut Cake 251
California Crispies 40
Canadian Split Pea Soup 67
Candied Fruit Cake 249
Candy
Chocolate Potato Chips 280
Christmas Chocolates 279
Christmas Tree Fudge 278
Easter Eggs 278
Failproof Chocolate Fudge ...276
Nana's Chocolate Fudge 276
Needhams 277
Peanut Butter Cups 275
Penuchi Fudge 276
Thelma's Ginger Fudge 277
Cape Shore Lobster Bake 134
Caponata Alla Siciliana 118
Carrots
Belgian Carrots 115
Carrot Bread 200
Carrot Cake 243

Glazed Carrots 116
Golden Carrots 115
Purée of Carrot Soup 68
Cassata Torte 237
Cathedral Windows 227
Cauliflower
Asparagus-Cauliflower Au
Gratin 109
Cocktail Cauliflower 60
Cauliflower Soufflé 116
Celery Seed Dressing 90
Champagne
Champagne Mold 80
Champagne Mustard 280
Champagne Punch 36
Cheese
Breakfast Soufflé 97
Cheddar Cheese Soup 72
Cheddar Spinach Salad 89
Cheese Bombay 50
Cheese Dressing 91
Cheese Meat Loaf 176
Cheese Stuffed Mushrooms . . 54
Cheesecake Bars 223
Cherry Jubilee Ring 82
Cherry Liqueur Salonika 284
Chestnut Bacon Rolls 58
Chicken
Apricot-Glazed Chicken
Breasts 148
Bengal Chicken Curry 150
Brunswick Stew 160
Chicken Boursin 151
Chicken Breasts and
Mushrooms in
Madeira Sauce 148
Chicken Breasts Vautier 153
Chicken Broccoli Casserole . . 152
Chicken Chablis 152
Chicken Curry 150
Chicken Cutlets in Vermouth
Sauce 149
Chicken Dijon 158
Chicken Divan 151
Chicken Florentine 153
Chicken Geraldine 155

Chicken in Puff Pastry 154
Chicken L'Indienne 157
Chicken Livers and
Mushrooms in
Madeira Sauce 95
Chicken Marsala 154
Chicken Mushroom Crêpes
with Mock Mornay Sauce . . 94
Chicken and Corned Beef 149
Chicken Pie Foie Gras 160
Chicken Vegetable Pilaf 155
Citrus Chicken 156
Curried Chicken a L'orange . . . 157
Italian Boneless Chicken 158
Mexico City Tamale Pie 162
Murgh Masallam (Indian
Chicken with Rice) 163
Oriental Chicken 159
Penny's Chicken Breasts 156
Piquant Chicken 159
White Lasagna 161
Chili 178
Chili Con Queso 62
Chili Rellenos 43
Chinese Almond Cookies 218
Chinese Barbecued Spareribs . . . 52
Chinese Beef and Radishes 173
Chinese Chicken Wings 52
Chinese Curried Beef 169
Chinese Delights 53
Chocochip Paté 58
Chocolate Apple Walnut Cake . . 244
Chocolate Cheesecake 254
Chocolate Coconut Cookies 210
Chocolate Hungarian Torte 239
Chocolate Mousse 264
Chocolate Potato Chips 280
Chocolate Ripple Cheesecake . . . 253
Chocolate Zucchini Cake 245
Chopped Chicken Livers
Hollister 57
Christmas
Christmas Breakfast 98
Christmas Chocolates 279
Christmas Cranberry Cake . . . 204
Christmas Sausage 105

Christmas Tree Fudge 278
Cinnamon Crescents 207
Citrus Chicken 156
Clams
   Clam Fritters 138
   Maine Sea Burger 143
   Pantry Clam Chowder 71
Clarke's Corn and Cheddar
   Cheese Chowder 73
Cocktail Cauliflower 60
Coconut Butter Balls 218
Coconut Crisps 211
Cold Cucumber Soup 64
Cold Filet of Beef with Sour
   Cream Filling 167
Contrefilet 168
Cookies
   Apricot Bars 221
   Beacon Hill Cookies 210
   Blue Ribbon Brownies 221
   Blueberry Drop Cookies 210
   Cathedral Windows 227
   Cheese Cake Bars 223
   Chinese Almond Cookies 218
   Chocolate Coconut Cookies .. 210
   Coconut Butter Balls 218
   Coconut Crisps 211
   Crunchy Chip Cookies 211
   Crunchy Fudge "Sinwiches" ..228
   Finnish Sour Cream Rings ...220
   French Ginger Molasses
     Cookies 219
   Frosted Almond Cookies 219
   Frosted Coffee Bars 224
   Frosted Praline Bars 227
   German Chocolate Bars 226
   Gingerbread House 286
   Gretchen's Soft Ginger
     Coffee Cookies 212
   Henry Bars 223
   Holiday Billy Goats 212
   Hope's Apple Squares 224
   Lemon Bonbon Cookies 217
   Lemon Lovenotes 222
   Lemon Zucchini Cookies 213

McGinty Cookies 213
Meringue Cookies 214
Oatmeal Cookies 214
Peanut Butter Roundups 215
Pecan Crisps 216
Pumpkin Cookies 215
Rocks 217
Rum Balls 275
Sir Walter Raleighs 228
Southern Spice Cookies 218
Spiked Chocolate Squares 225
Thumb Cookies 216
Tollhouse Brownies 222
Whoopie Pies 220
Coquille St. Jacques 142
Corn
   Clarke's Corn and Cheddar
     Cheese Chowder 73
   Corn Bread 197
   Corn Cakes 117
   Corn Chowder 73
   Spider Corn Cake 198
Corn Chowder 73
Cousin Molly's Pepper Jam 47
Crab
   Baked Crab 140
   Crab Open-Faced Sandwiches 100
   "Crocked" and Sherried Crab . 140
   Oeufs Avec Crabe 97
Cranberry
   Cranberry Cordial 285
   Cranberry Damsel 33
   Cranberry Rosé Soup 64
   Cranberry Salad 83
   Cranberry Surprise Pie 235
Crazy Quiche 103
Cream of Asparagus Soup 65
Creme De Menthe Pie 233
Crepes
   Chicken Mushroom Crepes
     with Mock Mornay Sauce .. 94
Crispy Cucumber Pickles 271
"Crocked" and Sherried Crab ...140
Crunchy Chip Cookies 211
Crunchy Fudge "Sinwiches" 228

INDEX

I N D E X

Cucumber Ring Supreme 78
Cumberland Sauce 188
Curried Cheese on Rye 49
Curried Chicken A L'Orange 157
Curry Dip for Raw Vegetables .. 59

D

Danish Coffee Cake 204
Danish Stuffing 164
Date Bran Muffins 206
Deb's Blueberry Buckle 264
Delicious Molded Fruit Salad ... 80

Desserts *(See Also Cakes,*
Candies, Cookies and Pies)
  Almond Tortoni Frenning 267
  Baklava 255
  Banana Split Dessert 266
  Bavarian Apple Torte 250
  Blueberry Mousse 261
  Chocolate Cheesecake 254
  Chocolate Hungarian Torte ...239
  Chocolate Mousse 264
  Chocolate Ripple Cheesecake .253
  Deb's Blueberry Buckle 264
  French Chocolate Nut Soufflé .258
  Galactoburiko (Custard Filled
      Diamonds) 256
  Gingerbread House 286
  Great Vanilla Ice Cream 258
  Guy's Cheesecake with
      Strawberry Glaze 252
  Kela Ka Rayta 265
  Lime Soufflé 259
  Marshmallow Mint Fidelio ...262
  Mount Katahdin 257
  New York Cheesecake 252
  Orange Soufflé 259
  Oranges Supreme 265
  Pie in a Pan 266
  Pots de Creme 263
  Rhubarb Torte 238
  Sour Cream Brulée 261
  Strawberry Blitz Torte 257
  Strudel 238
  Vanilla Almond Crunch 254
  White Wine Sherbet 263

Dilled Green Beans 110
Dolmathes 46
Dutch Salad 272

E

Easter Eggs 278
Easy Play Clay 282
Eggplant
  Caponata Alla Siciliana 118
  Moussaka 184
  Ratatouille with Sausage 182
  Vegetable Stuffed Eggplant ...117
Eggrolls 54

Eggs
  Christmas Breakfast 99
  Eggs-A-Plenty 98
  Eggs Augenstein 96
  Egg Nog 37
  Kelsey's Christening Brunch .. 99
  Mushroom Roulades 119
  Oeufs Avec Crabe 97
Ellen's Herbert Hotel Rolls 196
Escarole Navonna 118

F

Failproof Chocolate Fudge 276
Father Kerr's Christmas Punch . 34
Favorite Quiche 102
Finnish Sour Cream Rings 220
Fish House Punch 36

Fish
  Baked Haddock 141
  Baked Haddock with
      Crabmeat 146
  Baked Haddock with Curry
      Sauce 146
  Baked Swordfish and
      Mushrooms 144
  Filet of Sole with Crabmeat ..145
  Filet of Sole Rive Gauche 144
  Fish Chowder 71
  Fish Dip 61
  Fishmonger's Kettle 70
  Fiskebollar I Saus 139
  Lemony Baked Stuffed
      Halibut Steaks 143
  Viennese Fish 145

Filet of Sole with Crabmeat 145
Filet of Sole Rive Gauche 144
Fiskelbollar I Saus 139
Foolproof Roast Beef 166
Four Star Hot Fudge Sauce 267
French Chocolate Nut Soufflé ... 258
French Coconut Pie 235
French Doughnut Muffins 207
French Ginger Molasses
    Cookies 219
Fresh Apple Pound Cake 248
Fresh Strawberry Pie 232
Fried Rice 125
Frosted Almond Cookies 219
Frosted Coffee Bars 224
Frosted Praline Bars 227
Frozen Chocolate Walnut Pie ... 234
Frozen Fruit Salad 79
Frozen Lime Mint Salad 83
Frozen Pumpkin Pie 234
Fruit Brandy 285
Fruit Compote 105
Fruited Eggnog Bread 202
Fudge Ribbon Pie 233
Fudge Sauce 268

G

Galactoburiko (Custard Filled
    Diamonds) 256
German Chocolate Bars 226
Gingerbread House 286
Gingered Rhubarb Jam 275
Glazed Carrots 116
Golden Carrots 115
Goombay Smash 33
Gram's Date and Nut Bread 201
Grandmother Muskie's Polish
    Meatloaf 174
Grandmother Olson's French
    Dressing 92
Great Vanilla Ice Cream 258
Greek Zucchini 51
Green Beans Clarion 111
Green Pelican Cheese 50
Green Pepper Jelly 273
Green Tomato Relish 274

Gretchen's Soft Ginger Coffee
    Cookies 212
Grilled Apple Sandwiches 100
Guy's Cheesecake with
    Strawberry Glaze 252

H

Ham
    Austrian Ham Strudels 98
    Breakfast Soufflé 97
Harvest Apple Pie 230
Henry Bars 223
Herbed Brussels Sprouts 114
Herbed Potatoes 121
Hobo Steak 169
Holiday Billy Goats 212
Holiday Mashed Potatoes 122
Hope's Apple Squares 224
Hot Artichoke Dip 62
Hot Crabmeat Dip 60
Hot Cranberry-Raisin Sauce 187
Hummus 62
Hundred Dollar Chocolate Cake . 245

I

Indian Fried Shrimp 138
Indian Pudding 263
Inebriated Pork 180
Italian Boneless Chicken 158
Italian Meat Pie 176
Italian Stuffed Zucchini 130
Italian Style String Beans 111

J

Jalapeño Pepper Spread 47

Jam
    Gingered Rhubarb Jam 275
    Rose Hip Jam 274
Jane's Cheese Puffs 49

Jelly
    Green Pepper Jelly 273
    Parsleyed Vermouth Jelly ... 274
"Joe's" Yummy Special 177
Julienne of Parsnip and Leek ... 120

K

Kela Ka Rayta 265
Kelsey's Christening Brunch 99
Key Lime Pie 231

I N D E X

Kingfield Whole Wheat Rolls 197
Korean Salad 85

L

Lamb
Apricot Sauce for Lamb 187
Athenian Lamb 185
Lamb Curry 185
Moussaka 184
Lamb Shanks in Red Wine 186
Lasagna Alla Carola 174
Layered Meat Loaf 175

Lemon
Lemon Bonbon Cookies 217
Lemon Coconut Cooler 32
Lemon Lovenotes 222
Lemon Tea Cake 203
Lemon-Zucchini Cookies 213
Lemony Baked Stuffed Halibut
Steaks 143
Lentil Soup 74
Lime Soufflé 259

Liqueur
Cherry Liqueur Salonika 284
Cranberry Cordial 285
Orange Liqueur 284
Vodka Coffee Liqueur 285
Liver Paté 57

Lobster
Cape Shore Lobster Bake 134
Lobster Dip 61
Lobster Newburg 135
Pasta with Lobster and
Shrimp 136
Scalloped Lobster 135
Louisiana Beef Stew 178

M

Macadamia Nut Pie 232
Magic Morning Surprise 32
Maine Potato Bread 194
Maine Sea Burger 143
Marce's Scalloped Oysters 141
Marge's Bleu Cheese Dressing . 90
Maria's Squash Casserole 126
Marie's Oatmeal Cake 240
Marinade for Beef 187

Marinated Broccoli 51
Marion Beeson's Party Cake . . . 247
Marshmallow Mint Fidello 262
Maste Balls 283
Matchless Meat Loaf 175
McLellan Cake 237
McGinty Cookies 213
Melon Balls with Rum Lime
Sauce 78

Menus
After the Game Dinner 26
Anniversary Party Buffet 18
Before the Hockey Game
Supper 8
Bridal Shower 17
Cape Shore Lobster Bake 25
Christmas Dinner 29
Christmas Party 30
Cocktails for 24—A Double
Dozen 19
Cross Country Ski Dinner 7
Cupid's Choice 13
Eighteenth Century Tavern
Dinner 9
Engagement Champagne
Buffet 14
Fireside Dinner 10
Graduation Dinner 16
Greek Dinner 10
Harvest Dinner 27
Holiday Family Brunch 28
Independence Day Dinner . . . 21
Italian Dinner 11
Jubilee Dinner 20
Midnight Buffet After the
Symphony 12
New Year's Eve Gala 6
Opening Night Buffet 12
Patio Supper 24
Rehearsal Dinner 14
Special Occasion Dinner 16
Spring Fever or Easter Brunch 15
Summer Brunch 22
Summer Luncheon 22
Super Bowl Party 6

Supper After the Monhegan
  Race 23
Meringue Cookies 214
Mexican Chef Salad 89
Mexico City Tamale Pie 162
Mom's Eggnog Sauce 268
Mom's German Potato Salad 87
Morning Cup 33
Mount Kafahdin 257
Moussaka 184
Mud Pie 236
Mulled Wine 35
Murgh Masallam (Indian
  Chicken with Rice) 163

Mushrooms
  Best Marinated Mushrooms
    Ever 55
  Cheese Stuffed Mushrooms .. 54
  Chicken Mushroom Crepes
    with Mock Mornay Sauce .. 94
  Mushroom Chowder 68
  Mushroom Roulades 119
  Mushroom Soufflé 119
  Rice and Pecan Casserole 124
  Stuffed Mushrooms 55
Mustard, Honey..............281
Mustard Ring 82

N
Nana Carey's Nutmeg Sauce 106
Nana's Chocolate Fudge 276
Nasty Nacho Casserole 177
Needhams 277
New England Boiled Dinner 170
New Orleans Salad Dressing ... 91
New York Cheesecake 252
No-Fail Whole Wheat Bread 191
Nuts
  Salty Topaz 270
  Spiced Nuts 270
  Sugared Nuts 270

O
Oatmeal Cookies 214
Oatmeal-Sesame Bread 195
Oeufs Avec Crabe 97
Old Fashioned Blueberry Cake ..236
Old French Fruit Pound Cake ...250

Onions
  Julienne of Parsnip and Leek .120
  Onions Au Gratin 120
  Soupe A L'oignon Gratineé ... 66
Orange
  Orange Cake 246
  Orange French Toast 101
  Orange Liqueur 284
  Orange Pineapple Delight 81
  Orange Ring Cake 246
  Orange Soufflé 259
  Oranges Supreme 265
Oriental Chicken 159

P
Pancake Allemagne 101
Pantry Clam Chowder 71
Parsleyed Vermouth Jelly 274
Parsnips
  Candied Parsnips 121
  Julienne of Parsnips and Leek .120
  Parsnip Chowder 70
Party Casserole 128
Party Punch 37
Party Salad Loaf 101
Pasta with Lobster and Shrimp ..136
Peach Fuzzies 32
Peach Melba 45
Peanut Butter Cups 275
Peanut Butter Pie 230
Peanut Butter Roundups 215
Peanut Kisses 43
Pecan Crisps 216
Penny's Chicken Breasts 156
Penuchi Fudge 276
Perfect Pound Cake 253
Perked Pot Roast 172
Pickled Beets 112
Pickled Pineapple 53

Pickles
  Bread and Butter Pickles 271
  Crispy Cucumber Pickles 271
  Sherried Peppers 271
  Summer Squash Pickle 273
Pies
  Bakie's Pecan Pie 235

I N D E X

Cranberry Surprise Pie 235
Creme De Menthe Pie 233
French Coconut Pie 235
Fresh Strawberry Pie 232
Frozen Chocolate Walnut Pie .234
Frozen Pumpkin Pie 234
Fudge Ribbon Pie 233
Harvest Apple Pie 230
Key Lime Pie 231
Macadamia Nut Pie 232
Mud Pie 236
Peanut Butter Pie 230
Pie in a Pan 266
Sour Cream Custard
   Apple Pie 231
Pineapple
Baked Pineapple 106
Pickled Pineapple 53
Piquant Chicken 159
Plaza Suite 32
Plum Pudding 260
Polynesian Pork 180
Poor Man's Salmon Mousse 47
Popovers 205
Poppy Seed Tea Bread 202
Pork
Austrian Ham Strudels 98
Christmas Sausage 105
Escarole Navonna 118
Inebriated Pork 180
Polynesian Pork 180
Pork Chops with Orange
   Sauce 181
Pork Tenderloin for Two 179
Rice Giralda 125
Sausage Biscuits 124
Sweet Irene's Ham Loaf 181
Portland Country Club's
   Blueberry Cake 205
Pot Roast Autrichienne 171
Pot Roast Indienne 172
Potatoes
Art's Elegant Potato Soup 74
Baked Stuffed Potatoes 122
Herbed Potatoes 121
Holiday Mashed Potatoes 122

Mom's German Potato Salad .. 87
Potatoes O'Brien 121
Potted Shrimp 60
Pots de Creme 263
Puddings
Blueberry Shaker Pudding ...261
Britt's Holiday Pudding 260
Brownie Pudding 262
Indian Pudding 263
Pecan Pudding 262
Plum Pudding 260
Yorkshire Pudding 132
Prune Cake 249
Pughie's Seasoned Salt 280
Pumpkin
Baked Pumpkin 123
Pumpkin Bread 199
Pumpkin Cake Roll 247
Pumpkin Cookies 215
Purée of Carrot Soup 68

Q
Queen Elizabeth Cake 251
Quiche
Crazy Quiche 103
Favorite Quiche 102
Spinach Pie 102
Spinach Quiche 103
Tomato Pie 104

R
Ratatouille with Sausage 182
Refrigerator-Rise Oatmeal
   Bread 190
Reine De Saba 241
Rhubarb Coffee Cake 203
Rhubarb Torte 238
Relishes
Dutch Salad 272
Green Tomato Relish 274
Tomato Marmalade 273
Zucchini Relish 272
Rice
Rice and Pecan Casserole 124
Fried Rice 125
Rice Giralda 125
Rice Supreme 124

298

Rocks 217
Roquefort Salad Dressing 91
Rose Hip Jam 274
Rum Balls 275
Russian Black Bread 193
Russian Chicken Livers 56
Russian Tea 38
Ruth Howard's Boeuf
    Bourguignon 166

S

Saint Nick Salad Ring 81
Salad
    Artichoke Pimento Salad 85
    Bean Salad 90
    Caesar Salad 86
    Champagne Mold 80
    Cheddar Spinach Salad 89
    Cherry Jubilee Ring 82
    Cranberry Salad 83
    Cucumber Ring Supreme 78
    Delicious Molded Fruit Salad . 80
    Frozen Fruit Salad 79
    Frozen Lime Mint Salad 83
    Korean Salad 85
    Melon Balls with Rum Lime
        Sauce 78
    Mexican Chef Salad 89
    Mom's German Potato Salad . . 87
    Mustard Ring 82
    Orange Pineapple Delight 81
    Saint Nick Salad Ring 81
    Seven Layer Salad 86
    Shrimp Salade Bombay 84
    Spinach and Bleu Cheese Salad 88
    Tabbouleh 88
    Tania's Broccoli Salad 84
    Wine Jelly Ring with Seedless
        Grapes 79
    Zesty Slaw 87
Salad Dressings
    Celery Seed Dressing 90
    Cheese Dressing 91
    Grandmother Olson's French
        Dressing 92
    Marge's Bleu Cheese Dressing 90
    New Orleans Salad Dressing . 91

Roquefort Salad Dressing 91
Vinaigrette Dressing 92
Vinaigrette Dressing Supreme 92
Salmon Chowder 72
Salmon Party Log 44
Salty Topaz 270
Sandwiches
    Crab Open-Faced Sandwiches 101
    Grilled Apple Sandwiches 100
    Party Salad Loaf 101
Saturday Night Soup 75
Sauces
    Apricot Sauce for Lamb 187
    Barbecue Sauce 283
    Blender Bérnaise Sauce 188
    Blender Hollandaise Sauce . . . 132
    Butterscotch Sauce 268
    Cumberland Sauce 188
    Four Star Hot Fudge Sauce . . 267
    Fudge Sauce 268
    Hot Cranberry-Raisin Sauce . . 187
    Mom's Eggnog Sauce 268
    Nana Carey's Nutmeg Sauce . . 106
Sauerkraut Bake 126
Sausage Biscuits 104
Savory Minestrone 66
Scalloped Lobster 135
Scallops
    Coquille St. Jacques 142
    Scallops with Vermouth 141
Scandanavian Baked Beans 110
Seafood (See Clams, Crab, Fish,
Lobster, Scallops & Shrimp)
Serendipity Cake 242
Seven Layer Salad 86
Sherried Peppers 271
Sherry Shrimp 139
Shredded Wheat Bread 190
Shrimp
    Indian Fried Shrimp 138
    Sherry Shrimp 139
    Shrimp Pentagon 137
    Shrimp Salade Bombay 84
    Sweet and Pungent Shrimp . . . 137
Sir Walter Raleighs 228
Smoked Oyster Dip 61

Soups

Art's Elegant Potato Soup 74
Avocado Soup 65
Bohemian Vegetable Soup
    (Cream) 75
Canadian Split Pea Soup 67
Cheddar Cheese Soup 72
Clarke's Corn and Cheddar
    Cheese Chowder 73
Cold Cucumber Soup 64
Corn Chowder 73
Cranberry Rosé Soup 64
Cream of Asparagus Soup 65
Fish Chowder 71
Fishmonger's Kettle 70
Lentil Soup 74
Mushroom Chowder 68
Pantry Clam Chowder 71
Parsnip Chowder 70
Purée of Carrot Soup 68
Salmon Chowder 72
Saturday Night Soup 75
Savory Minestrone 66
Soupe AL'oignon Gratinée 66
Soupe Aux Cerises 65
Soupe Provence 69
Squash Soup 76
Vegetable Soup Nivernaise ... 67
Winter Wooly Soup 76
Zucchini Soup with Sausage .. 69
Sour Cream Brulée 261
Sour Cream-Chocolate
    Chip Cake 236
Sour Cream Custard Apple Pie ..231
Southern Spice Cookies 218
Sparkling Rum Fruit Punch 36
Special Blueberry Muffins 206
Spiced Nuts 270
Spicy Cheese Twists 48
Spider Corn Cake 198
Spiked Chocolate Squares 225

Spinach

Artichoke and Spinach
    Casserole 108
Cheddar Spinach Salad 89

"Joe's" Yummy Special 177
Korean Salad 85
Spinach and Bleu Cheese
    Salad 88
Spinach and Cheese
    Casserole 127
Spinach Casserole 126
Spinach Pie 102
Spinach Quiche 103
Tomatoes with Spinach
    Mornay 128

Spreads

Champagne Mustard 280
Honey Mustard 281
Strawberry Butter 281

Squash

Baked Acorn Squash 127
Maria's Squash Casserole 126
Squash Soup 76

Strawberry

Strawberry Blitz Torte 257
Strawberry Butter 281
Strawberry Nut Bread 201
Strawberry Wine Slush 37
Strudel 238
Stuffed Cabbage A La
    Moosewood 114
Stuffed Mushrooms 55

Stuffing

Danish Stuffing 164
Vegetable Stuffing 164
Sugared Nuts 270
Summer Squash Pickles 273
Surprise Dip 58
Sweet and Pungent Shrimp 137
Sweet and Sour Meatballs 44
Sweet and Sour Zucchini 131
Sweet Irene's Ham Loaf 181
Sweet Potato Soufflé 130

T

Tabbouleh 88
Tania's Broccoli Salad 84
Teriyaki Steak 168

Thelma's Ginger Fudge 277
Three Cheese Squares 48
Thumb Cookies 216
Tollhouse Brownies 222
Tomato
   Tomato Bleu Cheese Timbale . 129
   Tomato Marmalade 273
   Tomato Pie 104
   Tomatoes with Spinach
      Mornay 128
Treasure Bits 45
Twenty-Four Hour Cocktails . . . 35
V
Vanilla Almond Crunch 254
Veal
   Veal and Mushrooms with
      Madeira Sauce 182
   Veal Cutlets Foyot 184
   Veal Ragout 183
   Veal Scallopine with Cheese . . 183
Vegetables *(See Also Individual
Listings)*
Vegetables
   Artichoke and Spinach
      Casserole 108
   Asparagus Au Naturel 109
   Asparagus-Cauliflower Au
      Gratin 109
   Asparagus Parmesan 108
   Baked Acorn Squash 127
   Baked Beans 110
   Baked Pumpkin 123
   Baked Stuffed Potatoes 122
   Baked Vegetable Casserole . . . 131
   Beets in Orange Sauce 112
   Belgian Carrots 115
   Broccoli and Bleu Cheese 112
   Broccoli Deluxe 113
   Broccoli Surprise 113
   Candied Parsnips 121
   Caponata Alla Sicilianna 118
   Cauliflower Souffle 116
   Corn Cakes 117
   Dilled Green Beans 110
   Escarole Navonna 118

Fried Rice 125
Glazed Carrots 116
Golden Carrots 115
Green Beans Clarion 111
Herbed Brussel Sprouts 114
Herbed Potatoes 121
Holiday Mashed Potatoes 122
Italian Stuffed Zucchini 130
Italian Style String Beans 111
Julienne of Parsnip and Leek . 120
Maria's Squash Casserole 126
Mushrooms Roulades 119
Mushroom Soufflé 119
Onions Au Gratin 120
Party Casserole 128
Pickled Beets 112
Potatoes O'Brien 121
Rice Giralda 125
Rice and Pecan Casserole 124
Rice Supreme 124
Sauerkraut Bake 126
Scandanavian Baked Beans . . . 110
Spinach and Cheese Casserole 127
Spinach Casserole 126
Stuffed Cabbage A La
   Moosewood 114
Sweet and Sour Zucchini 131
Sweet Potato Soufflé 130
Tomato Bleu Cheese Timbale . 129
Tomatoes with Spinach
   Mornay 128
Vegetable Platter 59
Vegetable Soup Nivernaise . . . 67
Vegetable Stuffed Eggplant . . . 117
Vegetable Stuffing 164
Vendor Pretzels 281
Vi's Moist Coconut Cake 251
Viennese Fish 145
Vinaigrette Dressing 92
Vinaigrette Dressing Supreme . . 92
Vodka Coffee Liqueur 285

W
White Lasagna 161
White Wine Sherbet 263

I N D E X

Whoopie Pies 220
Wild Duck with Orange Sauce .. 162
Willa Allen Dowling's Cinnamon
   Twists 208
Wine Jelly Ring with Seedless
   Grapes 79
Winter Wooly Soup 76

Y

Yarmouth Spiced Tea 38
Yorkshire Pudding 132
Youngstown Club Cheese 50

Z

Zesty Slaw 87
Zucchini
   Chocolate-Zucchini Cake 245
   Italian Stuffed Zucchini 130
   Sweet and Sour Zucchini 131
   Zucchini Bread 200
   Zucchini Relish 272
   Zucchini Soup with Sausage .. 69
   Zucchini Squares, Greek 51

R.S.V.P.
Junior League of Portland, Maine, Inc.
P.O. Box 677
Portland, Maine 04104

Please send me _____ copies of R.S.V.P. at $14.95 per copy plus $3.00 per copy for postage and handling. (Maine residents please add $.90 sales tax per book.)

Name _____

Address _____

City _____ State _____ Zip_____

Make checks payable to R.S.V.P.

Proceeds from the book will be used to finance projects and community activities of the Junior League of Portland, Maine.

R.S.V.P.
Junior League of Portland, Maine, Inc.
P.O. Box 677
Portland, Maine 04104

Please send me _____ copies of R.S.V.P. at $14.95 per copy plus $3.00 per copy for postage and handling. (Maine residents please add $.90 sales tax per book.)

Name _____

Address _____

City _____ State _____ Zip_____

Make checks payable to R.S.V.P.

Proceeds from the book will be used to finance projects and community activities of the Junior League of Portland, Maine.

Re-Order Additional Copies